To Randy, with love

Who Counts as an American?

The Boundaries of National Identity

ELIZABETH THEISS-MORSE
University of Nebraska–Lincoln

CAMBRIDGE
UNIVERSITY PRESS

CAMBRIDGE UNIVERSITY PRESS
Cambridge, New York, Melbourne, Madrid, Cape Town, Singapore,
São Paulo, Delhi

Cambridge University Press
32 Avenue of the Americas, New York, NY 10013-2473, USA

www.cambridge.org
Information on this title: www.cambridge.org/9780521756952

First published 2009

Printed in the United States of America

A catalog record for this publication is available from the British Library.

Library of Congress Cataloging in Publication data
Theiss-Morse, Elizabeth.
    Who counts as an American? The boundaries of national identity /
Elizabeth Theiss-Morse.
        p.   cm.
    Includes bibliographical references and index.
    ISBN 978-0-521-76013-3 (hbk.) – ISBN 978-0-521-75695-2 (pbk.)
    1. National characteristics, American – Social aspects.   2. National characteristics,
American – Psychological aspects.   3. Nationalism – Social aspects – United States.
4. Nationalism – United States – Psychological aspects.   5. Group identity – United
States.   6. Loyalty – Social aspects – United States.   7. United States – Social
conditions – 1980–   8. Social psychology – United States.   I. Title.
E169.1.T465 2009
305.800973–dc22   2008053276

ISBN 978-0-521-76013-3 hardback
ISBN 978-0-521-75695-2 paperback

Who Counts as an American?
The Boundaries of National Identity

Why is national identity such a potent force in people's lives? And is the force positive or negative? In this thoughtful and provocative book, Elizabeth Theiss-Morse develops a social theory of national identity and uses a national survey, focus groups, and experiments to answer these important questions in the American context. Her results show that the combination of group commitment and the setting of exclusive boundaries on the national group affects how people behave toward their fellow Americans. Strong identifiers care a great deal about their national group. They want to help and be loyal to their fellow Americans. By limiting who counts as an American, though, these strong identifiers place serious limits on who benefits from their pro-group behavior. Help and loyalty are offered only to "true Americans," not Americans who do not count and who are pushed to the periphery of the national group.

Elizabeth Theiss-Morse is Professor and Chair of Political Science at the University of Nebraska–Lincoln, where she has taught since 1988. She is the coauthor of two award-winning Cambridge University Press books: *Congress as Public Enemy: Public Attitudes toward American Political Institutions* (with John R. Hibbing), winner of the American Political Science Association's (APSA) Fenno Prize in 1996 for the best book on Congress, and *With Malice toward Some: How People Make Civil Liberties Judgments* (with George E. Marcus, John L. Sullivan, and Sandra L. Wood), winner of the APSA's Best Book in Political Psychology Prize in 1996. A second book written with John Hibbing, *Stealth Democracy: Americans' Beliefs about How Government Should Work* (Cambridge, UK, 2002), was named an "Outstanding Academic Title" by *Choice* magazine in 2003. She also co-edited with John Hibbing *What Is It about Government That Americans Dislike?* (Cambridge, UK, 2001). She has published articles in the *American Journal of Political Science*, *American Political Science Review*, *Perspectives on Politics*, *Political Psychology*, and *Political Behavior*, among others, and she has received five National Science Foundation grants.

Contents

Figures

Tables

Preface

In 1986, my husband Randy and I took a trip to New Zealand. We spent a couple of days in Queenstown, located in a breathtakingly beautiful spot on the edge of Lake Wakatipu looking out at The Remarkables mountain range. The area's natural beauty has made Queenstown a popular tourist destination, so it was no surprise that upon arriving in Queenstown we saw many tourists, like ourselves, from around the world. We especially noticed a lot of Americans, including a group of Americans singing "If You're Happy and You Know It Clap Your Hands" very loudly in the Skyline Restaurant atop Bobs Peak and another group of Americans emerging from a tourist bus complaining loudly that New Zealand sure wasn't like America ("And you have to ask for water in a restaurant and when they bring it, it doesn't even have ice in it, of all things!").

Sitting in The Cow, a pizza restaurant where multiple parties were seated together at each table, we heard some Americans at the next table complain that they didn't like having to sit with strangers. Shortly thereafter, our server came to our table and engaged us in a conversation. She asked us what we had seen and done in New Zealand thus far. After a pleasant conversation, she asked if we were Canadians. Since Randy and I at the time had more pronounced Minnesota accents, this question was not far-fetched, but it raised something of a dilemma. Did we want to tell the server we were Americans, fully placing ourselves within the group "the American people," or did we prefer not having that identity placed on us at that time? What did we think of the American people, and did we want to be seen as part of that social group?

A decade later, when John Hibbing and I began work on our book *Stealth Democracy*, I became intrigued with a particular aspect of our work on people's perceptions of democratic processes: What do Americans think of the American people? And what does it matter? John and I found in our research that people's desire to remove power from elected officials is in part a reflection of their views of "the American people." At the same time, however, these same people fully recognize the limitations of their fellow Americans – that they do not care much about politics, that they are not very well informed, and that they are too busy to pay much attention to politics in the first place – which leads to not wanting to put too much power in the people's hands. So Americans do not want elected officials to have too much power but they also are unwilling to endorse giving a lot of power to the American people. Many Americans therefore turn to "stealth democracy" as a viable alternative to a people-centered direct democracy and to the politician-centered representative democracy we currently have.

After finishing the work on *Stealth Democracy*, I began to think more deeply about Americans' perceptions of the American people. This thinking led me to research on national identity, which subsequently led me to engage more fully with what it means to hold a national identity. I was struck by the disjuncture between how European scholars think and write about national identity and how American scholars think and write about the concept. Is American identity really a different animal from, say, British identity or French identity or Polish identity? Is American identity "exceptional"? I don't think so. I therefore tried to draw out a theory of national identity that could encompass the American case along with any other case, which I call a social theory of national identity. National identity is about feeling part of a national group, being part of the "American people" or the "French people" or the "Polish people." National identity does not differ depending on from which country one comes.

If national identity is a social identity, which I am convinced it is, then much of the research from social psychology on group dynamics can be used to understand what national identity is and what its consequences will be. Many people identify with their national group, often strongly, and being part of that group affects their attitudes and behavior. This social group understanding of national identity opens up all sorts of interesting questions. What explains differences in how strongly people identify with their national group? How do people define who is in their national group and who is not? If there are differences in people's commitment to their national group and in the boundaries they set on that group, what are the consequences? I am especially interested in consequences that arise from group-oriented attitudes and behaviors. Who helps and who gets helped in the national group? How does national identity affect reactions to criticisms coming from fellow group members? In broad terms, how does national identity help or hurt the group – in this case, the American people?

My research on national identity has had a significant impact on my own thinking about American identity and the American people. In many ways, the negatives of a strong national identity outweigh the positives. Strong identifiers define their national group more narrowly than weak identifiers, setting strict boundaries on who is included in the group and who is excluded. They are also more likely to marginalize group members who aren't prototypical. Marginalized group members are less likely to be helped and less likely to be listened to when they raise concerns about the national group. The result is a large number of marginalized compatriots who feel tremendously frustrated and angry and strong identifiers who refuse to acknowledge the need to make changes that would actually strengthen the group in the long run.

But the positives are important and cannot be readily dismissed. The most positive consequence is strong identifiers' sense of responsibility to their national community. Strong identifiers are much more likely than weak identifiers to be motivated by concerns about what is in the best interest of the national group. Weak identifiers are not so motivated. Having group members who care deeply about their group and its well-being is essential to any group. The group is strengthened by having members who help each other, who willingly move beyond their own self-interests to think about the group's interests, who defend the group when it is under attack. Without these strong identifiers, groups are not really groups at all. They are simply a collection of atomistic individuals. The positives of national identity are unfortunately undermined by the strong tendency of strong identifiers to set hard, exclusive boundaries on their national group. When a strong commitment to the group combines with a narrow understanding of who counts as a "true American," the results are devastating for marginalized Americans and for the national group as a whole.

This project on national identity has benefited greatly from the help offered by several organizations and people. I am deeply grateful to the National Science Foundation, which provided most of the funding for this research (SES-0111887). It is such a luxury to be able to use original data collected specifically for the purposes of this research, and I thank the National Science Foundation for giving me this opportunity. I am also grateful to the U.S. Congress Fund, the University of Nebraska–Lincoln (UNL) Research Council, and the Gallup Research Center, all at the University of Nebraska–Lincoln, for providing me with additional resources to work on this project.

The multiple methods used in this study necessitated the help of many individuals. I thank the Ohio State University's Center for Survey Research, and especially Matthew Courser, for doing such a good job helping with and administering the national survey. Focus groups are great fun to conduct, but putting them together entails a tremendous amount of work. The focus groups used in this research could not have happened without the impressive efforts of Nelson Okuku Miruka, from the University of Nebraska–Lincoln, and Emily Sharum, from the University of Arkansas. Thank you for all of your help. And thanks to Todd Shields for recommending Emily to me.

The experiments demanded the services of the greatest number of people, often during odd hours and on weekends. I thank Dan Braaten, Eric French, Travis French, Eric Heinze, Mitch Herian, Brian Hernandez, Seema Kakran, Tina Mueller, Aaron Peeks, Ala' Qadi, Bennie Shobe, and Tyler White for all of the work they put into the experiments. I am especially grateful to Eric Whitaker, who served as my research assistant for much of this project. Eric's hard work and innovative approach to dealing with various problems that arose were extremely impressive. I was often able to focus my attention on other matters knowing that Eric was taking care of the everyday details of this project. Thanks to Ryan Lowry for his work on the final stage of this process. Finally, I am deeply indebted to Helen Sexton, the administrative assistant in the Department of Political Science at the

University of Nebraska–Lincoln. Helen made sure everyone got paid on time and always knew whom to call when a crisis arose or information was needed. I was also helped tremendously throughout this project with advice, suggestions, and insights from colleagues both at Nebraska and around the country. Some gave helpful feedback on conference papers that developed into chapters. Some read a part or all of the book manuscript. And some gave useful advice during the data-gathering phase of the project. The book was much improved by all of the intelligent and constructive comments I received. Thanks to the two anonymous reviewers at Cambridge University Press, John Fulwider, John Hibbing, Leonie Huddy, Debbie Schildkraut, John Transue, and Eric Whitaker. I am especially grateful to Jeff Spinner-Halev and Amy Fried for their time, effort, and extremely helpful comments on earlier drafts of the manuscript.

Finally, my life would be much less enjoyable and full without my family. My two kids, Nicholas and Christopher, always make me keep my work in perspective. Any feelings of frustration or anxiety I experienced working on this book were quickly washed away as soon as we were together and they regaled me with stories from school or the latest joke they had heard or the funny things their friends had done that day. I love them very much. My husband and best friend, Randy, is always there for me. I consciously tried very hard not to bring questions and concerns about this project home with me, and I never once asked him to read any part of the book. I wanted this book to be purely my gift to him.

The Need for a Social Theory of National Identity

Throughout the Iraq War, and even prior to its inception in March 2003, some Americans vigorously criticized the Bush administration for various aspects of the war, protesting that the reasons for starting the war were based on faulty intelligence; that the United States should have put together a strong, broad-based multinational force; that the administration had no real plan for what to do in Iraq once Saddam Hussein and his government fell. Counterprotesters and people who supported the Bush administration's foreign policy responded to these criticisms by calling the protesters "un-American" or "bad Americans" (O'Reilly 2007; "Pro-war Demonstrators Show Support for U.S. Troops" 2003; "Thousands Rally in Support of War" 2003). By implication, good Americans do not criticize, especially during times of war. If Americans do not like a policy being pursued by their government, they should remain silent or, at more of an extreme, move to another country, Canada perhaps, because they clearly aren't behaving like true Americans.

In the midst of the Iraq War, on August 29, 2005, Hurricane Katrina wreaked havoc on the Mississippi Delta region of the United States. Reactions to the U.S. government's response to the widespread destruction varied widely, with some people defending the government's response and others questioning whether the government would have responded as slowly if the majority of the hurricane's victims had been wealthy and white rather than poor and black. Some critics of the government's response focused on race, arguing that the

underlying racism in America explained the government's failure to
deal with the catastrophic effects of the hurricane quickly and effec-
tively. Others focused on poverty, arguing that "Poor people don't
count as much as other people, and that didn't start with the hurricane" (Large 2005: M1). Whether race or poverty was at the root
of the government's sluggish response, the concern was that people in
America get treated differently, that some Americans don't "count" as
much as other Americans.

About a year later, in the summer of 2006, the Gallup News Service
released a *USA Today*/Gallup poll outlining Americans' attitudes
toward Muslims and Arab Americans (Saad 2006). A large minority of respondents (39 percent) said they felt some prejudice toward
Muslims, with the same percentage saying that Muslim Americans
were not loyal to the United States. What ought to be done with
Muslim Americans? About 40 percent of the respondents supported
treating Muslims differently from other U.S. citizens by requiring them
to carry special identification cards (39 percent) or by making them
undergo more intensive security checks at U.S. airports (41 percent).
In 2007, a *Newsweek* poll found that just over half of the respondents (52 percent) thought that the FBI should wiretap mosques in the
United States to keep track of any radical preaching by Islamic clerics.
In that same poll, a quarter of respondents favored the mass detention
of U.S. Muslims if another attack like the one on September 11, 2001,
occurred in the United States (*Newsweek* Poll 2007). Americans are
guaranteed their basic civil liberties in the U.S. Constitution. Some
Americans question, however, whether they apply to all Americans.

And in September 2007, Senator John McCain, in an interview
with beliefnet, a web site covering religious issues, said that the United
States "was founded primarily on Christian principles" and that "the
Constitution established the United States of America as a Christian
nation" (Labaton 2007: 22). While McCain later tried to clarify his
comments, the views he expressed in the interview mimic those held
by a majority of the American people. A poll by the Pew Forum on
Religion & Public Life (2006) found that two-thirds of Americans
see the United States as a Christian nation and would like to see more
religion allowed in public spaces. The notion that the United States is
a Christian nation could certainly reflect the simple acknowledgment
that a large majority of Americans are Christian. It does not. Rather, a

majority of Americans (55 percent) believe the Constitution explicitly establishes the United States as a Christian nation, according to a First Amendment Center poll (Stone 2007). Contrary to the Constitution and the framers' intent, a majority of Americans mistakenly believe the framers placed within the Constitution a declaration stating that the United States is a Christian nation. Many political leaders, including McCain, Lieutenant General William Boykin, and the Republican Party of Texas, have fostered the misleading view that the United States is a country of and for Christians.

What do these stories about antiwar protesters, Hurricane Katrina victims, Muslim Americans, and Christian Americans have in common? They all share a concern with national identity and who the American people are as a national group. Who "counts" fully as an American? And how does being counted affect how Americans treat one another? This book explores the answers to these questions using a national random-sample survey, focus groups, and experiments. I develop what I call the social theory of national identity to explain Americans' behavior toward their fellow Americans. When Americans are considered "true Americans," fully included in the group "the American people," they have the opportunity to enjoy all of the benefits of group membership: being helped by fellow Americans during times of need, being treated fairly in the distribution of resources, and being listened to when they are critical of the group and its actions. Americans who are not accepted as fully part of the group, whom I refer to as marginalized Americans, are not given these same benefits of group membership. They are offered help only grudgingly, if at all, and their criticisms are rejected by those who consider themselves fully American. Whether a person is considered a prototypical, "true" American or a marginalized American has serious implications for how they are treated by their fellow Americans.

The social theory of national identity I propose explains why people treat fellow Americans the way they do. This theory rests on the notion that national identity, like other group identities, is inherently social and is centered on people's strong bond and sense of community with their fellow group members – in this case, their compatriots. It is this bond, this attachment, that is at the heart of national identity. People are deeply affected by their perceptions of fellow group members and by being part of a group of fellow nationals. To understand national identity and its effects, then, it is essential to examine the dynamics of social groups and how these dynamics affect members' attitudes and behaviors.

There are two aspects of national identity that are of primary importance to the social theory of national identity: the level of commitment people feel toward the national group and the boundaries they set to determine who is fully in the group and who is not. Group commitment is important because national identity concerns ascriptive groups; most people are born into a certain citizenship through no choice of their own and they retain that citizenship throughout their lifetime. Whether or not people like their national group, others label them as members and perceive them to be part of the group. Some people will be highly committed to their national group whereas others will do what they can to distance themselves from a group about which they feel ambivalent or which they disdain. How committed people feel to their national group can significantly influence their attitudes and behaviors.

Setting group boundaries is the second important aspect of group identity. All groups set boundaries between who is included in the group and who is excluded. A great deal of work has been done on the boundaries between ingroups and outgroups and the impact that these boundaries have on intergroup relations. A much less studied aspect of boundaries is the impact that the setting of boundaries has *within* the group. The setting of boundaries can be used to distinguish those who are full members of the group from those who are marginalized group members. Group members who fit the group prototype are fully accepted as members of the group and benefit from all of the positive ingroup behaviors, such as being helped by fellow group members in times of trouble. Group members who do not fit the prototype, however, are marginalized in the sense that often they are not fully accepted as full members of the group. They do not benefit from their group membership the way prototypical members do and must constantly struggle to be accepted by the group. These marginalized group members are still members of the group, but are not fully considered so.

When commitment and the setting of exclusive boundaries combine, the mixture is potentially explosive. Strong commitment to the national group can lead to a strong sense of community and fellowship, but when these strong identifiers set exclusive boundaries on their national group, the dynamics of marginalizing group members who don't fit the group prototype are invidious and detrimental. The sense of fellowship is powerful for those fully accepted as compatriots and is bitter for those not accepted as full members of the national community.

This chapter develops this social theory of national identity, drawing on political theory and social psychology to lay out the contours of national identity. But if this social theory of national identity is right, is the previous research on American identity all wrong? After developing the social theory of national identity, I address the contributions and limitations of past research on American national identity and place this research in the context of the social theory I propose. I finish the chapter by briefly discussing the consequences of national identity and by providing a road map for the rest of the book.

A SOCIAL THEORY OF NATIONAL IDENTITY

David Miller (1995) holds a social understanding of national identity, arguing that there are five aspects of this identity that play important parts in establishing the national community. The first is in many ways the most important, since without it the other four cannot follow, and it is the one I will focus on here.[1] According to Miller, national identity is based on people's belief that a national community exists and that the people within that national community share certain characteristics. People must "recognize one another as compatriots" (Miller 1995: 22) and share the belief that the members belong together as a group. As Miller says, "nations are not aggregates of people distinguished by their physical or cultural traits, but communities whose very existence depends upon mutual recognition" (Miller 1995: 23). It is people's shared belief that they constitute a group, a national group, that matters. Without that shared belief, there can be no national identity.

---

[1] Miller's five aspects of national identity are as follows: 1) a belief exists that a national community exists; 2) the identity embodies historical continuity; 3) the national community is an active community; 4) the identity is embedded in a geographical place; and 5) there is a common political culture with shared beliefs (1995: 22–6).

This understanding of national identity as a shared sense of belonging fits well Benedict Anderson's (1991) famous definition of nation as an "imagined community." Anderson defines nation as an imagined community that is both sovereign and limited. It is sovereign in the sense that the nation governs itself. It is limited in the sense that there are boundaries: Some people in the world are part of the community whereas others are not. Even though people within the nation have met only a small number of their fellow nationals, they can imagine the rest who fit within the boundaries of the national group. They feel a strong sense of comradeship even without the benefit of personal interaction. Again, it is the shared belief that one is a member of a group of compatriots that is at the core of the idea of a nation.

Miller (1995) and Anderson (1991) both think of national identity as an inherently social identity. People view themselves as entwined with other people in a community sharing a common bond, and it is this that defines the group. Most Americans share this sense of community with fellow Americans. Following the terrorist attacks on September 11, 2001, there was a dramatic increase in the number of flags one could see flying across the United States, but more important was the renewed sense of community these flags symbolized. As one commentator said, the American flag "evoked fellow feeling with Americans, for we had been attacked together" (Packer 2001: 15). Many people from across the United States claimed a deep connection with New Yorkers and, more broadly, with all Americans. But this sense of community with fellow Americans did not rise phoenix-like out of the tragedy. Americans have long felt a strong sense of attachment to their fellow Americans.

From the country's inception, astute observers have commented on the sense of fellowship among Americans. James Madison, in Federalist #14, warns his fellow citizens to beware of those who argue against a strong union:

Hearken not to the unnatural voice which tells you that the people of America, knit together as they are by so many cords of affection, can no longer live together as members of the same family; can no longer continue the mutual guardians of their mutual happiness; can no longer be fellow-citizens of one great, respectable, and flourishing empire. ... No, my countrymen, shut your ears against this unhallowed language. Shut your hearts against the poison which it conveys; the kindred blood which flows in the veins of American citizens, the mingled blood which they have shed in defense of their sacred rights, consecrate their Union and excite horror at the idea of their becoming aliens, rivals, enemies (Hamilton, Madison, and Jay 1961: 103–4).

Madison draws direct attention to the common bonds that hold Americans together as a people, the "cords of affection," the "kindred blood." The idea of breaking the union apart is repulsive because it would break the people apart.

This sense of fellowship among citizens is an important aspect of being part of the national community. Many people, though not all, feel a strong attachment to their fellow citizens. They feel part of a national community even though they have never met, and will never meet, more than a small fraction of compatriots in their lifetime. The ties that bind are strong and are reinforced by the history and culture citizens share. Charles Taylor even places the stability of democracies on this sense of attachment:

[A] nation can only ensure the stability of its legitimacy if its members are strongly committed to one another by means of a common allegiance to the political community. ... In other words, a modern democratic state demands a "people" with a strong collective identity. Democracy obliges us to show much more solidarity and much more commitment to one another in our joint political project than was demanded by the hierarchical and authoritarian societies of yesteryear (Taylor 1998: 144).

Democracies depend on a sense of cohesion among citizens because of the notion of popular sovereignty. A group of people – the citizens of a country – are the ultimate political authority and must therefore deliberate and make decisions. Taylor argues that to do so, people must feel a strong sense of commitment to one another, a collective identity.

What does it mean to have a collective identity? People can hold various identities, from the book group to which they belong to their racial group or national group. What these various identities have in common is that individuals place themselves within social groupings that are distinguishable from other social groupings. A person who identifies herself as an American establishes Americans as a group that is separate from other national groups, and one that makes up part of her sense of self. Identification with any group entails "the sense that one's conception or definition of who one is (one's identity)

is largely composed of self-descriptions in terms of the defining characteristics of social groups to which one belongs" (Hogg and Abrams
1988: 7). Social identity theorists argue that in the move from the
individual self to the collective self, people take on the concerns and
goals of the group as their own and act to increase the well-being of
the group (Brewer 2001).

According to Henri Tajfel (1978: 63), social identity is "that part of
an individual's self-concept which derives from his knowledge of his
membership of a social group (or groups), together with the value and
emotional significance attached to that membership." A social identity
therefore has three components: 1) a cognitive aspect, which refers to
a person's awareness of group membership or self-categorization; 2)
an evaluative aspect, which is how good or bad the person considers
the group to be; and 3) an emotional aspect, which is a person's feeling of attachment to the group. National identity includes all of these
components: People need to think they are a member of their national
group, evaluate their national group positively, and feel attached to
their national group.

When people identify with a group and their sense of self shifts from
the personal to the collective, certain group dynamics come into play
that explain much of group behavior. The group dynamics that play a
key role in the social theory of national identity are group commitment
and the setting of group boundaries. How strongly people feel committed to their group and how exclusively they set their group's boundaries
are natural group processes that heavily influence group members' attitudes and behaviors toward other group members. These two group
dynamics are the focus of this book. But groups also promote certain
norms that play an important part in understanding group behavior.
The norms tell group members what they ought to believe and how
they ought to behave as group members. Americans, for example, hold
strongly the norms of individualism and patriotism. I will discuss these
various group dynamics in turn.

Level of Commitment to the Group

While people hold all sorts of social identities, a key component for
understanding the effects of these identities on attitudes and behaviors
is the extent to which they feel committed to the group. Differences in

feelings of attachment drive many intergroup and intragroup processes, such as perceiving exaggerated differences between one's ingroup and the outgroup and seeing one's ingroup in a highly positive light (Ellemers, Spears, and Doosje 1999a). People who are "die-hard" group members are much more likely to merge their group membership with their sense of self, to behave in a group-oriented manner, and to hold and follow group norms than are people who are "fair-weather" group members (Doosje, Ellemers, and Spears 1999: 85). Because people are motivated to feel good about their group membership, they have an incentive to enhance the success of their group and to view their group positively. Being strongly committed to the group leads people to promote vigorously the well-being of the group.

People vary in how strongly they identify with any given group. Some groups command a tremendous amount of commitment and loyalty from group members whereas others do not. For example, groups that are more exclusive and that make prospective members experience more hardships to get into the group tend to command strong attachments (Brewer 2001). The more difficult it is to become a member of a group, the more people will want to become a member, the more strongly they will identify with the group, and the more the group will influence their behavior. A group that makes its new members go through initiation rites or pass difficult tests, for example, can command tremendous loyalty and extreme actions from members. It is no surprise that people who enter the military must go through grueling basic training. The notion is that once through the ordeal, a soldier will do almost anything for the good of the group, including giving his or her life.

Similarly, group memberships that are voluntary can expect to generate greater attachments than group memberships that are involuntary (Andrews 1991). People can choose to be members of groups they especially like, thereby increasing the likelihood that they will feel strongly attached to the group. When people are members of a group involuntarily, however, such as when they are born into their racial, gender, or national group, they may or may not like the group and they may or may not feel an attachment to that group. People who are born in the United States are Americans whether they want to be or not. Only taking the large step of emigrating to another country breaks this involuntary national group membership.

Recognizing the predominantly involuntary nature of national group membership opens up our understanding of group commitment. When group membership is voluntary, people can choose not to join a particular group. Voluntary group commitment levels are therefore likely to be consistently high. Involuntary group membership, on the other hand, means there will be wider variation in group commitment. Some people will feel strongly part of the group into which they were born, others will simply not think much about it, and still others will actively reject their group membership. They do not want to be a member of the group but are still members involuntarily, and they will be perceived by others to be part of the group. Many group memberships, including gender, race, and nationality, cannot simply be shaken off.

But some have suggested that national identity is a special case, that it commands greater commitment than other identities because it is so potent. While nationality is derived ascriptively, it is constantly reinforced through symbols, culture, language, and politics (Billig 1995). Politicians make frequent reference to "the American people" as a unified group and call on Americans to behave or think in certain ways or to make sacrifices for the good of the country. Unlike other identities, national identity is one for which people are willing to give their lives (Miller 1995). The ascriptive nature of national identity means that people will vary in their level of commitment to the group, but the potent nature of this identity means that many of those who identify with their national group will feel that commitment strongly.

National identity, like any social identity, is a continuum running from no sense of identity with the group to having the identity be fully and completely part of one's sense of self. The more strongly people identify with their group, the more the group affects their attitudes and behaviors. The less people identify with their group, the more they will act in idiosyncratic, and perhaps self-interested, ways. We therefore need to take level of commitment into account when examining the consequences of national identity.

The Setting of Group Boundaries

The second group dynamic relevant to the social theory of national identity is the setting of group boundaries. Making one's ingroup distinct from the outgroup, of setting boundaries, is precisely what Marilynn Brewer (2003) argues is at the heart of group identities. Her optimal distinctiveness theory states that people are drawn to groups that satisfy two social needs: a need for inclusion and a need for differentiation. People want to assimilate their individual selves into a larger group (inclusion) but they also want to distinguish themselves from others (differentiation). Being a member of an exclusive (rather than an inclusive) group satisfies both of these desires. People get to be included in a social group that has highly distinct boundaries that separate the ingroup members from all outgroup members.

[handwritten margin notes: JRH / connection]

National identity is interesting if looked at from this perspective. National groups establish clear, well-demarcated, objective, legal boundaries. At times these objective national group boundaries work well to distinguish the ingroup from the outgroup. When an American tourist in Brazil runs into another American in a local bar, the shared citizenship can create a connection that sets the pair off from the surrounding Brazilians. But if Anderson (1991) is right that the national group is an imagined community, then legal citizenship may not be the deciding factor. We might agree that everyone with U.S. citizenship is an American, but some U.S. citizens might not be imagined in the national group. According to Timothy L. Phillips (1996: 114), "Social groups may have full citizenship rights, but be located outside of … the 'national community.'" Democracies, even diverse democracies such as the United States, are not immune from the effects of marginalizing some ingroup members. Taylor (1998) raises the notion that there is a tension between inclusion and exclusion in democracies. Democracies must be inclusive to be deemed legitimate but they are pulled toward exclusion precisely because being too inclusive welcomes too much difference, tearing the consensus that helps to build a sense of community. "There is a standing temptation to exclusion, arising from the fact that democracies work well when people … trust one another, and feel a sense of commitment toward one another" (Taylor 1998: 146).

People can disagree over who is fully included in the national community and who is not, yet the general contours of the group boundaries are determined in part by constructions of the past. The past weighs heavily in collective memories (see, e.g., Anderson 1991; Schwartz 2000; Zerubavel 1995). The boundaries of national identity can shift over time – once Irish Catholics were marginalized but now they are not – yet the stereotypes that define a group, that indicate who are prototypical members of the group, are often difficult to change. If the stereotype of an American is someone who is cowboy-like – individualistic, gun-toting, white, and male – then people who are individualistic, gun-toting, white, and male are likely to be quickly deemed "American" whereas someone who does not share these characteristics will be less likely to call to mind "American." As Patricia G. Devine (1989) has convincingly shown, stereotypes come to mind automatically and must be actively put down if they are not to influence attitudes and behaviors. National identity, then, is linked to the characteristics of certain members, the dominant group members, and through that linkage acts to exclude or marginalize those members who do not fit the stereotype (Sidanius and Pratto 1999) .

Group boundaries are set and maintained based on the prototypical members of the group. Prototypical members are those who exemplify the group stereotypes, and it is these stereotypes that most differentiate the group from other groups. Americans might not see much difference between Norwegians and Swedes, but Norwegians and Swedes do based on the perceived characteristics of each national group. The stereotypes of a group, which are widely accepted, establish who is considered fully a member of the group and who just doesn't fit. The stereotypes are so deeply embedded that prototypical group members often do not think much about them. Marginalized group members, however, are reminded frequently that they are in the national group but not prototypical members of it (Sidanius and Petrocik 2001).

Much of the work on stereotypes focuses on the boundaries that these forces help to create and maintain between ingroups and out-groups. Little work has been done on the effects of boundaries on intragroup relations, especially the relations between prototypical group members and those who are marginalized because they are not accepted as full members of the group (but see Abrams, Hogg, and Marques 2005; Hogg 2005; Hogg, Fielding, and Darley 2005). Marginalized group members are part of the group in the sense that they are group members, but they are not always treated as members of the group. Boundaries therefore establish the distinction between the ingroup and the outgroup, but they also establish who falls right at the center of the group and who is pushed off to the periphery.

It is the most highly committed group members who will be motivated to set the strictest boundaries. Strong identifiers care deeply about the group. They want to keep the group alive and well, and one way to do this is to make sure the group is distinctive and exclusive. This suggests that strong identifiers will have a narrower, ethnocultural understanding of identity because such an understanding sets very strict boundaries on the national group. An ethnocultural view of identity emphasizes the racial, ethnic, and religious characteristics of a group. People who fit the demographic stereotype of the group are the "true" Americans – they are white, Northern European, and Christian. Strong identifiers are likely to hold a more ethnocultural view of their national identity because of a strong desire to maintain the group boundaries and therefore, they believe, to ensure the group's strength, vitality, and exclusivity.

But I argue that strong identifiers will be more likely to set *any* boundaries. Demographic boundaries are not the only boundaries that distinguish the national group. Even the belief that, for example, Americans must respect the institutions and laws of the United States or something as innocuous as the notion that Americans must feel American can work to make the national group distinct. My argument here is simply that strong identifiers are more likely to set boundaries than weak identifiers, whether the boundaries are strict and exclusionary (such as being white or Christian) or amorphous and permeable (such as feeling American). It is the act of separating the group from other groups that is important to strong identifiers.

Group Norms

All groups experience the basic group dynamics of members differing in their level of commitment to the group and in their setting of group boundaries. Social norms also play an important role in groups. Social norms are the expectations that guide behaviors and attitudes within a social group. They are consensual standards "that are understood by members of a group, and that guide and/or constrain social behavior without the force of law" (Cialdini and Trost 1998: 152). If a social norm for Americans is that they are patriotic, then Americans are likely to hold patriotic attitudes and to behave in patriotic ways because of social pressures to follow the norm. This is especially true of strong identifiers who want to behave like good group members. These group norms become stereotypes as Americans are widely assumed to be, for example, patriotic. Prototypical group members are guided by the norms important to the group so their behaviors fit well what is expected of the group. When people do not follow important group norms, they are considered deviants and are marginalized within the group. Being unpatriotic makes one a "bad American" or "un-American."

At the national level, these norms often remain unspoken, falling into what Michael Billig (1995) refers to as "banal nationalism." Every day all around us are the symbols and norms that create a national consciousness yet people remain unconscious of them. Some, however, are pervasive and widely recognized. National group members should love their country. They should hold dearly the values that define the nation. They should hold in esteem the history and political structures that established the nation. Even these presumably non-social aspects, though, have a social side. Group members are consciously or unconsciously aware of the norms that guide the group, and they are more likely to behave in accordance with those norms when their group identity is important to them. While all groups have norms, the content of the norms varies across groups. For example, Americans heavily emphasize the norm of individualism whereas the Japanese, for example, emphasize the norm of collectivism. Members of both national groups hold norms, but the content of the norms differs.

ALTERNATIVE VIEWS OF AMERICAN NATIONAL IDENTITY

The social theory of national identity can be used to understand any national identity, whether American or any other national group. It is a universal theory that I apply to the case of American identity, but I could just as easily apply it to German identity, Japanese identity, or Brazilian identity. This universal understanding does not, on its face, fit well the prevailing scholarship on national identity, especially American identity.[2] According to the prevailing wisdom, European

---

[2] Some scholars have applied social identity theory to national identity, as I do. See, e.g., Brewer 2004; Gibson 2006; Gibson and Gouws 2003; Huddy and Khatib 2007; Sniderman et al. 2000; Transue 2007.

and other national identities are based on religion, ethnicity, culture, history, and territory (Gellner 1983). A group of people has inhabited a particular piece of land for thousands, or at least hundreds, of years; they share a language and a culture; and they remember vividly the battle of the whatever in which their nation defeated, or perhaps was defeated by, another nation. The long-established national myths and the very real languages and territories are what make up national identity.

American identity is of necessity something different, or so the argument goes. The United States has its national myths, its distinct territory, and a shared language (immigrants are expected to learn English, and they do so quickly). However, it differs from other countries in that its history is short, its people are a hodgepodge of ethnic groups, and it does not have the same kinds of religious or ethnic cleavages as European countries do. American identity is therefore "exceptional" (Huntington 2004; Lipset 1996; Schlesinger 1993). If American identity is not deeply territorial or historical or based on language or culture or ethnicity, then what is it? Scholars have struggled over what constitutes American identity, usually accepting that it is unique or exceptional but disagreeing over what it actually is. The various understandings of American national identity generally fall into four camps: American identity as historically ethnocultural, American identity as a set of beliefs or principles, American identity as community, and American identity as patriotism. While these understandings are not mutually exclusive – many scholars combine these various elements in their work – I will discuss each in turn to clarify the arguments. I will also raise questions or concerns about each understanding and discuss how each fits in the social theory of national identity.

American Identity as Historically Ethnocultural

From the founding of the United States, American identity has contained an ethnocultural element. John Jay's famous quote depicts clearly this ethnocultural view of Americans: "Providence has been pleased to give this one connected country to one united people – a people descended from the same ancestors, speaking the same language, professing the same religion, attached to the same principles of government, very similar in their manners and customs ..." (Hamilton, Madison, and Jay 1961: 38). Since then, the ethnocultural view of American identity has gone through periods of widespread acceptance and of determined rejection. Race and ethnicity have been a key focus of nativist concerns, especially in connection with immigration policies. In 1882, Congress passed the Chinese Exclusion Act, which placed a ban on most Chinese immigration. As the officers of the Workingmen's Party stated, "we declare that the Chinamen must leave our shores. We declare that white men, and women, and boys, and girls, cannot live as the people of a great republic should and compete with the single Chinese coolies in the labor market" (Mink 1986: 82). The early twentieth century saw increased bans on Asian immigration so that by 1917 virtually all Asian immigration had been put to a stop. The Quota Act of 1921 and the National Origins Acts of 1924 and 1929 limited the number of immigrants allowed into the country and established from where immigrants could come. Nationality quotas were not abolished until 1965.[3]

Disputes over immigration in the early twenty-first century concern the number of Latinos and Latinas coming into the United States. Tom Tancredo, in his run for the Republican nomination for the 2008 presidential election, made immigration his major issue. While on the stump in Iowa, Tancredo said:

Sure, there's that nostalgic part of me that idealizes an America that probably never existed. But, an America more homogeneous, yes. It is not a white America, which is something I've heard people attacking me for all the time. We've always been a nation made up of so many different people, but it seemed to me there was more of an attempt to assimilate. So yeah, I long for that. Can we put this genie back in the bottle? I don't know. I have to try. ...

This is our home. ... But what happens when you come home and the house is full of people you don't even know? Is there nothing strange about this? Shouldn't I feel a little bit upset about this? This is my home, my country (Pappu 2007).

---

[3] The 1924 National Origins Act specifically set the admissions quota to 2 percent of a nationality group's population in the 1890 Census. The National Origins Act passed in 1929 established that 70 percent of immigrants would come from northern and western Europe and 30 percent from southern and eastern Europe. Information from http://www.closeup.org/immigrat.htm#overview, accessed May 25, 2005.

Explicit racial or ethnic prescriptions for being an American are much more rare today than in the past, but the desire to keep "strangers" out of the country is not so rare.

While scholars have primarily been interested in the racial and ethnic restrictions to American identity fostered by nativists over time, religion has also been an issue. Samuel Huntington (2004) has made a strong case that American identity rests on its Anglo-Protestant culture. Huntington does not argue in any way that Americans ought to be Protestant, but he does believe that any undermining of their Anglo-Protestant culture is detrimental to American identity and to the United States. The notion that America is Christian and specifically Protestant can be seen clearly in the waves of anti-Catholic and anti-Jewish sentiment that have swept across U.S. history. Nativists reacted strongly to the influx of the Irish beginning in the 1830s primarily because of their Roman Catholicism (Citrin et al. 1994; Reimers 1998). And in the early 1890s, members of the Iowa-based group American Protective Association took an oath never to vote for a Catholic, whether foreign or native born, and never to hire a Catholic (Reimers 1998: 12). Jews were banned from many private clubs and organizations, and covenants often restricted where they could live.

It is perhaps surprising that there is so little reticence today in claiming that the United States is a "Christian nation" or a "nation of Christians." The Republican Party of Texas included in its 2004 party platform the statement "The Republican Party of Texas affirms that the United States of America is a Christian nation."[4] Lieutenant General William Boykin, an intelligence official in the Pentagon, stated that international terrorists are "after us because we're a Christian nation."[5] In both instances, some outrage was expressed over the characterization of the United States as Christian, but the Texas Republican Party and General Boykin never suffered any repercussions for their statements. Americans widely accept the characterization of the United States as a "nation of Christians" since "more than 80 percent of our countrymen are Christian" (Kaplan 2005).[6]

---

[4] http://www.texasgop.org/library/RPTPlatform2004.pdf, accessed May 25, 2005.
[5] http://www.pbs.org/newshour/bb/military/july-dec03/boykin_10–21.html, accessed May 25, 2005.
[6] But see Meacham (2007) for an argument countering this view.

Much of the work that highlights ethnocultural understandings of American identity focuses on Americans' reactions to immigration (see, e.g., Citrin 1990; Citrin et al. 1994; Citrin et al. 1990a, 1990b; Citrin, Wong, and Duff 2001; Esses et al. 2001; Reimers 1998; Schildkraut 2003, 2005). Attitudes toward immigration are important. They directly address who is allowed to be considered an American. But ethnocultural understandings of who counts as an American are pervasive in American culture and have wide-ranging effects beyond immigration policy. Ethnocultural understandings can affect the boundaries that establish who counts as an American even among Americans who are fully citizens of the United States. In the social theory of national identity, people who strongly identify with the American people are significantly more likely than weak identifiers to set ethnocultural boundaries on their national group. The ethnocultural understanding of national identity therefore fits well the social theory outlined earlier in this section. It is part and parcel of the boundaries that Americans set on their national group.

American Identity as a Set of Principles

The most widely discussed and accepted view of American national identity rests on the set of beliefs Americans hold, especially their shared belief in liberalism (Smith 1988: 229–30). According to the liberal view, what unites Americans as a people and is the basis for what it means to them to be an American is a belief in the basic liberal values and principles upon which the United States was founded. Arthur Schlesinger, Jr., perhaps captures this view best when he says, "The genius of America lies in its capacity to forge a single nation from peoples of remarkably diverse racial, religious, and ethnic origins. It has done so because democratic principles provide both the philosophical bond of union and practical experience in civic participation" (Schlesinger 1993: 134). Democratic principles are at the heart of what makes Americans American and they are what make American identity exceptional.

Often this set of principles is referred to as "the American Creed." According to Huntington (1997: 29), the American Creed is "a set of universal ideas and principles articulated in the founding documents by American leaders: liberty, equality, democracy, constitutionalism, liberalism, limited government, private enterprise." These principles define the nation and allow it to incorporate immigrants into the national fabric. Immigrants could come from anywhere and still become Americans by believing in the American Creed. American identity, then, is simple and straightforward. What makes Americans American is their shared belief in equality, liberty, and democracy. As Franklin Delano Roosevelt said, "Americanism is a matter of mind and heart; Americanism is not, and never was, a matter of race and ancestry. A good American is one who is loyal to this country and to our creed of liberty and democracy" (quoted in Schlesinger 1993: 37).

The liberal understanding of American identity has not been without its critics. Multiculturalists, who applaud the cultural, ethnic, and racial diversity of the United States as a hallmark of American identity, are critical of liberalism because liberals expect all Americans to become Anglo-Saxon in word and deed if not in ethnicity. Liberals respond that multiculturalists promote group identities over a uniting American identity. "In sharp antithesis to liberal doctrine, multiculturalism construes racial group identity as the *preferred* choice of self-definition and validates the ongoing affirmation of ethnic distinctiveness" (Citrin et al. 1994: 9; emphasis in the original). If ethnic and racial identities are held more dearly than an American identity, then there is little that holds the diverse peoples of the United States together. "If separatist tendencies go on unchecked, the result can only be fragmentation, resegregation, and tribalization of American life" (Schlesinger 1993: 18).

If these liberal critics are right, multiculturalism does not promote an American identity but rather many racial and ethnic identities that supersede an American identity. But Deborah Schildkraut (2005) is able to salvage multiculturalism under her incorporationist view. A "hard" multicultural view holds that ethnicity and race preempt nationality (Citrin, Wong, and Duff 2001), but Schildkraut correctly argues that this view has never held much sway in the United States. Instead, many Americans have a view of their national group as one that has long accepted immigration and the novel mix of peoples who come to the United States. Americans are often tolerant and accepting of diversity and do not want everyone to be the same. The incorporationist view "allows for both differentialism and assimilationism, each to some degree" (Schildkraut 2005: 53). The United States is a country of hyphenated Americans, with the left side of the hyphen embodying one's ethnic or racial identity and the right side of the hyphen the shared identity of being an American (Walzer 1992).[7]

Both the liberal and the incorporationist understandings of American identity rest on a set of beliefs that Americans share and that act as a bond among fellow citizens. Americans are individualistic but their shared beliefs in themselves as a people and their liberal principles bring these disparate individuals together. There are two problems, however, with defining national identity as a set of beliefs, whether liberal or incorporationist. First, by highlighting beliefs or principles as the basis for American identity, scholars suggest that American national identity is something different from, for example, Italian identity and British identity, which are based on culture, territory, language, and so on. In essence, the definition of national identity in the United States is American-specific. But is American identity really different from other national identities? Don't *all* national identities contain sets of beliefs and principles that are thought to demarcate one national group from another and that are often taken as norms that ought to guide behavior? The United States is not unique in this regard. Many French people believe in freedom and equality; many Brits believe in liberalism. Does this make the French and Brits American? No. Americans believe that the American people should hold certain beliefs to be fully American, and that is what makes these beliefs important to American identity. The French and British also hold certain beliefs to be central to their national identity.

Second, a belief-based view of American identity ignores disagreements over what the beliefs or values mean.[8] While people might well agree that Americans must believe in freedom, equality, and diversity, it is not clear that they agree on what these beliefs mean or how they

---

[7] In Great Britain, on the other hand, many people of color do not feel British. Jenni I'Anson, a mental health aide and native-born British subject of Jamaican descent, said, "The only times I call myself British are when I go to get a passport and when someone asks me where my accent comes from. ... Otherwise I would never class myself as British. There is no sense of belonging here. I would only say that I am African-Caribbean" (Hoge 2002: A13). In contrast, people in the United States tend to refer to themselves comfortably as hyphenated Americans.

[8] Schildkraut (2005) is an exception. She emphasizes that people's interpretations of the beliefs that make up their national identity can vary widely, and that it is people's interpretations that explain their policy attitudes.

ought to be applied. The tolerance literature offers reason to be cautious.[9] Americans believe overwhelmingly in the abstract democratic principles of freedom of speech, freedom of assembly, due process, and so on, yet when asked to apply these principles in concrete situations, their support for these principles drops dramatically (McClosky and Brill 1983; Prothro and Grigg 1960; Sullivan, Fried, and Dietz 1982). It is easy to say that constitutional freedoms are wonderful and ought to be applied at all times. It is not so easy to apply them to disliked groups who want to say or do objectionable things. The same holds for the abstract values and principles that unite Americans. Everyone believes in freedom and equality, but not when it comes to applying them to marginalized groups in American society. Certainly African Americans have felt the brunt of the application of these values and beliefs, as have homosexuals and Arab Americans. Just because Americans believe in the abstract values does not mean that such values make any difference in real, concrete situations. Can such abstract principles that break down upon application really be the basis for American identity? I don't think they can.

Having said this, however, I fully recognize that beliefs play a part in national identity. The beliefs of group members help define a social group in terms of setting group boundaries, even if those boundaries are amorphous and permeable (anyone can believe in liberalism or multiculturalism), and constitute the group norms that play an important role in what behaviors are considered acceptable to the group members. If the norm is to fly the national flag or to give generously to charities, then people who are strongly committed to their group will be more likely to exhibit these behaviors. But group members can disagree over what the beliefs or norms really mean and their importance to the group, and they can choose which norms to apply in specific situations, leading to further disagreement. Equality and individualism are two norms held by Americans; when confronted with an issue such as affirmative action, some Americans will apply the equality norm and support affirmative action whereas others will

---

[9] Work on abstract views of good citizenship and citizenship in practice also shows that we ought to be cautious about interpreting what abstract beliefs really mean. Americans believe in a highly participatory good citizen but can offer many excuses for why they do not participate themselves (Theiss-Morse 1993).

apply the individualism norm and oppose affirmative action. Beliefs and principles are therefore important to national identity, but group dynamics affect their use within the group.

American Identity as Community

The third view of American identity that I will discuss is civic republicanism. This view is perhaps more prescriptive than the other two discussed previously, which instead focus on different aspects of American identity as practiced. Unlike liberalism, the civic republican view emphasizes commitment to the common good and to one's community. Civic republicanism emphasizes "achieving institutions and practices that make collective self-governance in pursuit of a common good possible for the community as a whole" (Smith 1988: 231). It also emphasizes an active, participatory citizenry. When people participate in their community, they value the common good over their private self-interests (Held 1996). Doing what is needed to promote the common good is therefore essential within one's community. Civic republicans feel an obligation to their fellow community members in a way that an isolated liberal individual does not.

But what is community? As Rogers Smith (1988) points out, civic republicans have underlined the need for homogeneous and small communities to make republicanism work. People who share the same values and culture are more likely to reach a consensus on the common good and to feel a part of the community. The United States, however, is neither small nor homogeneous, so what makes people feel a sense of attachment to the national community? The perhaps less-than-convincing answer to this question offered by civic republicans is that participation in the national community builds this sense of attachment. When people participate in the national community, they develop a sense of the common good and feel part of the whole. Participating in politics, however, is not the catalyst that makes people feel united within the national community. Many Americans would prefer not to participate in politics, and they especially disdain the conflict that politics naturally brings to the forefront (Hibbing and Theiss-Morse 2002). When people feel they have lost, they are especially likely to feel turned off of politics. Instead, feeling a sense of connection with and commitment to one's fellow nationals might well be the key. Even in a large country such as the United States, people can feel attached to the American people and a sense of obligation to that group.

The civic republican emphasis on community and the common good is important. People who have a strong sense of being part of their community are likely to take community concerns and goals seriously and to work for the betterment of the community. Without that sense of community and community betterment, people are just self-interested, atomistic individuals who feel little compulsion to help or responsibility for their community. But as some civic republicans have pointed out, group homogeneity matters. The more homogeneous the national group is in terms of its ethnocultural make-up and its set of shared principles and beliefs, the more likely Americans are to feel a sense of community with that group. As the social theory of national identity predicts, this sense of community is likely to be strongest among those who are highly committed to their national group, who set strict boundaries on the group, and who view their national group as homogeneous. Marginalizing group members who do not fit the prototype allows strong identifiers to imagine a homogeneous national community.

American Identity as Patriotism

Many political psychologists who discuss national identity meld the concept with patriotism, often invoking the concept of national attachment. For example, Qiong Li and Marilynn B. Brewer associate positive national identity with patriotism and negative national identity with nationalism, referring to high levels of national identification as "hypernationalism" (Li and Brewer 2004: 727–8). But national identity is not synonymous with patriotism (or nationalism, for that matter). Patriotism is love of country (which includes some mix of culture, values, the regime, the land, the national history and myths, the government and its policies, and, on rare occasions, the people), whereas national identity as I conceptualize it refers to feeling part of one's national group – in this case, the American people – and holding that national group as part of one's sense of self. Having a national identity is a social identity, which means identifying with a group of people, with ingroup members. Patriotism is a group norm among Americans.

The mixing of national identity and patriotism, however, is quite widespread. Scholars often include patriotism as either a major part of the definition of national identity, such as Stanley Renshon's (2005: 58) definition of national identity that includes three elements: attachment to what America stands for, psychological characteristics, and patriotism. The most important of these is patriotism ("the missing link of American national identity" [p. 65]). Patriotism and national identity are sometimes used interchangeably as basically the same concept (see, e.g., Bar-Tal and Staub 1997; Blank and Schmidt 2003; de Figueiredo and Elkins 2003; Kosterman and Feshbach 1989; Li and Brewer 2004; Mummendey, Klink, and Brown 2001). In this latter conception, patriotism and national identity both reflect attachment to one's nation or country. Often a distinction is further made between patriotism and nationalism, where patriotism is a positive attachment to country and nationalism additionally involves feeling superior to other countries.

I argue that national identity and patriotism are conceptually distinct and need to be studied as distinct concepts. National identity is a group identity, a group made up of fellow nationals, and consists of a cognitive, affective, and evaluative attachment to that group. Patriotism is most often defined as love of country but the definitional components of the term vary. Leonard W. Doob (1964), Seymour Feshbach and Noboru Sakano (1997), Jon Hurwitz and Mark Peffley (1990), Rick Kosterman and Seymour Feshbach (1989), and others define patriotism simply as love of country. Stephen Worchel and Dawna Coutant (1997) include the additional notion that patriotism involves putting the interests of the country above self-interests. Stephen Nathanson (1997: 312) provides a four-part definition: "1. a special affection for one's country, 2. a sense of personal identification with one's country, 3. a special concern for the well-being of one's country, and 4. a willingness to sacrifice to promote the country's good."

The common theme in most understandings of patriotism is that the target of patriotic feelings is the country, whether it includes the country's history, its territory, its culture, its symbols, or its governmental arrangements. Rarely does the definition involve attachment to the people within a country, and even more rarely is attachment to the people included in measures of patriotism (for example, the American National Election Studies [ANES] battery on patriotism and the comprehensive study of patriotism by Sullivan, Fried, and Dietz 1992 do not include this social component). Daniel Bar-Tal and Ervin Staub

(1997: 2; see also Renshon 2005), as an exception, define patriotism as "attachment by group members to their group and the land in which it resides," but certainly most scholars view patriotic feelings as aimed at the country and its symbols, not the people within the country.

The difference between the concepts of patriotism and national identity is important. People can love their country but not feel a strong sense of attachment to their national group. Similarly, people can have a strong sense of national identity and not feel patriotic. Why should scholars insist on conflating the two concepts? Group identity is different from love of country (at least conceptually), and we can gain greater insight into different types of national attachments if we keep the two concepts separate. This makes sense conceptually. It also makes sense empirically. In an important study, Leonie Huddy and Nadia Khatib (2007) examine the impact of national identity (as a social identity) and three understandings of patriotism – symbolic, constructive, and uncritical – on political participation. They find that national identity has a positive, significant, and robust relationship with the extent to which people pay attention to politics, their knowledge about politics, and voter turnout. Among the patriotism measures, only uncritical patriotism is significantly related to these political engagement variables and the relationship is always negative. That is, uncritical patriotism is related to less attentiveness, less knowledge, and lower voter turnout. Symbolic patriotism is negatively related to the engagement variables as well but is insignificant. Constructive patriotism was used only to predict attention to politics, because of data limitations, and the relationship was positive but insignificant.

These empirical results further support the conceptual distinction I am making. National identity is not the same as patriotism and the two concepts need to be kept distinct. People who hold a strong national identity feel a deep collective identity with their national group. Patriots feel a deep love for their country. While these two concepts are distinct, the social theory of national identity helps make sense of the relationship between them. As mentioned earlier, Americans hold strongly the norm of patriotism. Good Americans should be patriotic; they should love their country. People who strongly identify with their fellow Americans are more likely than weak identifiers to believe and act in ways that support group norms, including patriotism. Patriotism, like individualism, is a norm, and the group dynamics that drive how national identity works can also explain why strong identifiers should be much more likely than weak identifiers to hold the patriotism norm.

The various research traditions concerning national identity raise important questions: What is national identity? Is it a belief in national principles? Is it the use of racial or religious categories to determine who is in the national group, or is it the rejection that such categories should matter? Is it a sense of being part of the national group? Or is it simply another term for patriotism? This brief overview of scholars' depictions of national identity highlight important contributions to our understanding of American identity but they also raise some troubling considerations. On the positive side, they each pinpoint an important aspect of American identity that must be considered in any research on the topic. American identity rests on a strong set of beliefs – the American Creed – that delineates what Americans believe holds them together as a people. But these beliefs, especially equality and liberty, cannot belie the fact that the United States has a long history of treating certain groups in an inegalitarian way. Nativist visions of the American people crop up whenever there is a public debate about immigration or English language policies. Multiculturalism's emphasis on racial and ethnic identities points to the possible ramifications of ethnoculturalism: If whites have historically defined American identity, then minorities may well feel more comfortable situating their identity in their racial or ethnic group rather than in their national group (Sidanius et al. 1997; Sidanius and Petrocik 2001; Sidanius and Pratto 1999). Civic republicanism highlights the importance of feeling that one is part of a community and recognizing the obligations that promote the common good. Patriotism is a potent norm that guides expectations concerning Americans' attitudes and behaviors. All of these aspects of American identity are important and need to be considered in a theory of American identity. The social theory of national identity is able to include these arguments and determine what role they play in explaining why national identity has such a strong impact on Americans' beliefs about and actions toward their fellow compatriots.

THE CONSEQUENCES OF NATIONAL IDENTITY

Thinking about national identity as a social identity opens up all sorts of possibilities for how national identity affects people's attitudes and behaviors. Social psychologists have long understood the important impact that group dynamics have on people's behavior. Placing national identity into this group context points to certain expectations concerning how the group will affect what people think and do as Americans. Especially important in terms of consequences is the combination of the two group dynamics discussed earlier: commitment and the setting of group boundaries. I argue that the social dynamics of national identity lead to both beneficial and detrimental behaviors within the group. In this research, I am particularly interested in how the combination of commitment and the setting of boundaries affect two types of group behaviors: helping fellow group members and staying loyal to the group.

Helping Fellow Nationals

Miller's (1995) primary claim is that national identity generates a sense of obligation to fellow nationals. In particular, he contends that national identity makes people more supportive of a strong welfare system since they will be concerned about the well-being of their compatriots. Pushing Miller's argument further, this sense of obligation likely goes beyond support for welfare. If people feel a bond with the other members of their national community, even if they will never meet the vast majority of them face to face, they will likely feel obligated to help them in a variety of ways, including by giving to charities, helping in crises, and so on. Overall, then, national identity should be related to feeling an obligation to help one's compatriots in whatever way possible.

Research from social psychology suggests that these arguments might be right. People who strongly identify with their group tend to cooperate with fellow group members rather than going it alone or behaving uncooperatively (Turner 1999). They are willing to make personal sacrifices for the group, helping the group even at personal expense (Doosje, Ellemers, and Spears 1999) and exerting themselves on behalf of the group (Ellemers, Spears, and Doosje 1999b). Just as civic republicans contend, feeling that one is part of a community increases the desire to help the community and to pursue the common good rather than individual self-interest. A positive consequence of national identity, then, is likely to be a greater willingness to do what is necessary to help fellow Americans. Whether it is responding to a natural disaster, volunteering, giving to charity, or supporting a strong welfare system, people who strongly identify as Americans are likely to be the ones who do whatever it takes to help fellow Americans.

This rosy picture becomes murkier, however, when we take into account the setting of group boundaries. If strong identifiers are more likely to set stricter boundaries on the national group, then the question arises concerning who gets helped. Are all Americans equal recipients of the cooperative, community-oriented, helping behaviors? Or are prototypical members more likely to be the beneficiaries of helping behaviors than marginalized group members? Strong identifiers might be more likely to help their fellow Americans, but they set more exclusive boundaries on the group and therefore, I argue, are likely to help only a subset of Americans, those who are prototypical. Indeed, Timothy L. Phillips (1996) found that Australians who held a more exclusive understanding of their national group's boundaries were more opposed to government assistance to aboriginals than were those who held a more inclusive understanding. People who only weakly identify as Americans, on the other hand, are much less likely to help out fellow group members. They simply care less about the well-being of the group and its members than strong identifiers. When they are willing to help, though, their more inclusive boundaries for the American people mean they will be willing to help a broader range of people, both the prototypical and the marginalized. What this means, then, is that the people who are most likely to be helped in the national group are prototypical members because strong identifiers help more but set more exclusive boundaries on the group. When the positive benefits of group membership accrue primarily to prototypical members, marginalized group members are likely to feel anger and resentment. They are Americans too, so why shouldn't they get the same benefits?

Loyalty to the National Group

A second consequence of group identity relates to loyalty to the group, especially in terms of criticism directed at the group and how people respond to it. Strong identifiers are willing to stick by the group and remain loyal when it is going through hard times (Doosje, Ellemers, and Spears 1999). Their desire to protect their group's image manifests itself in being less willing to acknowledge negative information about the group's history and instead to focus on positive aspects of this history (Doosje, Ellemers, and Spears 1999; Ellemers, Spears, and Doosje 1999b). When forced to confront negative information, strong identifiers are more likely to defend the group's actions and to rationalize criticisms targeted at the group (Branscombe et al. 1999). Because of their tendency to focus on the positive and to discount negative information about the group, strong identifiers are also less likely to feel ashamed or guilty about the bad things their group has done (Doosje, Ellemers, and Spears 1999). Bertje Doosje and his colleagues (1998), for example, found that when Dutch subjects were given both positive and negative information about the colonization of Indonesia by the Dutch, strong identifiers were more likely to focus on the positive information and less likely to experience a sense of collective guilt than weak identifiers.

While strong identifiers generally react to criticism by trying to shore up the group and its image, their response likely depends on who is doing the criticizing. This is where group boundaries again become important. When the criticism comes from a marginalized group member, strong identifiers are likely to react by disregarding the criticism and further marginalizing the criticizer. The criticizer is a bad American – unpatriotic, disloyal – and therefore need not be taken seriously. What happens, though, when the critic is a prototypical American? It is likely to be easier to accept criticism of the national group when the criticism comes from a good American with legitimate concerns.

The extent to which people are committed to their group and whether they are inclusive or exclusive in setting group boundaries has important consequences, especially when the ingroup in question is the national group. I examine these two types of consequences of national identity: helping behaviors and group loyalty. The study of these consequences will help determine whether national identity is a good or bad influence on people's attitudes and behaviors.

THE BOOK'S ORGANIZATION

This book weaves together these various arguments to offer a social understanding of national identity, specifically applied to the case of

American national identity. If people truly are social beings who are heavily influenced by the groups to which they belong, then ignoring the social side of national identity provides a misleading picture of people's attachment to their national group. National identity is a social phenomenon, and we need to understand its social aspect to understand its profound influence.

Empirical research on American national identity has focused on people's support of national values and principles, such as egalitarianism, individualism, diversity, and patriotism, not on Americans' identification with the American people. Yet feeling a part of the national group, thinking of the American people as "we," has long been a central aspect of American national identity. Popular sovereignty places the people as a group at the center of the political system. The U.S. Constitution begins, "We the people of the United States ... do ordain and establish the Constitution of the United States of America." The people are the final authority. Discerning what the American people think of this group to which they belong is tremendously important and too often neglected.

My main thesis, that national identity is inherently a social phenomenon and that its social influence has serious political consequences, is heavily informed by work in social psychology and specifically by research from the social identity perspective. Chapter 2 begins to develop this social theory of national identity by focusing on people's level of commitment to their national group. Groups have a profound influence on people's behavior, and the more strongly people identify with a group, the more profound its influence will be. I develop a measure of American national identity that takes into account the social aspect of identity, and I use this measure to discover the extent to which Americans identify with their national group. I further show in a first cut at the data used in this research that national identity strength is strongly related to holding group norms, specifically individualism and patriotism. Finally, I briefly test how commitment relates to people's assessments of their fellow nationals' actions, specifically the choices they make in elections.

I more fully develop the social theory of national identity in Chapter 3 by addressing the setting of group boundaries. I argue that group norms and stereotypes reflect who are the prototypical members of the group and therefore who are the people most fully part of the group. Group members who do not fit the group norms and stereotypes potentially threaten the group boundaries that distinguish the ingroup from outgroups. These group members are pushed to the periphery of the group and marginalized as group members as a means of shoring up the group and its distinctiveness. Since they are marginalized, they don't quite count and can more easily be ignored. Using this argument, I examine empirically where Americans set the boundary on the group "the American people" by determining who fits the group prototype. I also empirically test how people's level of commitment to the group affects the degree of exclusivity of the boundaries they set.

Chapters 4 and 5 provide the main brunt of the empirical analyses concerning the consequences of national identity. Chapter 4 focuses on the obligation to help fellow citizens. I examine the impact of commitment and the setting of boundaries on Americans' sense of obligation to help their fellow Americans. I offer compelling evidence that while people who strongly identify with the American people hold the helping norm more strongly than weak identifiers, their tendency to set harder, more exclusive boundaries on the national group restricts whom they are willing to help. The beneficiaries of this help are not marginalized Americans, yet they are the people who are often most in need of that help. Weak identifiers are less likely to help fellow Americans than strong identifiers, but when they do help, they are especially likely to help marginalized Americans.

Chapter 5 focuses on another prevalent norm in group behavior: loyalty. Specifically, I consider two ways that people can exhibit loyalty toward their national group: Good group members should feel pride in their nation, and they should not criticize the group. Again, I examine the impact of commitment and boundary setting on group loyalty. Strong identifiers are more likely to feel pride and less likely to accept criticism of the group, whereas weak identifiers recognize the value of constructive criticism. But strong identifiers are willing to accept criticism from prototypical group members, just not from marginalized group members. These results reinforce the argument that strong identifiers feel a pronounced compulsion to protect the group, even from its own members. Such behavior, however, does not allow any opportunity for the group to learn from its mistakes.

Chapter 6, the concluding chapter, makes an argument for the social theory of national identity by pointing out the interesting contributions such an approach can make toward our understanding of national identity. It also addresses the normative question, "Is national identity good or bad?" The answer to this question is complex, but I argue that the negatives of national identity outweigh its benefits. I conclude the chapter by offering possible solutions to the problems that arise from national identity that take into account the potent group dynamics that underlie all national, and group, identities.

2

Commitment to the National Group

Americans like the American people. They generally think highly of them, even while acknowledging a few negative characteristics. According to a 2005 Pew Global Attitudes Project poll, the vast majority of Americans thought the American people were hardworking (85 percent), inventive (81 percent), and honest (63 percent). Granted, they also thought Americans were greedy (70 percent) and not religious enough (58 percent), but overall, Americans were significantly more positive about their fellow Americans than they were negative (Pew Research Center 2005). In the Democratic Processes Survey, in 1998, a majority of Americans thought the United States would be better off if Americans made the decisions, not politicians (56 percent), and that Americans could solve the country's problems if they were just given a chance (63 percent) (Hibbing and Theiss-Morse 2002: 112). And in a national random-sample survey of American citizens conducted in the spring of 2002, more Americans agreed (46 percent) with the statement, "the world would be a better place if people from other countries were more like people in the U.S.," than disagreed (37 percent).[1]

Liking one's fellow nationals is important, and these poll results suggest that most Americans hold a very high opinion of their compatriots. But liking the group isn't enough. For people to identify with a group, any group, they need to evaluate the group positively, but they

[1] See the appendix for more information on the survey.

also need to be cognitively aware that they are members of the group
and they need to feel a sense of attachment to the group (Tajfel 1978).
The evaluative component is obviously important. People want to be
part of a good group, a group that in important ways is able to make
them feel better about themselves. Cognitive awareness of membership
is also important. If people do not think they are a member of a group,
it is difficult to identify with the group. The affective component is
the feeling of attachment. The more people feel strongly attached to a
group, the more likely they are to identify with it. The combination of
these components leads to group identities having an important influence on people's attitudes and behaviors. "[G]roups have a profound
impact on us. They influence the attitudes we hold, and the way we
perceive, feel, and act. For example, our ethnic, cultural, and national
group background influences language, accent, dress, cuisine, and a
range of other attributes including profoundly different ways of thinking" (Hogg 2001b: 124).

Thinking of national identity as based in national group membership, rather than as beliefs, history, territory, culture, or ethnicity, as
is often done, raises a number of interesting questions. First, many
groups to which people belong are small, face-to-face groups, making
it easy to know who the other group members are. National groups, on
the other hand, are extremely large and amorphous, and people will
never meet all or even a large portion of their fellow nationals. Can
large groups, such as national groups, influence members' attitudes,
feelings, and behaviors like small groups can? Are people even able to
identify with such large groups where it is shared group membership
that matters, not personally knowing the people in the group?

Second, if people can identify with such a large group, how much
does the strength of their identification vary and what impact does this
variation have? Some people might think of themselves as Americans
frequently, evaluate Americans as a group very positively, and feel a
very deep sense of attachment to fellow Americans. Being an American
is essential to their sense of self. Others, however, might feel much less
of a sense of American identity: They might think of themselves rarely
as an American, evaluate the American people neutrally or negatively,
and feel little if any attachment to their fellow Americans. Who identifies most strongly with their national group and who feels neutral or
actively distances themselves from this same group? And what effect

does a strong commitment have on group members? I argue that the more strongly committed people feel to their national group, the more likely they are to hold strongly the group's norms and the more likely they are to judge group outcomes positively.

This chapter examines these aspects of American national identity by drawing out the social dynamics behind national identity. If we think of the American people as a social group, we can begin to uncover why American identity is such a strong force on people's attitudes and behavior. I begin, therefore, with a discussion of social psychological research on the influence of groups on individuals. I then move to an analysis of commitment. Do people identify strongly with their fellow Americans? I will show in this chapter that people vary in the strength of their national identity, and this variation in commitment will prove to be important throughout the rest of the book. I look at who tends to identify more strongly with the American people and how national identity relates to the American norms of individualism, egalitarianism, and patriotism. Finally, I will briefly address how commitment to the national group affects Americans' assessments of election outcomes. Since it is the American people, as a group, who determine their leaders, then what they think of their fellow citizens should have a significant impact on the legitimacy they accord election outcomes and the politicians they elect.

THE INFLUENCE OF OTHERS ON HUMAN BEHAVIOR

Thinking of the American people as a social group brings into play many of the dynamics of social group behavior examined by evolutionary and social psychologists. Groups place subtle, and often not-so-subtle, pressure on their members to think or act in certain ways. And people accordingly often think and act differently when they are in a group compared to when they are alone. Study after study shows that people's attitudes and behaviors are influenced by those around them. For example, people conform to group judgments (Asch 1958), they obey authority figures (Milgram 1974), they do what needs to be done to uphold a positive reputation (Hoffman, McCabe, and Smith 1996; Larimer 2003), they look for social cues to determine when to help someone in trouble (Darley and Latané 1968), they are less likely to litter when others are around (Reno, Cialdini, and Kallgren 1993),

and even the size of the tip they leave in a restaurant is affected by
whether they are eating alone or in a group (Bodvarsson and Gibson
1997; Freeman et al. 1975). Several factors affect whether people are
influenced by group pressures (Latané 1981), but one of the most significant is how important the group is to the person. Pressures to follow social norms are extremely strong in groups with which people
identify, primarily because the members care deeply about what other
members think of them. The social world matters, and group attachments matter even more.

Take, for example, Solomon E. Asch's conformity research. Asch
(1958) examined whether people would conform to group pressure in
situations where there was a factually correct answer. Participants in
the experiment were asked to determine which of three lines of different lengths matched the test line. All but one of the participants
were confederates in the experiment and on many rounds they gave
an incorrect answer. The experimental participant, faced with the
socially difficult position of going against the group consensus, often
gave the group's answer rather than the factually correct answer. In
an intriguing modification of this experiment, Dominic Abrams and
his colleagues (1990) led some participants to believe that the other
people in the room (the confederates) were in their ingroup (psychology majors) whereas others were led to believe that the confederates
were members of an outgroup (ancient history majors). Conformity
was dramatically higher in the ingroup condition than in the outgroup
condition.

Another example is the polarization effect. Research has found that
people's attitudes become significantly more extreme when they are in a
group of like-minded people (Isenberg 1986; Moscovici and Zavalloni
1969; Myers and Lamm 1976). What happens, though, when we take
into account ingroups and outgroups? Diane M. Mackie and Joel Cooper
(1984) asked participants to offer their opinion on the use of standardized
tests for university admissions, an idea that the participants somewhat
favored. They then listened to a tape offering arguments for retention
or abolition of the tests that were attributed either to their ingroup or
to an outgroup. The results are strong and telling. Participants who listened to an outgroup argument generally took the opposite stance (that
is, if the outgroup made a pro-retention argument, participants became
more pro-abolitionist in their opinion, and the opposite occurred when

they heard a pro-abolition argument). The strongest polarization effects, however, were found in the ingroup condition. Participants who heard a pro-retention argument from their ingroup became much more pro-retention. When they heard a pro-abolition argument from their ingroup, they became much more pro-abolition.

Why are ingroups so important? One answer to this question is that strong ingroup attachments have been essential for human survival. We are, in essence, hard-wired to be social. In the past, living on one's own meant almost certain death, whereas living in groups increased the likelihood that people would survive but also led to potentially fractious relations between ingroups and outgroups (Barkow, Cosmides, and Toobey 1992). As groups became larger, moving from bands to tribes to chiefdoms to states and empires, conflicts between groups, often violent, were common.[2] People needed to figure out quickly who was in the ingroup, and could therefore be trusted, and who was in the outgroup, and therefore needed to be treated warily.

Discerning ingroup members from outgroup members quickly and efficiently places tremendous weight on the cognitive ability of categorization. According to Jerome Bruner (1957), humans have an inescapable need to categorize the world around them. The world is far too complex for people to be able to make sense of it without imposing categories on it. People automatically categorize what they see and thereby simplify and order the world. The category most likely to be used in a particular situation depends on which category is accessible in memory and which category best fits the situation (Bruner 1957). By categorizing the world, though, they also change it. Once people place

---

[2] Small bands had trouble surviving on their own and therefore needed to interact with other bands to exchange goods, people, and information (Caporael 2001). So bands created broader social networks. Over time, in certain environments, these social networks – or tribes – expanded, became agriculturally based, and developed defined hierarchies and task specialization (Diamond 1997). Chiefdoms developed and, in this phase of human existence, social groupings continued their preeminence. Even though people did not interact face to face with all members of the group, being a member of the group still dominated their existence. Finally, these chiefdoms often developed into states, which were larger, more impersonal, and more specialized. The large empires, such as the Roman Empire, expanded across an extended geographical area and incorporated a multi-ethnic mix of peoples (Diamond 1997). These diverse peoples shared a common bond as subjects of the same state even as they differed along numerous dimensions. Fellow ingroup members shared this bond even if they never met face to face.

an object into a category, they tend to see sharper differences *between* categories (accentuation) and diminished differences *within* categories (assimilation) (see, e.g., Tajfel and Wilkes 1963). Because of the strong tendency to accentuate and assimilate, people perceive the members of a category as more similar than they are while at the same time they see differences between the categories as wider than they are (Hogg and Abrams 1988). For example, if four people – two men and two women – are holding a discussion and the two women agree on a particular point whereas the men disagree, the people's sex becomes a salient categorization. The discussion participants are likely to think that the women are similar in many ways, more than just agreeing on the one issue, just as they are likely to believe that the men are similar in many ways. They are also likely to think that the differences between the men and women are much more pronounced than they really are.

According to self-categorization theory, a big difference between categorizing objects and categorizing people is that the self is heavily implicated in the latter. That is, when people categorize people, they are themselves included in the judgment simply by being a fellow ingroup member or a member of the outgroup. All social categorization is done in relation to the self. Upon walking into a room and seeing an African American woman, a white woman can easily categorize her as a woman or as an African American.[3] If she categorizes her as a woman, then they are in the same ingroup (women). The white woman, as the perceiver, views the black woman as similar in many ways because they are both women. She highlights the similarities and downplays the differences. If the white woman categorizes the black woman as an African American, on the other hand, then the black woman is in an outgroup (black rather than white) and is viewed as different in many ways. Differences are accentuated; similarities are downplayed.

Social identity theorists have found that this simple act of placing oneself and others in an ingroup or in an outgroup has profound effects on people's attitudes and behaviors. People are biased in favor of their fellow ingroup members, think more highly of fellow ingroup members than of outgroup members, and at times are more inclined to derogate the outgroup (for a general overview, see Brewer 2003;

---

[3] She could also be categorized as an African American woman, but I'll leave that possibility aside for now.

Hewstone, Rubin, and Willis 2002; Hogg and Abrams 1988). Ingroup members are also more likely to think in terms of the group, moving outside of their individual interests and sense of self. Social identity clearly has strong effects on attitudes and behaviors.

Varying Degrees of Group Commitment

Thus far I have discussed the influence of ingroups on people as if all group members were equally influenced by their group attachment. These general effects of group membership are significant and telling, but it is obvious in the real world of social groups that some group members more strongly identify with their group than other members do. The strength of group identities varies. Anyone who has witnessed a sporting event can see the differences across fans. Nebraska football fans are a good example. Some people enjoy going to a Husker game on a sunny afternoon and hope the Huskers win. Others are in a different stratosphere altogether. Their lives revolve around those Saturday afternoons. They care desperately who wins and will sit through a game from beginning to end regardless of the weather. As a former student of mine once said, "The Huskers are my life." These are the people who are fully committed to their Husker identity.

With a few exceptions, scholars in the social identity research tradition have tended to ignore variation in identity strength. People either identify with a group or they do not. The reason that social identity researchers often conceptualize identity as being either on or off is partly theoretical. According to self-categorization theory, a certain identity becomes salient within a particular context. Granted, what makes a certain identity salient is its fit and its accessibility in memory, and accessibility suggests that certain categories might be more prominent in a person's thinking than others. But most social identity scholars have discussed accessibility as a purely cognitive aspect of identity: People have experienced or are aware of a variety of categories and these are the categories that are accessible at any given time.[4]

---

[4] For example, New Guinean hunters and gatherers have, out of necessity, been deeply aware of the plant life around them, including all of the properties that signify edible versus inedible plants, and therefore have traditionally had numerous highly accessible categories for plant life (Diamond 1997). People living in modern-day Manhattan do not share this same range of categories. The New Guinean has a

From the social identity perspective, then, salient identities reflect the situation at hand. A person can identify as a gardener in one situation and as an American in another. Identities are fluid. But this approach to understanding group identity ignores individual differences in the extent to which people identify with a particular group, what Ellemers, Spears, and Doosje (1999a) call "commitment" and Huddy (2001) calls "shades of identity." As Kay Deaux (2000: 5) states, "Although people may share a common cognitive category, their identification with the category can vary substantially, and these variations have important consequences for behaviour." Social categories are not neutral. They are affectively charged, and the potent affective tags attached to ingroups and outgroups affect accessibility, perceived fit, and ingroup bias (Lodge, Taber, and Burdein 2003; on hot cognitions, see Lodge and Taber 2000, 2005).

Huddy (2001) convincingly argues that many political identifications are long-standing and quite stable, and when an identity is long-standing and stable, it is more likely to be integral to a person's sense of self and to be accessible across many different contexts, even when the fit is poor. For example, strong partisans maintain their party identification over much of their lifetime (Green, Palmquist, and Schickler 2002; Weisberg and Hasecke 1999), and their identification affects a variety of attitudes and behaviors. Weak identifiers, on the other hand, often act as if they have no party identification at all (Petrocik 1974). National groups are another type of political group that invite strong commitments. People are even willing to die for their country. Strong identifiers, those who are highly committed to their national group, do not have a transitory group identity dependent only on context for its existence. In fact, people who strongly identify with a group are less affected by context than people who only weakly identify with a group (Kinket and Verkuyten 1997).[5]

---

wider variety of available categories for plants that might become salient in a given context than the New Yorker does.

[5] Research shows that strength of identification can be influenced by a number of factors, including minority group status, less permeable group boundaries, acquired identities (rather than ascribed), and similarity to the group prototype (see Huddy 2001 for a discussion of these factors). Stephane Perreault and Richard Y. Bourhis (1999) also found that personality factors – ethnocentrism, authoritarianism, and personal need for structure – were significantly related to strength of group identity, with ethnocentrism being the strongest factor. More work needs to be done to

Aside from theoretical considerations, viewing identity salience as fluid and context dependent is also due to the methodological foundation of social identity theory (see, e.g., Huddy 2001). Henri Tajfel's (Tajfel et al. 1971) early work that established the theory used the minimal group paradigm. Tajfel made the important discovery that even in the most minimal of groups, based on an alleged preference for the paintings of Paul Klee or Wassily Kandinsky, a large majority of participants allocated rewards in a way that benefited their group over the other group, even when it meant that their group received a smaller reward in absolute terms than would have been the case if they had been more fair to the other group. The rather arbitrary categorization based on painter preference led to both ingroup favoritism and outgroup discrimination: "the mere act of allocating people to arbitrary social categories is sufficient to elicit biased judgements and discriminatory behavior" (Brown 2000: 283).

Attachments to real groups may well have different properties from minimal group attachments. If the sole salient categorization in a minimal group experiment is an arbitrary one, then people will grab on to that single distinction. But in the real world, categorization is a much more complex process. Any number of categories may be salient at a given time, and crosscutting group memberships may well mollify the effects of any one identity. For example, in the situation in which two men and two women hold a discussion and the people's sex becomes a salient identity, further discussion could reveal that one man and one woman are Democrats and the other two people are Republicans. And the male Republican and the female Democrat might both be native Minnesotans. Of all these various identities, we may find that some of the discussion participants hold a certain identity particularly strongly. One participant might be especially committed to his party identification, another to Minnesotans, and so on. Having a choice of identities and different levels of commitment to those identities makes the real world of group identities potentially quite different from the minimal group laboratory experiment where only one identity is salient.

discover the factors that explain why some people hold a strong identity whereas others only weakly identify with a group.

Discerning a person's level of commitment to a group becomes especially important when we distinguish between voluntary and involuntary group memberships. It makes sense that a person who chooses to join a group will tend to identify strongly with that group (Perreault and Bourhis 1999). Group membership is voluntary and people will likely join groups they value. A gardener will join a gardening club, not a bowling league. But not all group memberships are voluntary. What happens when a person is born into a group and therefore becomes a member through no choice of his or her own? Even if the person does not feel part of the group, others will categorize her as a member of the group. The social view of the person is as a member of the group even if the person does not identify with the group and does not see herself as a group member.

This problem is potentially faced by anyone who is a member of an involuntary group but does not identify with the group. In most studies of social identity, researchers have either assumed a group identification or have ensured it by studying small groups with which members feel a strong attachment. In the real world, though, being a member of a group, especially an involuntary group, does not guarantee identification with the group. Indeed, some people might actively reject membership in a group to which they ascriptively belong. National groups are a good example. National group membership is for the most part involuntary, yet national groups also elicit identities that are clearly stable, long-standing, and often potent. Many Americans will likely identify strongly with their national group but others will not. All of them are Americans, though, whether they want to be or not.

AMERICANS' COMMITMENT TO THEIR NATIONAL IDENTITY

While there is likely to be significant variation in Americans' identification with the American people, overall we can expect their national identity to be strong. National groups are largely involuntary, but national symbols that reinforce identity are pervasive and national groups can command greater sacrifices from members than most other groups (Billig 1995). American national identity is likely to be especially strong following the attacks on the World Trade Center and the Pentagon on September 11, 2001. Threat to a group increases commitment to the group (Branscombe et al. 1999; Thompson et al.

1997), and Americans felt a deep sense of threat after the attacks (Huddy et al. 2002; Huddy et al. 2005).

This sense of increased unity among the American people after September 11 was expressed by several focus group participants in the focus group discussions held for this project.[6] Focus group discussions, consisting of five to ten adults, were held in three locations in early 2002: two in Lincoln, Nebraska (one primarily consisting of white participants and the other consisting solely of African American participants), and one each in Rogers, Arkansas, and Fort Smith, Arkansas (both consisting primarily or solely of whites). In Lincoln, Nebraska, the following exchange reflects a common response when the terrorist attacks were mentioned:

Rachel: ...The nation has become, there is a sense of solidarity, there's a sense of commitment, there is a higher level of pride to be an American, to think in terms of what it means to be an American. ... We have that sense of one nation under God, ... whether it's been prayers, whether it's been churches, people have become less committed to those different, the differences that we have.

John: How long will it last? It won't last that long. How long did it last after Pearl Harbor?

Penny: ... I know that before 9/11, a lot of attitudes were a lot different, even my own. As to today everyone is, you know, is my neighbor, everyone is an American. It's like the lines erase themselves.

In all four focus groups, some participants shared the view that the September 11 attacks changed Americans, making them more united. As one participant in Fort Smith, Arkansas, said, the attacks made Americans mad, and when "you make everyone mad, then they are united."

Some participants, however, disagreed with this view and argued instead that September 11 did not change Americans. On the positive side, Daniel from Lincoln said, "I think Americans have always been good at pulling together." The September 11 events did not bring together a highly disunited group since Americans have always come together easily. Other participants thought that while the terrorist attacks increased patriotic behaviors like flag waving, there was little change in how Americans treated fellow Americans. In the focus

---

[6] See the appendix for details concerning the focus groups.

group in Lincoln, Nebraska, consisting only of African Americans, the following exchange capped a fairly lengthy discussion of patriotism in the black community:

Diane: Why should we throw up flags because of something that just happened September 11th, when a lot of stuff has been going on way before that. I mean I just don't understand why we need to throw up flags and just "Hurray, hurray" to the United States, just throw up a flag because of something that happened on September 11th.

Jim: So you don't buy that "united we are"?

Diane: No. Why should I?

Vanessa: It's been on our currency for how many years? They need another spanking.

This sentiment that Americans were more patriotic but not more united as a group after September 11 was not a prevailing view, but it did come up in all of the focus groups. The African American participants were the most outspoken in these views, but whites in other focus groups raised similar concerns. For example, in the predominantly white focus group in Lincoln, several participants mentioned that America cannot be much of a united community when so many people are living in poverty and are homeless. Overall, however, most of the focus group participants felt a strong sense of attachment to their fellow Americans, whether because of September 11 or not.

To determine the strength of Americans' national identity, a good measure of the concept is needed. There is no clear-cut, straightforward, accepted way to measure national identity. Some scholars have relied on the set of questions asking about the importance of a variety of characteristics for being a "true American" (see, e.g., Citrin et al. 1994; Citrin, Wong, and Duff 2001). This set of questions, used in some surveys from the American National Election Studies and General Social Survey, allows scholars to determine whether people emphasize a belief in democratic principles as key to being an American or if they emphasize demographic characteristics such as race, religion, and being native born. The problem, from my perspective, is that these questions do not measure identity directly. Rather, they measure the boundaries of the national group. These questions also do not get at the social nature of national identity. If national identity entails identifying with one's national group, then a measure of national identity needs to take into account a sense of membership with the national group.

Social psychologists have expended more effort than political scientists in trying to find a good measure of group identity. For example, Tom R. Tyler and Steven Blader (2000) break down group identity into three parts: cognitive identification, pride, and respect (see also Smith and Tyler 1997). Their measures of cognitive identification fully engage the notion that group identification entails having the group be part of one's sense of self. A person who identifies with a group thinks of himself or herself in group terms, and the experiences of the group become the person's experiences. Tyler and Blader therefore ask people in a work setting, for example, if "being a [occupation] is important to the way I think of myself as a person," and, "I feel that the problems of the [company or organization] are my own 'personal' problems," among many other questions. Karen Trew and Denny E. Benson (1996) discuss identity in terms of salience, commitment, and sense of authenticity. Salience refers to how important the group identity is to the person, commitment refers to the perceived social pressures that increase commitment to the group, and sense of authenticity refers to the idea that the identity genuinely reflects who the person is.

Drawing on this social psychological literature on measuring group identity, I measured American national identity using four items that get at the cognitive, evaluative, and affective components of a social identity that Tajfel argued are the components of a social identity. A national random-sample telephone survey, the Public Perceptions of the American People survey, was specially commissioned in mid-2002 to examine in depth Americans' identification with their fellow citizens.[7] Respondents – 1,254 adult American citizens – were asked a series of questions about their perceptions of the American people as well as various demographic and political attitude questions. One of the first questions respondents were asked concerned their identification with a variety of social groups, including "the American people":

People differ in how attached they feel to, or how much they identify with, the various social groups they belong to. For instance, being male or female

[7] See the appendix for information on the national survey.

puts people in the group of "men" or "women," but people may differ in how much they feel part of that group. I'd like to know how much you feel part of the following groups. Let's say "1" means you do not feel part of the group at all and "7" means you feel very strongly part of the group, while 2 through 6 indicate something in between.

Respondents were then asked about a variety of social groups (in randomized order): people in your racial or ethnic group, people who are the same sex as you, people who do the same kind of work as you, people who share your religious beliefs, people from your region of the country, people from your state, and the American people. Overall, people said they identified strongly with all of the groups. The mean responses ranged from 5.24 (for region of the country) to 5.82 (for the American people), where 7 signifies the strongest identification with the group. The variation across the groups in the percentage of people giving the extreme response of 7 is more telling. Figure 2.1 provides data on the percentage of people who said they feel very strongly part of the group (7) for each type of group. Whereas less than a third of respondents said they strongly identify with their state, about half said they felt the strongest identification possible with the American people. Americans obviously feel a strong sense of being part of their national group.

This question on identifying with the American people is a good one, but to get at the various components of a social identity, more questions are needed. The national identity measure that I created also includes responses to other questions, two of which get at the cognitive and affective components of social identity: "Being an American is important to the way I think of myself as a person" (the cognitive component), and, "I am a person who feels strong ties to the American people" (the affective component). Response options ranged from strongly disagree to strongly agree. As was true with the first identity question, Americans responded generally positively to these questions. The means were 4.0 for the cognitive component and 4.2 for the affective component (where 1 is strongly disagree and 5 is strongly agree with the statement). To measure the final – evaluative – component, I used a series of questions asking respondents to rate the American people on several polar adjectives: "I would like you to tell me what you think of the American people as a group. Let's think about being informed about politics. If 1 is extremely uninformed and

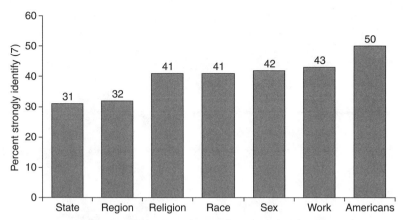

FIGURE 2.1. Percentage of respondents who strongly identify with various social groups

7 is extremely informed, with 2 through 6 in between, where would you place the American people?" Respondents were also asked to rate the American people on how unselfish or selfish, tolerant or intolerant, and untrustworthy or trustworthy they are. Responses to these items were added together to create one evaluative component ranging from 4 to 28. The mean score for the evaluative component was 18.

The American national identity index was created by rescaling the responses to the four American identity items so that they ranged from 0 to 1 and then adding those items together. The American identity scale ranges from 0 to 4, where 0 means that respondents reject an identity with the American people and 4 means they have a very strong identification with their national group. As was obvious from the single indicators, Americans tend to identify strongly with the American people (see Figure 2.2). Just over half of all respondents scored 3 or higher on the index, and the average score was 2.9. Only a handful of people – seventeen in all – received a score of less than 1. In the post–September 11 world, Americans identify strongly with their national group.

While Americans overall tend to hold a strong national identity, there is variation in commitment to the national group. Who among the diverse array of Americans is most likely to hold a strong national identity? To answer this question, I regressed the American identity index on a battery of demographic and political attitude

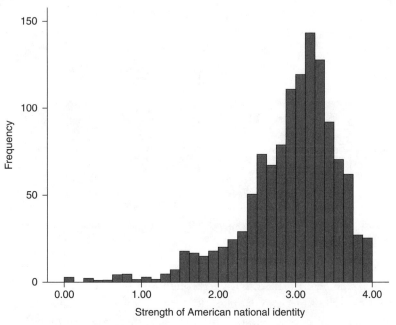

FIGURE 2.2. Respondents' American identity strength (using the American identity scale)

variables. Some expectations concerning who is most likely and who is least likely to identify with the American people come readily to mind. Given the racial stereotype that Americans are white, it is likely that people of color will feel less committed to an American national identity than whites who are not Hispanic. Similarly, if Americans are assumed to be Christian, then non-Christians might well feel alienated from such a Christian-hued national identity. Expectations concerning political attitudes come less readily to mind. Huddy and Khatib (2007) argue that national identity, which they measure as feeling American, should not have an ideological bent since feeling American does not carry any ideological baggage (whereas patriotism does, with uncritical patriots being conservative and constructive patriots liberal). Simply feeling American, however, does not take into account all three components of identity used in my measure. Nonetheless, I have no reason to expect my measure of national identity to be ideological in nature. Huddy and Khatib (2007) further show that national identity is negatively related to education. Given this negative relationship, it might also be the case that national identity is negatively related to political knowledge. Finally, since national identity is a social identity, attitudes toward people in general and toward group attachments in particular might affect attachments to the American people as a group. I therefore included two additional variables: interpersonal trust (more trusting people are likely to identify more strongly with their national group) and the tendency to identify with groups (people who tend to identify with any number of groups are more likely to identify with their national group).

The results of the regression analysis are shown in Table 2.1.[8] In terms of demographics, religion and race are indeed significant predictors of holding a strong national identity. Christians are significantly more likely than non-Christians to identify strongly with the American people, whereas blacks are significantly less likely than whites, the dropped category, to identify with the American people. Hispanics and other people of color, on the other hand, do not significantly differ from whites in their national identity. In general, not being considered a prototypical American – and, as I'll argue in the next chapter, being marginalized as an American – affects the extent to which people feel connected to their national group. Non-Christians and blacks tend to distance themselves from their American identity, an identity that often excludes them. Age is the second-best predictor of national identity, with older people being much stronger identifiers than younger people. Whether this is a life-cycle effect or a generational effect cannot be parsed out with cross-sectional data, but the relationship between age and national identity strength is very strong. The only other significant demographic predictor is education, with the highly educated having weaker identities. Perhaps surprisingly, income is not related to having a strong American identity. The stereotype of Americans as relatively wealthy, or at least comfortable, is widespread, yet the poor and wealthy alike identify strongly as Americans.

Moving on to the political attitude variables, Huddy and Khatib (2007) found that ideology was unrelated to national identity, but ideology matters in this study. Conservatives of whatever stripe do

---

[8] See the appendix for the measures used in the following analysis.

TABLE 2.1. *What explains commitment to an American national identity?*

	American identity
Sex (male)	.010 (.009)
Age	.106*** (.023)
Native-born	.021 (.023)
Race (whites excluded category):	
Black	−.038** (.014)
Hispanic	.027 (.016)
Other race	−.015 (.019)
Christian	.027* (.011)
Education	−.050** (.016)
Income	.011 (.019)
Ideology (moderates excluded category):	
Extremely conservative	−.009 (.017)
Somewhat conservative	.003 (.013)
Somewhat liberal	−.005 (.017)
Extremely liberal	−.078*** (.024)
Party identification (Independents excluded category):	
Strong Republican	.026 (.014)
Weak Republican	.006 (.013)
Weak Democrat	−.013 (.013)
Strong Democrat	.011 (.013)
Political knowledge	−.036* (.016)
Interpersonal trust	.048*** (.011)
Tendency to identify with groups	.330*** (.021)
Constant	.424*** (.033)
F	21.98***
Adj. R^2	.32
N	898

Source: Perceptions of the American People Survey, 2002
Note: * $p < .05$; ** $p < .01$; *** $p < .001$. Results are from ordinary least squares (OLS) regression analyses. Cell entries are unstandardized regression coefficients with standard errors in parentheses. All dependent and independent variables have been transformed to range from 0 to 1. See the appendix for variable details.

not differ significantly from moderates (the dropped category) in their national identity strength, nor do those who say they are somewhat liberal. But those who say they are extremely liberal do. The extremely liberal are much less likely to hold a strong national identity than moderates, conservatives, or more moderate liberals. While extreme conservatives and the somewhat liberal are less likely than moderates to identify with their fellow Americans, the relationships are far from significant. Extreme liberals stand alone from all other ideological groups in the extent to which they are willing to distance themselves from their national identity. The differences in how national identity is measured in the two studies might well explain the different findings. Rather than focusing on only one component of identity, I include all three components in my measure, which might affect the results. It also might be that breaking ideology into categories matters since the relationship between ideology and national identity strength is not linear.[9] Extreme conservatives are not the reverse of extreme liberals. They are instead very similar to moderates. The results also show that while national identity is related to ideology, it is not related to party identification.

People's engagement in the political system and with other people also has a pronounced effect on the extent to which Americans identify with their fellow Americans. People who are more knowledgeable about politics are significantly less likely to identify with the American people than are the less knowledgeable. Interestingly, it is engagement with other people that matters the most. Interpersonal trust is strongly related to commitment to the American people. People who are trusting of others are much more likely to be strong identifiers. The best predictor of American identity, though, is the tendency to identify with any group. Whether it is a matter of personality or social orientation, some people are more likely than others to identify with a wide range of groups, including the group the American people.

An interesting aspect of the characteristics related to national identity is that an obvious consistent pattern does not emerge. In studies

---

[9] When the seven-point ideology scale is included in the model, rather than the dummy ideology variables, ideology is not significant at the .05 level or even the more permissive .10 level.

of political participation or political knowledge, for example, having higher socioeconomic status and holding a more privileged position in society are related to participating more and knowing more (Delli Carpini and Keeter 1996; Verba, Schlozman, and Brady 1995). When it comes to national identity, socioeconomic status is not a consistent predictor of national identity. The less educated identify more with their national group, but income is insignificant. Social engagement increases national identity strength but political engagement, as measured by political knowledge, decreases this identity. A pattern that does emerge, however, is that people who fit the stereotype of the prototypical American identify more strongly with the American people than those who do not. Whites identify more strongly whereas blacks do not. Christians identify more strongly than people who are not Christians. This pattern will be explored more fully in the next chapter.

NATIONAL IDENTITY, AMERICAN PRINCIPLES, AND PATRIOTISM

In Chapter 1, I argued that national identity needs to be conceptualized differently from several popular understandings of the term, especially the notion that national identity is about believing in a certain set of principles. National identity is not adherence to a set of principles or beliefs, although strong identifiers are more likely to hold group norms, and some of these norms might be certain beliefs or principles. A person who holds a strong American identity, for example, is more likely than a weak identifier to believe in individualism and to be patriotic because these are normative beliefs associated with Americans. The beliefs are not national identity but norms promoted by the national group, and holding those norms is what good Americans do. The group is much more a part of strong identifiers' sense of self, and therefore the group norms are a much stronger guide for their attitudes and behavior than is true for weak identifiers.

To test the relationship between national identity and people's belief in American principles and patriotism, I again used the Perceptions of the American People Survey. Individualism was measured using a single question: "Any person who is willing to work hard has a good chance of succeeding." Response options were strongly disagree, disagree, neither agree nor disagree, agree, and strongly agree. I also analyze whether strong identifiers are more likely to be patriotic than weak identifiers. I measured patriotism using three questions: "I feel proud to be an American," "Generally the U.S. is a better country than most other countries," and, "I cannot think of another country in which I would rather live." Response options ranged from strongly disagree to strongly agree.

I also examine beliefs in equality, although the questions I used to measure this concept are less than ideal, a problem that will crop up in later chapters as well. Respondents were asked, "If people were treated more equally in this country, we would have many fewer problems," and, "One of the big problems in this country is that we do not give everyone an equal chance," with the same strongly disagree to strongly agree range of response options. Responses to these two questions were combined to create one egalitarianism measure. The problem with these equality questions is that they do not measure whether people hold a belief in equality. Instead, they measure whether people think the United States has achieved an acceptable level of equality. People who strongly believe in equality can strongly agree with these statements, believing the United States needs to do more in its pursuit of equality, or they can strongly disagree, believing that the United States has already achieved equality. In both cases, equality is held as a principle, but how successfully the principle has been put into practice is open for debate. I use this measure of equality here to determine whether a strong national identity is related to egalitarianism, but I fully recognize the measure has limitations.

Do strong identifiers follow their group norms more than weak identifiers? Are they more likely to espouse the American beliefs and principles held dear by the American people? Figure 2.3 suggests that, in general, they are. I divided the American identity scale into three groups – weak, medium, and strong identity – corresponding to the one-third of respondents who scored lowest on the scale, the one-third who scored in the middle range, and the one-third who scored highest. I then determined how each group fared compared to the means on the individualism, egalitarianism, and patriotism scales. As the figure shows, only the egalitarianism results are counter to expectations. Weak identifiers score higher than the mean on this measure

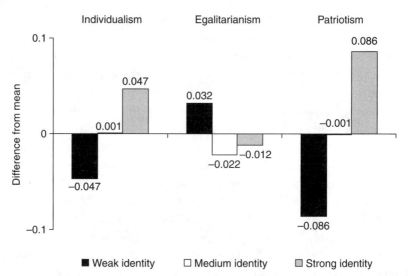

FIGURE 2.3. Differences from mean support for individualism, egalitarianism, and patriotism by strength of American identity

whereas strong identifiers score slightly lower than the mean.[10] Both individualism and patriotism are significantly related to national identity strength, as expected. Strong identifiers are much more likely than weak identifiers to believe in individualism and to be patriotic. Good Americans hold dearly the group norms of individualism and patriotism. Weak identifiers, on the other hand, are much more likely to shun these norms.

To test these arguments more fully, I regressed individualism, egalitarianism, and patriotism on American identity and a variety of standard control variables (demographics and political attitudes). I expect to find that even when these possible predictors of American principles are controlled, American identity remains the most potent predictor of these beliefs. Americans whose sense of self is fully embedded in the group "the American people" subscribe fully to the group

---

[10] In Chapter 5, I examine the reactions of strong and weak identifiers to criticisms of the United States. The problem of the wording of the egalitarianism measure becomes especially salient in this context. The measure could be taken as a criticism of the United States, that it has not done enough in achieving equality, and strong identifiers tend to react negatively to criticisms of the United States and the American people.

norms. Being a good American demands believing in individualism and patriotism. It also means believing in equality, but not in a critical sense. For the egalitarianism measure, then, I expect to find a negative relationship with identity strength.

Table 2.2 provides clear, unequivocal evidence that feeling a strong attachment to the American people increases the likelihood that Americans will hold strongly the norms of individualism and patriotism. Even controlling various sociodemographic variables, ideology, and party identification, national identity has a pronounced impact on the extent to which Americans are individualistic and patriotic. Moving from the weakest to the strongest identity increases belief in individualism by almost half the scale (.413 on a 0 to 1 scale) and patriotic beliefs by over half of the scale (.625 on a 0 to 1 scale). National identity is far and away the best predictor of these two sets of beliefs, far outstripping all of the other variables in the model. The same cannot be said for egalitarianism, however. American identity is negatively related to beliefs about equality in the United States, with weak identifiers believing more needs to be done to increase equality. The relationship, however, is much weaker than for individualism and patriotism, although it is still significant. A change from the weakest to the strongest identity decreases egalitarianism beliefs by only .12, a much smaller effect than was the case for individualism and patriotism.

THE AMERICAN PEOPLE AND THEIR CHOICES
ON ELECTION DAY

People who are strongly committed to their national identity tightly merge their sense of self with their national group. They often think of themselves as Americans, they have a positive regard for the American people, and they feel a deep sense of attachment to their group. According to the social identity perspective, people want to be part of a group they like because it increases their sense of self-esteem. Being a member of the group makes them feel good. Being a member of a higher status group makes them feel even better (Tajfel and Turner 1986). It is not surprising, then, that people tend to exhibit an ingroup positivity bias (Brewer 1999; Spears, Doojse, and Ellemers 1999). That is, they favor their ingroup over outgroups in many different ways.

TABLE 2.2. *American national identity, American principles, and patriotism*

	Individualism	Egalitarianism	Patriotism
American identity	.413*** (.049)	−.120* (.050)	.625*** (.029)
Sex (male)	.015 (.015)	−.048** (.015)	−.007 (.009)
Age	−.105** (.037)	.041 (.038)	−.041 (.022)
Race (whites excluded category):			
Black	−.038 (.024)	.107*** (.025)	−.013 (.014)
Hispanic	.037 (.028)	.050 (.028)	.009 (.016)
Other race	−.101*** (.032)	.051 (.032)	.013 (.019)
Education	−.006 (.027)	−.046 (.028)	−.038* (.016)
Income	.027 (.031)	−.001 (.032)	.039* (.018)
Christian	−.018 (.019)	−.035 (.019)	.008 (.011)
Political knowledge	.056* (.027)	−.128*** (.027)	.024 (.016)
Ideology (moderates excluded category):			
Extremely conservative	.017 (.029)	−.036 (.030)	.008 (.017)
Somewhat conservative	.003 (.022)	−.023 (.022)	.027* (.013)
Somewhat liberal	.012 (.029)	.023 (.029)	−.005 (.017)
Extremely liberal	−.115** (.037)	.164*** (.038)	−.029 (.022)
Party identification (Independents excluded category):			
Strong Republican	.037 (.024)	−.108*** (.024)	.016 (.014)
Weak Republican	.025 (.022)	−.101*** (.023)	.012 (.013)
Weak Democrat	−.048* (.022)	−.007 (.022)	−.014 (.013)
Strong Democrat	−.023 (.022)	.032 (.023)	−.010 (.013)
Constant	.483*** (.043)	.829*** (.044)	.375*** (.025)
F	8.06***	12.94***	33.38***
Adj. R²	.12	.18	.38
N	975	971	972

Source: Perceptions of the American People Survey, 2002
Note: * p < .05; ** p < .01; *** p < .001. Results are from OLS regression analyses. All of the dependent and independent variables have been transformed to range from 0 to 1. See the appendix for variable details

Marilynn B. Brewer and Donald T. Campbell (1976), for example, found that almost all of the East African ethnic groups studied rated their ingroup higher than outgroups in terms of such characteristics as trustworthiness, obedience, honesty, and friendliness. People who strongly identify with their group are especially likely to favor it. They are more likely to view their group in a positive, group-oriented light, and they are more attracted to fellow group members than weak identifiers (Turner 1999). Fellow group members are a good bunch of people in many ways, and the strong identifier is one of them. Assessments of the group, then, are assessments of the strong identifiers themselves. Strong identifiers are therefore more likely to think well of their fellow Americans than are weak identifiers.

Believing that fellow group members share positive traits is important, especially when the group is one's national group. In a democratic political system such as that of the United States, the people are sovereign and as such they make collective decisions that have an impact on the polity. If people view the American people, the sovereign collective, as holding the qualities necessary to make good political decisions, then they will view those decisions as more legitimate and as simply better than if the qualities of the collective are questionable. Decisions made by a good group of people must surely be better than decisions made by people whose qualities are questionable. An important area where a positivity bias toward fellow Americans likely makes a big difference is in people's judgments concerning election outcomes. Since it is Americans as a group who vote in elections, perceiving fellow Americans in a positive or negative light can affect evaluations of election outcomes and the perceived legitimacy of those outcomes. A national group held in a negative light would likely elect bad, or at least mediocre, people to office.

Beyond the positivity bias, though, people who strongly identify with their group are significantly more likely than weak identifiers to show deference to the group's leaders (Branscombe et al. 1999; Hogg 2001a). Conflict over the leaders decreases the group's consensus, thereby weakening the group. Since strong identifiers want their group to be strong and healthy, they are likely to refrain from being too critical of their leaders or of the process that leads to the selection of those leaders. Strong identifiers are also likely to view group leaders as embodying the group's norms and values (Ellemers, Spears, and

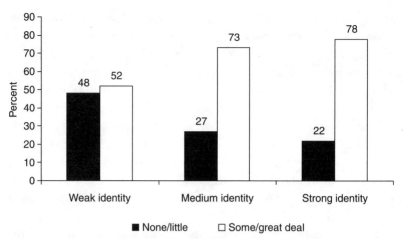

FIGURE 2.4. Strength of American identity and level of confidence in the wisdom of the American people on Election Day

Doosje 1999a). Group members, who hold these norms and values, will select the best group leaders possible. I therefore expect, for both reasons, to find that national identity strength is significantly related to positive evaluations of electoral choices.

Survey respondents were asked, "How much trust and confidence do you have in the wisdom of the American people when it comes to making choices on Election Day – a great deal, some, a little, or none?" Figure 2.4 shows that strong identifiers are much more likely than weak identifiers to judge Americans' electoral choices positively. Over three-quarters of strong identifiers (78 percent) have "some" or "a great deal" of trust and confidence in the wisdom of the American people on Election Day. Their fellow Americans make good vote choices. In contrast, weak identifiers are much less likely to give their fellow Americans this benefit of the doubt. Only half of weak identifiers (52 percent) have the same level of trust and confidence in Americans' vote choices.

This simple bivariate result, however, might be due to the characteristics of those who tend to be strong identifiers or weak identifiers. To test for this possibility, I regressed the wisdom of the vote question on various demographic and political attitude variables and the American identity scale. The election that took place closest to the survey was the controversial presidential election of 2000. Perhaps because of the nature of that election, with the popular vote going to Al Gore and the electoral college vote to George W. Bush, party identification is a less strong predictor than might normally be the case (see Table 2.3). Strong Republicans are much more likely than Independents (the dropped category) to have confidence in Americans' vote choices, but all other partisan groups do not differ significantly from Independents in their assessments. And while strong Republicans have a positive reaction to Americans' electoral choices, people who are extremely conservative are decidedly negative. The more highly educated and males are also more critical of Americans' wisdom on Election Day, whereas people of color and those who are more trusting of people in general are more positive.

The variable of interest, though, is national identity. As expected, American identity strength shows up as the strongest predictor in the model, far surpassing all other variables. Strong identifiers think highly of their fellow Americans and this translates into more positive assessments of the choices these people make. Strong identifiers also want their group to be successful, and choosing the best leaders for the national group is essential for group maintenance. Strong identifiers are motivated to believe group leadership choice is the best possible, and clearly the American people as a group are well able to make that choice on election day.[11]

CONCLUSION

If we think of national identity as a social identity, rather than as a simple manifestation of patriotism or the national principles that people hold or people's nativist tendencies, the concept takes on important dimensions that have been largely ignored in previous research.

---

[11] I ran the same regression analysis including patriotism in the model (data not shown) to see whether a simple love of country was driving these results. The results of the enlarged model are strikingly similar to those shown in Table 2.3. All of the signs and significance levels of the control variables are the same in the two models. American identity also remains the strongest predictor of people's confidence in Americans' electoral choices (b = .403, se = .067). Patriotism, on the other hand, is insignificant (b = .07, se = .061). It is feeling that one is a part of the national group that affects assessments of election outcomes, not love of country.

TABLE 2.3. *American identity and the wisdom of the vote on Election Day*

	Confidence in wisdom of Americans on Election Day
American identity	.454*** (.054)
Sex (male)	−.042* (.016)
Age	.008 (.042)
Race (people of color)	.042* (.020)
Education	−.076* (.030)
Income	−.026 (.034)
Political knowledge	−.021 (.031)
Political interest	.026 (.030)
Interpersonal trust	.075*** (.021)
Ideology (moderates excluded category):	
Extremely conservative	−.122*** (.033)
Somewhat conservative	−.006 (.024)
Somewhat liberal	.048 (.031)
Extremely liberal	−.016 (.042)
Party identification (Independents excluded category):	
Strong Republican	.053* (.026)
Weak Republican	.044 (.025)
Weak Democrat	.012 (.024)
Strong Democrat	.027 (.024)
Constant	.236*** (.047)
F	9.13***
Adj. R^2	.13
N	953

Source: Perceptions of the American People Survey, 2002
Note: * $p < .05$; ** $p < .01$; *** $p < .001$. The results are based on OLS regression analyses. The dependent variable and all of the independent variables have been transformed to range from 0 to 1. See the appendix for variable details.

People are members of their national group. Any understanding of national identity needs to take into account both the social influences and pressures that affect national group members and the largely involuntary nature of national group membership. This chapter has addressed these two essential features of national identity. People's level of commitment to their national group varies, and that variation helps explain key attitudes of the American people. People think and behave differently when their sense of self is deeply enmeshed with their national group. They behave and think like good group members.

Who identifies most strongly with the American people? Strong identifiers tend to be older, Christian, less educated, less politically knowledgeable, trusting of other people, and likely to identify with many social groups. They also tend not to be black or extremely liberal. Some of these characteristics suggest that strong identifiers tend to be more in the mainstream of American society, that they are what might be considered "typical Americans." Christians, for example, live in a society that many consider a "Christian nation." That they feel more attached to this national group flows from being fully accepted as typical Americans. Blacks, on the other hand, have frequently been reminded of their marginal status as Americans across U.S. history. It is perhaps not surprising that African Americans put some distance between themselves and this national group to which they belong. In the next chapter, I will use social identity theory to argue why these results make sense. Group dynamics lead to certain members fully embracing their involuntary group membership whereas others feel a need to distance themselves from their national group.

Yet overall, in post-9/11 America and the atmosphere of threat that pervaded American society after the attacks, Americans feel a strong sense of identity with their fellow Americans. They think of themselves as Americans, they think the American people are good as a group, and they feel strongly attached to their national group. The more strongly people hold these three components of national identity, the more eagerly they embrace the principles that constitute American norms. People who strongly identify with their national group want to be good group members, and this means believing in what the group deems important. Individualism and patriotism are certainly beliefs that Americans hold dearly. It is no surprise, then, that strong identifiers are much more individualistic and patriotic than weak identifiers. Weak identifiers want to distance themselves from their national group. Not holding the group norms, or holding them in a lukewarm fashion, is one way to let others know that they are not typically American, that they are not fully in the national group.

Group dynamics also play a role in how positively people evaluate their group's collective decisions. Strong identifiers think positively of their fellow group members and they want to be members of a good group. These positive assessments of the national group and its members are especially important when it comes to election outcomes. Even controlling party identification and ideology, people who strongly identify with the American people are much more likely to think Americans' choices during elections are wise than people who only weakly identify with their fellow Americans. This finding suggests that they would view election outcomes as more legitimate than weak identifiers: The people make wise decisions concerning the leadership of their national group and therefore the leaders are given a deeper legitimacy than would be the case if people thought Americans' electoral choices were bad.

Throughout this chapter, I have skirted key aspects of group identification: group stereotypes, prototypicality, and the setting of group boundaries. Group commitment is heavily intertwined with these aspects of the group. I devote the next chapter to laying out why and how groups set boundaries and what this means for national groups in particular. In doing so, I will pull together the various aspects of national identity that have been raised in the existing research. American principles and values, ethnocultural understandings of the American people, and the perception of the American people as a national community all play a role in who gets included in the group and who is marginalized.

3

The Setting of National Group Boundaries

On February 9, 1950, Joseph McCarthy, the junior senator from Wisconsin, gave a speech to a Republican women's club in Wheeling, West Virginia. McCarthy used the speech to unveil a list of 205 individuals he alleged were communists working in the U.S. government. The major theme of the speech, though, was that the United States, a Christian nation, was under attack from godless communists:

Today we are engaged in a final, all-out battle between communistic atheism and Christianity. The modern champions of communism have selected this as the time, and ladies and gentlemen, the chips are down – they are truly down. ... Can there be anyone who fails to realize that ... this is the time for the show-down between the democratic Christian world and the communistic atheistic world? (McCarthy 1950).

The battle was a moral one between good Christian Americans and godless communist traitors who had been "born with silver spoons in their mouths" right in America. It was McCarthy's moral duty to cleanse the United States of these atheistic traitors.

McCarthy's short but potent career hunting down supposed communists in the United States government is revealing. He was a highly controversial figure during his time largely because his lists of supposed communist sympathizers were rarely backed up with any evidence, but most people agreed with his basic message if not his tactics: Communists were bad and, more important for the purposes of this research, America was a Christian nation. If the United States

was – and is, as some argue – a Christian nation, then it makes sense to
view Americans as Christian. What happens, then, to Americans who
are not Christians? Are they not Americans, or not quite Americans?
Or are they just bad Americans?

This chapter examines some of the dynamics especially important to national identity: group norms, group stereotypes, prototypical members, and the setting of group boundaries.[1] Drawing on the
social identity approach, especially self-categorization theory, I argue
that group norms and stereotypes are exemplified by prototypical
group members who most clearly help to distinguish the ingroup from
outgroups. They are therefore fundamental to understanding where
people set group boundaries, that is, the boundaries that demarcate
who is included in or excluded from the group. If the United States is
a Christian nation, for example, and communist countries are athe-
ist, then Joseph McCarthy and others could use this characteristic to
demarcate Americans from communists.

But boundaries are important not just to intergroup relations. They
are also important to intragroup dynamics. The historical context
makes certain characteristics more prototypical than others, but political leaders and other elites also expend a great deal of effort defining
the American people in a way that suits them politically. Historical
context and elite behavior resound with people's psychological desire
for distinctiveness to make the setting of group boundaries an important political force. Group members who deviate from what is prototypical are potentially threatening to the group because they make the
group appear less exclusive and less distinctive. In essence, they muddy
the group boundaries and that raises questions about the group's viability. It's one thing to have Russians be atheists. It's another thing
to have Americans be atheists because what, then, differentiates the
two national groups? The ingroup's boundaries must be shored up.

---

[1] Many other group dynamics are important to understanding social identities and, in
particular, national identity, such as the impact of group leadership. Future research
should examine how political leaders affect people's understandings of their national
identity. In this regard, it is important to note that political leaders often refer to "the
American people" as if they were a cohesive, single-minded group. It is also clearly
the case that political leaders influence group norms, what is considered prototypical, and where the boundaries of the group are drawn. I focus on Americans' views
of these dynamics and leave the impact of group leadership to other researchers.

Group members who are not prototypical because they do not fit the norms and stereotypes are marginalized, pushed to the periphery of the group, and treated differently from prototypical members.

These issues of prototypicality and group boundaries raise fundamental issues for understanding the American people as a social group. Who are prototypical Americans? Who gets marginalized? Political theorists have made a distinction between civic and ethnic nations: Civic nations are based on shared beliefs and principles, whereas ethnic nations are based on shared ascriptive characteristics and ancestry (Greenfeld 1992; Ignatieff 1994). I argue that in the United States, both civic and ethnic concerns come into play when defining who is an American. Americans widely believe in liberal principles such as equality and freedom, but they also tend to believe that being an American entails certain ascriptive characteristics. The boundaries based on ascriptive concerns make group membership more difficult to attain and establish more clearly who the prototypical versus marginalized group members are. I further argue that the more strongly people identify with their national group, the more likely they are to set clearer and more exclusionary boundaries on the group. It is strong identifiers who care the most about their national group's viability.

I test these theoretical arguments about the setting of boundaries in two ways. First, I examine people's perceptions of whether they are typical Americans and how homogeneous they think their national group is. When people view Americans as a homogeneous group of people like them, their own characteristics are telling about who they consider to be full members of the group and who doesn't fit. Second, I ask people what makes someone "truly American." Even if people do not like the norms and stereotypes associated with their national group, they are aware of how others perceive the group and who fits as the prototypical member. These two alternative methods offer a picture of the boundaries that determine who is prototypical as an American and who is not. These two methods therefore bring us closer to determining who people perceive to be full members of the national group and who is marginalized. I end the chapter with an analysis of the effects of level of commitment on who sets more exclusive boundaries for the group and what this means for understanding American national identity and its effects.

THE SETTING OF GROUP BOUNDARIES

The United States has established clear, well-demarcated, objective boundaries concerning who is and who is not an American citizen. People who are born in the United States are U.S. citizens, as are children born to U.S. citizens who are residing overseas at the time of birth. For people not born in the United States or to U.S. citizens, the requirements to become a U.S. citizen are straightforward: Applicants for naturalization must be at least eighteen years old, have resided in the United States for at least five years, not have committed certain crimes, read and speak English, be attached to the Constitution and its principles, demonstrate basic knowledge concerning U.S. history and government, and take the Oath of Allegiance.[2] At times, these objective national group boundaries work well for determining the ingroup from the outgroup. American citizens carry a U.S. passport when traveling overseas and anyone waiting in line at Customs can see who is an American and who is not. American citizens also have the right to do certain things that non-citizens cannot, such as voting in elections. Everyone waiting in line to vote on Election Day is likely a U.S. citizen.

But if the national group is an imagined community, as Benedict Anderson (1991) says, then the setting of group boundaries is an important phenomenon to study. The boundaries of a social group determine who is in the group and who is not. Hard and fast boundaries make the distinction clear. Boundaries that are murky make it much more difficult to discern group members from those who do not belong in the group. The setting of boundaries therefore plays an extremely important role in the life of social groups, especially national groups. Whereas most research on group boundaries focuses on distinguishing the ingroup from outgroups, I argue that boundaries affect internal group dynamics and these effects have not been studied enough.[3] Some members who are objectively in the group might be marginalized because they are not imagined fully in the group.

---

[2] These requirements are outlined on the U.S. Citizenship and Immigration Services web site (http://www.uscis.gov/graphics/services/natz/general.htm), accessed June 8, 2006.

[3] But see George Lakoff's (1987) arguments concerning prototype theory and recent work by Michael Hogg and his colleagues (Hogg 2005; Hogg, Fielding, and Darley 2005; Hogg and Reid 2006) on inclusion and exclusion.

What determines who is marginalized and who is fully included in the group? The setting of group boundaries is not a neutral process and is influenced both by the collective memories of the group and by political elites who work hard to define the national group (see, e.g., Stuckey 2004). A brief look at a country's history reveals many of the boundaries set, but salient boundaries can also change over time. It was not all that long ago in U.S. history that Irish Americans and Italian Americans were not fully included in the national community. Now they are. But some people have long been marginalized – African Americans are a good example. It is group norms and stereotypes that establish the central characteristics, beliefs, and behaviors that distinguish the status of group members. Members who best exemplify these norms and stereotypes are the prototypical members, the ones who hold a central place within the group. Members who are atypical, by deviating from the group norms and stereotypes, are often marginalized, pushed to the group's periphery, and treated differently from prototypical members. They are members of the group but not fully accepted as such. I will begin by discussing group norms and stereotypes and then move on to filling out how prototypical members function to establish the distinctiveness of the group and hence the group's boundaries.

Group Norms

Michael A. Hogg and Dominic Abrams (1988: 159) define norms as "the set of expectations concerning the attitudes, beliefs, and behaviour of a particular group of people. They are the social uniformities within groups which also distinguish between groups. They are the stereotypic perceptions, beliefs, and modes of conduct associated with a group." Norms act to constrain behavior by delineating what group members ought to believe or how they ought to behave. The more strongly people identify with a group, the more they will exhibit the group's norms, but it is the norms that determine the content of their identity.

The substantive content of norms, then, is of primary importance in the study of group identity. Early research on intergroup behavior argued that ingroups exhibited a bias toward their own group and discriminatory behavior against outgroups. Identifying with a group would therefore lead to hostile intergroup relations. Yet many studies found that group identification leads to ingroup bias but not necessarily to hostility toward the outgroup (see Ashmore, Jussim, and Wilder 2001; Brewer 2001; Brewer and Kramer 1985; Oakes 2003). One explanation for this finding is that the norms of a group influence intergroup relations. If a group holds norms that are hostile and discriminatory toward outgroups, then it will treat outgroups just that way. But if a group holds norms that are friendly and fair toward others, then group members will treat outgroups well. As Stephen Reicher and Nick Hopkins (2001: 34) state, "It may well be true that in many cases group culture prioritizes such things as dominance, affluence and aggression such that differentiation from the outgroup entails negative and discriminatory behaviours towards them. However, one could also differentiate oneself by being more charitable or more generous or more caring towards the other." It is essential, then, to understand the content of group norms and the central role they play in group identity. Predictions about group behavior will be wide of the mark if group norms are ignored.

A perfect example of group norms playing a decisive role in people's behavior comes from research on individualistic versus collectivist cultures. Some countries, such as the United States and Great Britain, are strongly individualistic, whereas others, such as Japan and Brazil, are more collectivist. Hazel Rose Markus and Shinobu Kitayama (1994) have argued that group identity and its effects on behavior are stronger in collectivist than in individualistic cultures. In collectivist cultures, people are more oriented toward the group and therefore their behaviors are more directed by the group than in cultures that are individualistic. The implied argument is that the phenomenon of conformity to group norms matters more in collectivist than in individualistic cultures. In individualistic cultures, people are free to behave idiosyncratically without being pressured by the group, and conforming to group pressure is considered a negative. Some researchers, however, have questioned the interpretation of these results. If a group's norms are heavily individualistic, then behaving in an individualistic manner actually reflects group members conforming to the group norm. Those who strongly identify with their group "actually can become more individualistic, or work more for individual interests, when they perceive this to be group normative" (Spears 2001: 186).

The paradox, then, is that group identity can foster greater individualism if the group holds an individualistic norm, and the strongest individualists are conforming the most strongly to group norms (see Jetten, Postmes, and McAuliffee 2002). The content of group norms determines attitudes and behaviors whether in an individualistic or collectivist culture.

Because norms are basically the content of group identity, they help us to predict group behavior.[4] But it is erroneous to think that all group norms precisely dictate particular behaviors. Rather, norms reflect tendencies to behave in certain ways. To use Muzafer Sherif's social judgment theory language (Sherif and Hovland 1961; Sherif and Sherif 1969; Sherif, Sherif, and Nebergall 1965), norms have "latitudes of acceptance" that vary depending on the centrality of the norm to the group. Rupert Brown (2000) avers that some norms, those that are peripheral to the group or that are general, have wide latitudes of acceptance. A wide range of attitudes and behaviors are acceptable to the group and still fit the norm. Other norms are central to the group

---

[4] Social psychologists have studied extensively the development and influence of group norms. For example, Muzafer Sherif's (1958) autokinetic experiments, in which participants judged the distance that a pinpoint of light moved, provide important insights into how norms operate within a group (see Hogg and Abrams 1988). First, norms develop through social interaction since norms are inherently social. Second, norms are not arbitrary in the sense that they can defy reality. Rather, norms must be consonant at least with perceptions of the physical and social worlds. As Sherif's experiments showed, extreme norms are moderated over time to become more congruent with modal responses. Third, norms persist even after the norm setters have left the group, suggesting that norms are a quality of the group rather than of individual group members. Fourth, there is social pressure, subtle or not so subtle, that pushes group members to conform to the group norms. People want to fit in with a group they like, and fitting in means conforming to the group norms. Fifth, the impact of the norms persists even when members are not in the presence of fellow group members. When Sherif's subjects were asked to give their estimate of the movement of the light in private after having been in the group, they continued to give answers consistent with the group norm rather than with their initial private decisions. And finally, the group norm is not simply the mean response of the group. Some people in the group have more influence over the group's norms than others and they can push the norm closer to their own position. All of these aspects of group norms combined tell us a great deal about how norms operate within groups. And they do not apply only to physical reality. Other studies have found that the same features hold in groups establishing social norms. For example, Theodore Newcomb's (Alwin, Cohen, and Newcomb 1991; Newcomb 1943; Newcomb et al. 1967) studies of students at Bennington College revealed how conservative incoming students conformed to the liberal political norms of the campus.

and carry narrower latitudes of acceptance. An example is loyalty to the group. Group members are expected to be loyal to the group by, for example, supporting the group through thick and through thin and by taking actions that symbolize this loyalty, such as by being patriotic, by fighting in a war for one's country, or by defending the national group when it is criticized by an outgroup member. Norms that are central to the group are likely to be the most predictive of attitudes and behavior, at least among those who strongly identify with the group. Weak identifiers or those who actually disidentify with the group will be less concerned about following the norms, making the norms less predictive of their behavior.

People who identify strongly with a group tend to behave in accordance with the perceived norms, especially norms that are central to the group. Since these central norms have narrower latitudes of acceptance and interpretation, group members will share certain attitudes and behaviors that are established by the central norms. When members of a group behave similarly or hold similar attitudes, it is no wonder that group members perceive themselves to be, and are perceived by others as, homogeneous. The group norms establish what is appropriate, good group members follow the norms, and people inside and outside the group see these consistencies across group members. These group norms can therefore become stereotypic of the group.

Group Stereotypes

A stereotype "is a generalization about a group of people in which identical characteristics are assigned to virtually all members of the group, regardless of actual variation among the members" (Aronson, Wilson, and Akert 2002: 461). Stereotypes can be positive or negative and do not change easily once they have been associated with a group. Even if the group has changed over time or disconfirming evidence is rampant, people tend to hold on to the existing stereotypes.[5] For example, if people hold the stereotype that women are nurturing, then they will apply that stereotype to *all* women, not just the nurturing ones, and encountering many women who are not nurturing will not

---

[5] There is an extensive literature on stereotyping in social psychology, which I will not delve into here. See Hilton and von Hippel (1996) for a good overview of the social psychology literature on stereotyping.

lead to dropping the stereotype. Stereotyping is not just focused on others, though. People include themselves in the stereotype as well when they apply a stereotype to their ingroup.

Stereotyping allows for greater accentuation between groups. People want their ingroup to be distinctive, and stereotypes clearly separate the ingroup from the outgroup. This drive to stereotype the group to make it distinctive makes perfect sense when the stereotype is positive. People identify with groups because of a need for positive distinctiveness (Tajfel 1982) and they want to be a good member, which basically means that they want to behave the way a good member behaves.[6] But this drive for distinctiveness is so strong that ingroup members will even emphasize negative stereotypes of the group if doing so more clearly distinguishes the ingroup from an outgroup.[7] Street gangs can get kids who privately express a reluctance to use violence to behave very violently if the group norms demand such behavior, the group is stereotyped to be violent, and the kids want to be good group members (Sun 1993).

The people most likely to embrace the group stereotypes, whether positive or negative, are strong identifiers. Some group members, however, will dislike being in a group characterized by certain stereotypes, but it is often not possible to flat out deny their existence. Naomi Ellemers and her colleagues state, "consensual views about the traits or abilities that characterize a particular group limit the extent to which its members feel free to claim that their group is superior" (Ellemers, Spears, and Doosje 1999a: 2). What these group members

---

[6] When a person's individual identity is salient, then he or she will behave according to his or her sense of individual self. When a group identity is salient, however, it is the group norms and stereotypes that influence behaviors, and the collective sense of self takes precedence over the individual sense of self (Sedikides and Brewer 2001).

[7] An example of this comes from an experiment by Russell Spears (2001). Subjects in the experimental condition were primed to believe that an outgroup was especially neat. Subjects in the control condition were not led to make the ingroup-outgroup distinction. Then, in a seemingly separate study, subjects were asked to color a picture. The subjects in the experimental condition were significantly more sloppy in their coloring – by coloring outside the lines – than the subjects in the control condition. In other words, subjects behaved in a way that clearly distinguished their (messy) ingroup from the (neat) outgroup. Other research has found a similar tendency for people to play up negative stereotypes if it serves to distinguish the ingroup from an outgroup (Branscombe et al. 1999; Ellemers, Spears, and Doosje 1999b; Mlicki and Ellemers 1996).

can do is distance themselves from the group either physically or psychologically. If group boundaries are permeable and it is possible to change groups, an individual group member can choose to leave the negatively stereotyped group and join a positively stereotyped group. Abandoning one's group, however, is not always possible. Some groups have impermeable boundaries that make movement between them impossible or extremely difficult. Ethnic, racial, gender, and national groups are good examples. A woman who does not like the negative stereotypes associated with women cannot simply shift her group membership to the other group (men). Similarly, an African American who does not like the stereotypes associated with blacks cannot simply move to another racial group.[8] And while it is possible to change one's national identity, it is not easy to do so. Changing a national identity often entails learning a new language and acclimating to a new culture, not to mention the costs of moving, finding a job, leaving friends and family, and so on. In the wake of the 2004 presidential election, cries of "I'm moving to Canada" could be heard among demoralized liberal Democrats. On the day John Kerry gave his concession speech, six times more Americans accessed the web site of Canada's immigration ministry than usual (Boyd Bell 2004). But did Democrats leave the United States in droves to become Canadians? No, not because they did not want to, but because doing so is difficult. The vast majority of people are born into their national group and, whether they like it or not, they are members of that national group for their whole life.

Group Prototypes and the Setting of Group Boundaries

Norms and stereotypes are key to defining the group prototypes. When people think of a social group, they think of the categories into which the group fits. These social categories are represented as prototypes. Prototypes are

fuzzy sets, not checklists, of attributes (e.g., attitudes and behaviors) that define one group and distinguish it from other groups. These category

---

[8] There are, of course, exceptions to these claims. The Brandon Teena/Teena Brandon case, made famous in the movie *Boys Don't Cry*, is a perfect example. John Howard Griffin's experiences that led to the book *Black Like Me* offer a glimpse at changing racial identities.

representations capture similarities among people within the same group and differences between groups. In other words, they accentuate intragroup similarities (assimilation) and intergroup differences (contrast). ... [Prototypes] also enhance perceived *entitativity* – the property of a group that makes it appear to be a coherent and distinct entity that is homogeneous and well structured, has clear boundaries, and whose members share a common fate (Hogg and Reid 2006: 10).

The prototypical group member is someone who clearly reflects the stereotypes and normative tendencies of the group (Hogg and Abrams 1988), especially the norms that are central to the group.

People who strongly identify with their group want to be prototypical of the group, which means that they want to see themselves as clearly embodying the group's norms and stereotypes. Since group norms both describe and prescribe group attitudes and behaviors, strong identifiers can learn how they need to behave and what they need to believe to fit the prototype. "People know, and strive to know, with some precision how well they themselves match the prototype, how well others match the prototype, and how prototypical others think one is" (Hogg and Reid 2006: 13–14). Prototypical members – especially the group's leaders, who must be prototypical on the central norms – are most able to force conformity among other members precisely because they are prototypical. They reflect the standard, and they do what they can to enforce that standard.

Work in social psychology on re-fencing and on subtyping offers clues concerning the psychological processes that underlie how group prototypes affect the setting of group boundaries (see, e.g., Allport 1954; Maurer, Park, and Rothbart 1995; Richards and Hewstone 2001; Rothbart 2001). The prototypical group member exemplifies the central norms and stereotypes of the group, which have deep roots and are not easily altered. Witness the situation where, for example, an anti-Semitic person becomes friends with a Jew and doesn't recognize the obvious evidence that disconfirms the stereotype he holds of Jews. Gordon W. Allport calls this device "re-fencing." When confronted with disconfirming individuals – that is, with people perceived to be atypical of the group – "the exception is acknowledged, but the field is hastily fenced in again and not allowed to remain dangerously open" (Allport 1954: 23). The group boundaries remain as firm as ever.

Allport discusses re-fencing specifically in relation to the stereo-typing of minority outgroups. The same device is used on ingroup members as well, as the work on subtyping shows.[9] Groups are rarely completely homogeneous. There will always be subcategories of members within the larger group. For example, a sorority might include women from rural and from urban communities, from different states, and from a variety of ethnic or religious backgrounds. They will also likely differ in their attitudes, interests, and habits. The sorority contains all women, but these women could easily be subcategorized along a variety of dimensions. When considering all of these subcategories, clearly some ingroup members are more prototypical than others. To protect the ingroup stereotype, ingroup members subtype atypical members as a means of re-fencing. Subtyping:

refers to the process by which group members who disconfirm, or are at odds with, the group stereotype are mentally clustered together and essentially set aside as "exceptions to the rule." Subtyping as a process may serve to insulate the stereotype from change by isolating those category members who "don't fit" the stereotype, resulting in a representation of the group that does not reflect its actual diversity (Maurer, Park, and Rothbart 1995: 812).

Ingroup members readily box up atypical ingroup members and push them aside. The atypical group members "don't count," then, and can be readily ignored. Prototypical ingroup members leave the stereotype intact and can comfortably continue to hold their stereotype of the ingroup. Subtyping therefore allows people to imagine that the group is more homogeneous, and therefore more of a community, than it really is.

When atypical group members are boxed up and pushed to the side, the group marginalizes them. A comparison of marginalized and

---

[9] Researchers distinguish between subtyping and subgrouping. Subgrouping is when people think about a variety of subcategories and the similarities and differences across subcategories of members. When subgrouping occurs, the superordinate group is viewed as more heterogeneous because all of the subcategories are kept in the mix. When people are involved in subtyping, on the other hand, they think about who fits and who doesn't fit the group stereotype. The members who are placed in the don't-fit category are excluded from the boundaries of the superordinate group. The superordinate group is then viewed as more homogeneous because atypical members have been excluded (see, e.g., Maurer, Park, and Rothbart 1995; Richards and Hewstone 2001).

prototypical members is revealing (see Hogg, Fielding, and Darley 2005; Hogg and Reid 2006; Marques et al. 2001; Marques, Abrams, and Serodio 2001; Marques and Paez 1994). Prototypical members are well liked, which increases conformity and compliance with their wishes. They tend to identify more strongly with the group, behave in a way that enhances and supports the group, generate trust because of their group-oriented behavior, and are most often chosen as leaders of the group (Hogg and Reid 2006: 19–20). Marginalized members, on the other hand, are less well liked or even strongly disliked, are often less committed to the group, behave in ways that are considered deviant, and jeopardize the group's distinctiveness by being too much like the outgroup and not enough like the ingroup (Hogg, Fielding, and Darley 2005; Marques et al. 2001). Marginalized group members therefore generate less trust within the group. "Since loyalty and a sense that you can trust your fellow members to act in the group's best interests lie at the core of group life ..., betrayal of these expectations is a cardinal violation that invites severe punishment by the group" (Hogg, Fielding, and Darley 2005: 193).

Group members, especially strong identifiers, perceive the group to be homogeneous along the norms and stereotypes they deem significant. Two dynamics are important here. First, since group identity means immersing the self in the collective, and people then think and behave in terms of the group, they behave in a way that is consistent with the group norms. Strong identifiers are more likely to do this than weak identifiers, so it is no surprise that they are also more likely than weak identifiers to *be* good group members, to comply with the norms, and to internalize those norms (Ellemers, Spears, and Doosje 1999a). This may in part explain their greater tendency to view themselves as prototypical of the group. Strong identifiers are indeed more prototypical than weak identifiers – they, in essence, set the standard – so their view of themselves as such is not unrealistic. If strong identifiers view themselves as prototypical and they view the group as homogeneous, and these perceptions are based on people fusing their sense of self with the group, then people's sense of their group's membership will be that they are "people like me." In other words, when strong identifiers think of the group "the American people," they will think of people like themselves who share the same characteristics, attributes, and behaviors.

Second, prototypes demarcate the group's boundaries by establishing who is typical and who is atypical. A good example of this phenomenon is race as a prototype in national groups. John Jay (Hamilton, Madison, and Jay 1961) included race as a characteristic of the American people, as did many people in early American history (Smith 1988). The prototypical American in these early days was white. Convincing evidence exists that this continues to be the case in the United States today. Thierry Devos and Mahzarin R. Banaji (2005), in a brilliant series of experiments, established that "To be American is to be White" (p. 463), and that "White Americans are construed as prototypical exemplars of the category 'American'" (p. 464). While experimental subjects were egalitarian when explicit measures of group membership were used, implicit measures demonstrated over and over again that Americans hold an automatic "American = White" association (p. 453).[10] If the prototypical American is white, as these experiments show, then any American who is not white is atypical and therefore potentially subtyped and marginalized.

People of color in Canada face the same situation. Minelle Mahtani (2002) recounts the moving stories of mixed-race women in Canada, whose experiences led them to agree that "To be a real Canadian, it is assumed that one must be white" (Hill 2001: 77; cited in Mahtani 2002). Anyone who is not white, then, is an outsider, not quite Canadian. When Julia, a mixed-race Canadian, "tells others, 'I'm Canadian,' she discovers that her response is interrogated, her identity distanced" (Mahtani 2002: 78). A group of people can hold a national identity, but if others refuse, consciously or unconsciously, to include them in the national community, then the group's claims are not legitimized. The imagined community assumes a certain type of people, and when some people do not fit the image, they are distanced from their national identity.

Race is not the only characteristic that demarcates the American group boundary. Americans have a long history of using a variety of demographic characteristics to set their national group boundaries. John Jay (Hamilton, Madison, and Jay 1961) characterized the

---

[10] An exception is African Americans who viewed themselves as equally American as whites in an implicit study. White Americans always viewed themselves as more American than other racial groups (Devos and Banaji 2005: Study 5).

American people not just by race but by language, religion, and culture. Rogers Smith also includes a variety of accepted characteristics that defined who was an American in early American history:

> ... from the outset of the nation many Americans chiefly identified membership in their political community not with freedom for personal liberal callings or republican self-governance *per se*, but with a whole array of particular cultural origins and customs – with Northern European, if not English, ancestry; with Christianity, especially dissenting Protestantism, and its message for the world; with the white race; with patriarchal familial leadership and female domesticity; and with all the economic and social arrangements that came to be seen as the true, traditional "American way of life" (Smith: 1988: 234).

The prototypical American was, and likely still is, white, Christian, English-speaking, and a believer in liberalism and economic individualism. The extent to which these prototypes still hold today will be tested in the rest of this chapter, but clearly some people fit well the prototypical American whereas others do not. In essence, some Americans are more American than others.

To sum up this argument, strong identifiers are more likely to view themselves as prototypical (and actually to be prototypical), to view their group as homogeneous, and to establish clear boundaries for their national group that distinguish it from other national groups. They are the most motivated to establish strong group boundaries and to view their group as homogeneous and characterized by consensus because they want to keep the group strong. Atypical group members threaten the stereotype of the group and are therefore marginalized. People who more weakly identify with the group are not motivated to protect the group's boundaries, are more likely to see the group as being heterogeneous, and are more likely to view the group boundaries as porous.

SETTING BOUNDARIES ON A HOMOGENEOUS GROUP OF TYPICAL AMERICANS

I have implicitly made two separate but related arguments about how to determine where group boundaries are set:

- Prototypical members see fellow group members as people like them and view the group as homogeneous along central group characteristics. Since people who view themselves as prototypical often *are* prototypical, we can begin to determine group prototypes by finding out which Americans think of themselves as typical. These characteristics, then, help establish group boundaries by signifying who is typical and who is atypical.

- Strong identifiers are more likely to set group boundaries in general and to set more exclusive boundaries in particular, especially those that distinguish the group clearly from other groups. Paying close attention to the boundaries set by strong identifiers is therefore revealing, as they will set boundaries that secure the group prototypes.

I will examine evidence concerning the first argument in this section and the second argument in the next section.

To what extent do American citizens believe themselves to be typical members of their national group? As social psychologists have pointed out, the more strongly people identify with a group, the more motivated they are to see themselves deeply embedded in the group (see, e.g., Ellemers, Spears, and Doosje 1999b). If they are prototypical, they can rest assured that they are full-fledged, vital members of the group. Believing that they are prototypical and that group members are "people like me," though, also acts to set boundaries. People who are not "like me" are subtyped as atypical and therefore easily marginalized or excluded. Perceptions of typicality, then, help establish the characteristics that set Americans off from other national groups.

Using the Perceptions of the American People survey data, I examine first whether strong identifiers are more likely than weak identifiers to believe they are typical of the American people and that the American people are "people like me." Respondents were asked four questions that measure how typically American they think they are: "When I think of the American people, I think of people who are a lot like me," "I would feel good if I were described as a typical American," "On the important issues, I find I often agree with the American people," and, "In many respects, I am different from most Americans." Response options ranged from strongly disagree to strongly agree on a five-point Likert scale. If strong identifiers are motivated to believe they are typical and therefore full members of the group, then we

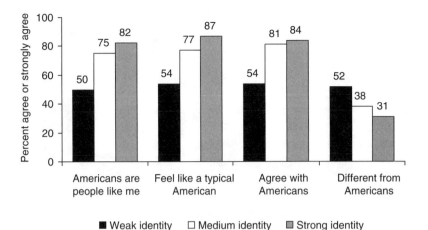

FIGURE 3.1. American national identity and the sense of being a typical American

should see a strong relationship between national identity strength and the belief that they are typical.

Figure 3.1 shows that strong identifiers are significantly more likely than weak identifiers to think of Americans as people like them and to think of themselves as typical Americans. Over four-fifths of strong identifiers think that Americans are like them (82 percent), that they are typical Americans (87 percent), and that they agree with the American people on important issues (84 percent), whereas only about half of the weak identifiers agree or strongly agree with these sentiments. The only question that garners less support among all respondents is the one that is worded so that they had to disagree with the statement to be considered typical. When asked whether they are different from most Americans, 31 percent of strong identifiers agreed or strongly agreed (whereas 55 percent disagreed, indicating that they thought they were not different). Nonetheless, strong identifiers are significantly less likely than weak identifiers to view themselves as different from their fellow Americans.

I created an overall typicality scale by adding together responses to the four questions, reverse coding the "different from me" question (see the appendix for information on this scale). I then divided the scale into three roughly equal categories: those who think of themselves as atypical, those who think of themselves as moderately typical, and

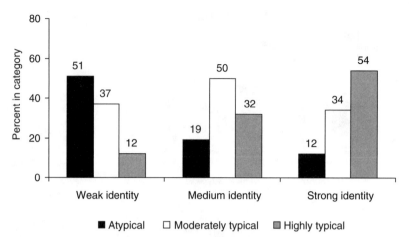

FIGURE 3.2. American national identity and overall typicality index

those who think of themselves as highly typical Americans. Figure 3.2 gives the overall picture of the relationship between level of commitment and perceptions of typicality. Among weak identifiers, about half – 51 percent – think of themselves as atypical and only 12 percent as highly typical. The response of strong identifiers is almost reversed: Only 12 percent think of themselves as atypical compared to 54 percent who think of themselves as highly typical.

Determining the characteristics of those who think they are the most typical helps to gauge the prototypical American. If there is a tendency for certain types of people to see themselves as much more typical than others, as more typically American, then we get a sense of who considers themselves fully American and therefore prototypical of the American people. If historical depictions of what an American is still hold today, we should find that Americans who think themselves prototypical are white, Christian, native-born, individualistic, and egalitarian.[11] Do these characterizations still hold today? I also include in the analysis political attitude variables that might be revealing. Americans, compared to many Europeans, are often seen as

[11] I do not have measures of some of the characterizations associated with prototypical Americans, such as beliefs in freedom and the republican form of government. Since the survey was administered only in English, everyone in the sample speaks English.

moderate or slightly right-leaning when it comes to politics. It might well be, then, that liberals of any stripe and extreme conservatives perceive themselves as atypical and moderates as typical. Party identification is more difficult to judge, but given that the United States has a two-party system, Independents might consider themselves atypical. I also include political knowledge – with the expectation that since Americans are not generally seen as highly informed about politics, the politically knowledgeable will see themselves as atypical – and patriotism, since patriotism is a norm widely held to be important to Americans.

To test these expectations, I regressed the typicality index on a variety of demographic and political attitude variables to see which characteristics are shared by those who think they are prototypical. People who say they are typical Americans are placing themselves fully in the group "the American people." Through their judgments of their own typicality, they reveal at the aggregate level what characteristics are associated with typical Americans, or at least with Americans who think they are typical. So what are these characteristics? Table 3.1 gives the ordinary least squares (OLS) regression results and Figure 3.3 provides a summary of these results. Proponents of the view that a belief in basic American principles is deeply enmeshed in what it means to be an American are right in the sense that Americans who hold such beliefs – in particular, patriotism and individualism – are significantly more likely to view themselves as typically American. On the other hand, the egalitarianism measure that emphasizes the need for greater equality is not associated with typicality.

Aside from these American principles, Americans who believe they are prototypical are less knowledgeable about politics and more likely to be moderate or somewhat ideological, either liberal or conservative. People who claim to be extremely liberal or conservative think of themselves as atypical. Demographically, those who think they are prototypical are significantly more likely to be older, female, not Southerners, and less educated. It is interesting to note that income is not related to considering oneself a typical American. Given the emphasis among political elites on the American middle class, however, it might be that the poor and the wealthy think of themselves as atypical whereas middle-income Americans view themselves as typical. The data do not support this argument, though. Among those

TABLE 3.1. *What explains feeling typical as an American: demographic and political attitudinal explanatory variables*

	Typical American	Typical American with American identity
American identity	–	.502*** (.037)
Individualism	.090*** (.022)	.055** (.020)
Egalitarianism	–.020 (.021)	–.017 (.020)
Patriotism	.375*** (.031)	.127*** (.034)
Sex (male)	–.022* (.010)	–.021* (.009)
Age	.117*** (.025)	.063** (.023)
Native-born	–.009 (.025)	–.011 (.023)
South	–.026* (.010)	–.024* (.010)
Race (whites excluded category):		
Black	–.034* (.016)	–.030 (.015)
Hispanic	–.006 (.019)	–.013 (.017)
Other race	–.011 (.022)	.003 (.020)
Education	–.048** (.018)	–.039* (.017)
Income	.019 (.021)	.019 (.019)
Christian	.009 (.012)	–.005 (.012)
Political knowledge	–.056** (.018)	–.040* (.017)
Ideology (moderates excluded category):		
Extremely conservative	–.076*** (.020)	–.072*** (.018)
Somewhat conservative	–.018 (.015)	–.020 (.013)
Somewhat liberal	–.037 (.019)	–.032 (.018)
Extremely liberal	–.126*** (.025)	–.115*** (.023)
Party identification (Independents excluded category):		
Strong Republican	.031 (.016)	.023 (.015)
Weak Republican	.043** (.015)	.038** (.014)
Weak Democrat	.036* (.015)	.026 (.013)
Strong Democrat	.013 (.015)	–.002 (.014)
Constant	.278*** (.046)	.167*** (.043)
F	18.74***	29.28***
Adj. R²	.29	.40
N	975	961

Source: Perceptions of the American People Survey, 2002
Note: * p < .05; ** p < .01; *** p < .001. Results are from OLS regression analyses. Cell entries are unstandardized regression coefficients with standard errors in parentheses. The dependent and independent variables have been transformed to range from 0 to 1. See the appendix for variable details.

Self-identify as a typical American	Self-identify as an atypical American
Strong identifier	Weak identifier
Believes in patriotism or individualism	Does not believe in patriotism or individualism
Politically moderate or somewhat ideological	Extreme liberal or extreme conservative
Older	Younger
Less educated	Better educated
Less politically knowledgeable	More politically knowledgeable
Weak partisan	
Not from the South	Southerner
Female	Male
Not black	Black

FIGURE 3.3. Defining the American prototype – characteristics of people who consider themselves typical or atypical Americans

who consider themselves atypical, one-third (33 percent) have a lower income and one-third (33 percent) a higher income. Among those who consider themselves typical, it is again the case that about one-third (32 percent) are lower income and one-third (32 percent) are higher income. Being Christian is also not related to feeling typically American. This finding is surprising given my argument. I further broke down Christians into Protestants and Catholics and included them as separate dummy variables in the regression analysis. Neither variable is significant. While Christians are not more (or less) likely to view themselves as prototypical, it will become clear in the next section that being Christian is a salient, widely held boundary placed on the American people.

Race, on the other hand, is a significant predictor of typicality. Whites are no more likely than Hispanics, Native Americans, Asian Americans, Pacific Islanders, or other smaller groups of people of color to consider themselves typical Americans. The one racial group that stands out is blacks, who are significantly more likely than whites to believe they are atypical.[12] The history of blacks in the United States, from the beginning of slavery and the encoding of slavery in the Constitution to the persistence of race as a defining and dividing

---

[12] Being black does not quite reach the standard level of significance ($p < .05$) when American identity is included in the model, but it comes very close ($p = .053$).

issue in twenty-first century America, has created a situation where African Americans today still do not feel prototypically American. Devos and Banaji's (2005) finding that being American means being white is certainly felt in the black community. Participants in the all–African American focus group held in Lincoln, Nebraska, rarely used the pronoun "we" when talking about the American people, preferring instead to use "they." In all of the other focus groups, participants used "we" almost without fail.

Not surprisingly, strength of identity and typicality are highly correlated (Pearson's r = .60, p<.001), and when American identity is included in the regression model, it is by far the best predictor of feeling typical. Strong identifiers view themselves as typical Americans, and as prototypical Americans they have more sway in establishing the boundaries of the national group than weak identifiers. Not only do strong identifiers think of themselves as typical Americans, they also are more likely than weak identifiers to view the group as homogeneous and as having reached a consensus. Respondents were asked the degree to which they agreed or disagreed with the statement, "Americans are similar to each other, sharing the same values and outlooks," which measures belief in homogeneity. Respondents were also asked how much of a consensus Americans had reached on major issues of the day: "On the major issues of the day, do Americans agree almost all of the time, agree sometimes, or agree almost none of the time?" Figure 3.4 demonstrates that, as with typicality, strong identifiers are significantly more likely than weak identifiers to view the American people as homogeneous and as having reached a consensus on important issues of the day. Only 27 percent of weak identifiers think Americans are similar to each other, compared to 41 percent of strong identifiers. Almost three times as many strong identifiers as weak identifiers think Americans agree on issues almost all of the time (48 percent compared to 17 percent).

Strong identifiers are more likely than weak identifiers to believe the American people are homogeneous and in agreement on important issues. Viewing the group as homogeneous and consensual allows strong identifiers to believe that the group is tight-knit and cohesive. Group members who are atypical raise questions about the distinctiveness and the cohesiveness of the group. Strong identifiers marginalize atypical members to reduce the muddying of the group boundaries and

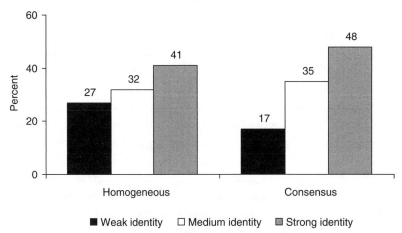

FIGURE 3.4. American national identity and perceived homogeneity and consensus among the American people

to allow them to continue to believe that the group is a homogeneous, cohesive community of people like them. Strong identifiers view themselves as highly typical members of a homogeneous group that agrees on the important issues of the day. Atypical members are easy to discern and easily pushed to the group's periphery, where they can be ignored or treated differently from full, prototypical members.

SETTING HARD AND SOFT BOUNDARIES ON THE NATIONAL GROUP

The second argument addresses whether strong identifiers are indeed more likely to set more exclusionary boundaries for their national group than are weak identifiers. Some boundaries are more definitive and impermeable than others. For example, if you have to be white to be considered a full-fledged member of the national group, then anyone who is not white is excluded. Boundaries based on belief, on the other hand, are potentially less definitive and less easy to apply to fellow group members. Anyone can believe in equality or freedom, even, for example, the French. Yet because interpretations of beliefs are subjective, people can define them and apply them as they see fit. A weak identifier might well agree that French people also believe in freedom and equality whereas a strong identifier might say that the

French don't believe in these principles as strongly as Americans do or that they don't believe in *American* freedom and equality.

I argue that strong identifiers are more likely to hold an ethnocultural view of their national identity because of a strong desire to maintain the group boundaries and therefore, they believe, to ensure the group's strength, vitality, and exclusivity. Setting exclusive boundaries maintains the group better than porous or inclusive boundaries. But I also argue that strong identifiers will be more likely to set *any* boundaries. Demographic boundaries are not the only boundaries that distinguish the national group. Even the belief that Americans must respect the institutions and laws of the United States or something as innocuous as the notion that Americans must feel American can work to make the national group distinct, depending on one's interpretation of these attributes. My argument here is simply that strong identifiers are more likely to set boundaries than weak identifiers, whether the boundaries are strict and exclusionary (such as being white or Christian) or amorphous and permeable (such as feeling American). It is the act of separating the group from other groups that is important to strong identifiers.

The hypothesis that strong identifiers are more likely than weak identifiers to set both hard and soft boundaries within their national group can be tested using the Perceptions of the American People survey data. Respondents were asked, "Some people say each of the following things is important for being truly American. Others say they are not important. How important do you think each of the following is?"[13] Respondents were asked about the following characteristics: to have been born in the United States, to have U.S. citizenship, to have lived in the United States for most of one's life, to be able to speak English, to be a Christian, to be white, to respect the U.S. political institutions

---

[13] This basic question series is in the 1996 General Social Survey. Because the question does not ask people what they *personally* think is characteristic of true Americans, they might answer what they think most Americans believe without believing it themselves. Given how I am using these questions here, I do not think this is a problem. Even if people personally do not think that true Americans must be, for example, Christian, their perception that this is what others think is important because it helps define what Americans think is prototypical. An individual might not personally think it is necessary for a true American to be Christian, but the belief that others think so contributes significantly to understanding what is considered prototypical by a random sample of American citizens.

and laws, to feel American, and to value freedom and equality. The response options were *not important at all*, *not very important*, *fairly important*, and *very important*. What I call hard boundaries are those characteristics that are impossible, or at least difficult, for people to obtain if they were not born into them: being born in the U.S., being Christian, being white, having U.S. citizenship, living in the United States a long time, and speaking English. Soft boundaries, on the other hand, are more porous because anyone can potentially claim the characteristics. Soft boundaries include feeling American, respecting laws and institutions, and valuing freedom and equality.

Figure 3.5 shows the mean responses of weak, medium, and strong identifiers for each of the "true American" questions. While some differences are bigger than others, the data clearly and consistently show that strong identifiers view the boundary characteristics as more important than weak identifiers.[14] The hard boundaries exhibit especially pronounced differences, as Figure 3.5(a) shows. Strong identifiers are much more likely to believe that to be a true American – to be fully accepted into the national group – people must be fully immersed in and deeply a part of the United States by being native born, having U.S. citizenship, and living in the United States most of their lives. They also believe that true Americans should speak English. Finally, strong identifiers are significantly more likely than weak identifiers to hold an ethnocultural view of citizenship: They are more likely to believe that true Americans ought to be Christian and are less inclined to dismiss the necessity of being white.[15] Weak identifiers, on the other hand, believe it is important to speak English and have U.S. citizenship, but they are less likely to view as important being native born, Christian, and living in the United States for most of one's life.

---

[14] All of the between-group differences in means are significant at the $p < .001$ level, although the substantive group differences on valuing freedom and equality are almost nonexistent.

[15] Recall that Devos and Banaji (2005) found the "American = white" association in their implicit measure, not their explicit measure. They argue that this racial prototype can be held either consciously or unconsciously. Implicit measures clearly tap these unconscious associations. Social desirability is another possible explanation. It is socially unacceptable to be explicitly racist in twenty-first-century America, and respondents know this when answering straightforward survey questions. The implicit measures bypass conscious efforts to give socially desirable answers. In Chapters 4 and 5, I provide further evidence that race matters to strong identifiers.

a. Hard boundaries

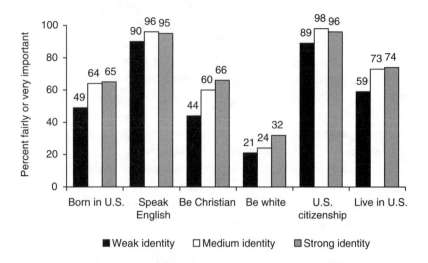

b. Soft boundaries

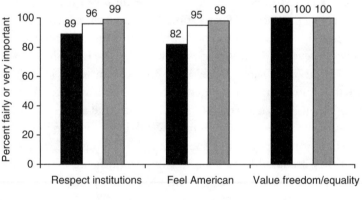

FIGURE 3.5. National identity and the setting of hard and soft boundaries for Americans

As expected, strong identifiers also distinguish themselves from weak identifiers on the soft boundary characteristics (see Figure 3.5(b)), although the differences are much less pronounced because weak identifiers are more likely to set soft boundaries themselves. All of the respondents thought it important that true Americans respect the institutions and laws of the land, feel American, and value freedom and equality. Indeed, valuing freedom and equality was the one characteristic that almost all respondents overwhelmingly held to be very important. But even when the boundaries are highly permeable – anyone can respect American institutions and laws, feel American, and value freedom and equality, not just Americans – strong identifiers are significantly more likely than weak identifiers to believe that the characteristics are very important to be considered a full member of the national group. Americans must have the right characteristics, both demographic and belief-based, to be considered true Americans.

To test the relationship between national identity and the setting of group boundaries in a more rigorous way, I created a hard boundaries scale and a soft boundaries scale and regressed them on national identity while controlling demographic characteristics (age, race, sex, native-born, region, education, income, and religious preference) and political attitudes (ideology, party identification, and political knowledge). Does national identity continue to play a significant role in establishing group boundaries even in a fully specified model? Table 3.2 provides the results of the OLS regression analyses for the establishment of hard and soft boundaries. The model does a somewhat better job explaining the setting of hard boundaries than of soft boundaries, perhaps because there is more variance to explain in the former.

The result that stands out starkly in both models is that the stronger people's national identity, the more motivated they will be to set boundaries on their national group, whether they be soft or hard boundaries. The national identity scale is by far the best predictor of the setting of boundaries. People with a strong national identity are much more likely to believe that true Americans must fit a variety of characteristics to be fully accepted in the national group. These include characteristics that are inherently exclusionary, such as being white or Christian or native-born, but also those that are much more porous and potentially more inclusive, such as feeling American or valuing freedom. Strong identifiers set the boundaries of the group more strictly, such that certain people are viewed as full members of the group. Those who are not prototypical are marginalized because they do not fit squarely within the group. Weak identifiers are less likely to think fellow Americans must possess certain qualities to be part of the national group.

Who Counts as an American?

TABLE 3.2. *Explaining the setting of hard and soft boundaries*

	Hard boundaries	Soft boundaries
American identity	.283*** (.042)	.402*** (.026)
Sex (male)	−.005 (.013)	−.021** (.008)
Age	.226*** (.032)	.041* (.020)
Native-born	−.022 (.033)	−.025 (.020)
South	.017 (.013)	.009 (.008)
Race (whites excluded category):		
Black	.120*** (.021)	.006 (.013)
Hispanic	.021 (.024)	−.006 (.015)
Other race	−.023 (.028)	−.033 (.017)
Education	−.136*** (.023)	−.029* (.015)
Income	−.091*** (.026)	−.033 (.017)
Christian	.080*** (.016)	.012 (.010)
Political knowledge	−.109*** (.023)	−.006 (.014)
Ideology (moderates excluded category):		
Extremely conservative	−.023 (.025)	−.019 (.016)
Somewhat conservative	−.008 (.018)	−.001 (.012)
Somewhat liberal	−.043 (.024)	−.018 (.016)
Extremely liberal	−.069* (.033)	−.044* (.020)
Party identification (Independents excluded category):		
Strong Republican	−.016 (.021)	.024 (.013)
Weak Republican	−.014 (.019)	.029* (.012)
Weak Democrat	−.017 (.018)	.008 (.012)
Strong Democrat	.022 (.019)	.027* (.012)
Constant	.471*** (.050)	.636*** (.031)
F	23.30***	19.44***
Adj. R²	.32	.28
N	943	966

Source: Perceptions of the American People Survey, 2002
Note: * p < .05; ** p < .01; *** p < .001. Results are from OLS regression analyses. Cell entries are unstandardized regression coefficients with standard errors in parentheses. All of the dependent and independent variables have been transformed to range from 0 to 1. See the appendix for variable details.

These results hold even controlling the effects of demographic and attitudinal variables. The demographic and attitudinal control variables give some clues concerning who is more likely to set stricter boundaries than others. Aside from the effects of national identity, people who are more likely to establish hard group boundaries are older, less educated, less wealthy, and Christian. They are also more likely to be black, although Hispanics and other people of color are no different from whites in the setting of hard boundaries. This finding concerning African Americans at first blush is surprising. An explanation for the result comes from a poll conducted by the Pew Research Center in 2006 on attitudes concerning immigration (Doherty 2006). African Americans are more likely than whites to view immigrants as competitors for much needed jobs. Since some of the hard boundaries directly relate to immigration – speaking English, being born in the United States – African Americans might react positively to setting these boundaries because of concerns about immigrants taking jobs away from blacks. In terms of political attitudes, people who are less politically knowledgeable are more likely to set hard group boundaries. Only extreme liberals are significantly less likely than moderates to set hard boundaries. The somewhat liberal and conservatives in general do not differ from moderates in how exclusively they set the boundaries of their national group.

The demographic and attitudinal variables are less predictive of the setting of soft boundaries, but there is some overlap. Older people and the less educated tend to set not only hard boundaries but soft boundaries as well. The extremely liberal are unlikely to set either hard or soft boundaries. And while males and females do not differ in their setting of hard boundaries, men are much less likely than women to set soft boundaries on the group the American people.

CONCLUSION

The boundaries set on national groups are in part historically constructed and in part the result of contested claims made by politicians and other political elites. It would make no sense in the United States to claim that people of English ancestry are not considered fully American. Similarly, there is historical precedent to consider seriously the notion that to be fully American means to be white and Christian.

While it is rare today to hear Americans say that to be American means to be white, they hesitate hardly at all when they say Americans must be Christian or native-born.

Group dynamics play an important role in the setting of boundaries as well. Group members, especially those who are highly committed to their group, are motivated to ensure that their group is distinct from other groups and that the group is a cohesive, homogeneous community. The setting of strong group boundaries both clearly demarcates the ingroup from outgroups and pressures group members to behave like good group members. The more viable the group is, the more that group members can pressure fellow group members to conform and the more they can view the group as being homogeneous. Atypical group members can be boxed up and pushed aside. The setting of group boundaries tells a great deal, then, about how group members ought to behave and think, who is fully included in the group, who is excluded from the group, and who is marginalized.

The findings in this chapter suggest that Americans associate being prototypical with holding certain beliefs, especially beliefs in patriotism, individualism, freedom, and respect for American laws and institutions. In this sense, scholars of American identity who have argued that core beliefs – the "American Creed" – are central to American identity are correct. They are also correct to emphasize that these core beliefs have a unifying effect in the sense that the vast majority of Americans hold these fundamental American norms. While these beliefs are widely held, it is strong identifiers who hold them as fundamental to being American. Good Americans are patriotic and individualistic; they value freedom; they honor American laws and institutions. Bad Americans do not hold these beliefs. In this way, the beliefs people hold, and presumably the actions generated by these beliefs, help separate true, prototypical Americans from those who don't quite fit.

The interpretation of the findings on shared beliefs, however, must be placed within the context of the other results concerning the demographic characteristics of who is a prototypical American. Basing national group boundaries on demographic characteristics is always more limiting than basing those boundaries solely on shared beliefs. The results on the setting of exclusive boundaries show that prototypical Americans are native born, have U.S. citizenship, speak English, live in the United States for most of their lives, are Christian, and are probably white. These characteristics establish strict boundaries for who is an American and make being a full-fledged American more difficult for those who do not fit the prototype.

That Americans would so willingly place exclusive boundaries on their national group is perhaps surprising given the timing of the survey, which was administered in 2002. I could not have picked a tougher time to test my arguments concerning boundaries. Americans were highly united after the September 11, 2001, attacks. If there should be any time when simple citizenship is all that matters, it should have been at the time that these data were collected. The ingroup was attacked by an outgroup. As the focus group participant said in Chapter 2, "Everyone is, you know, is my neighbor, everyone is an American. It's like the lines erase themselves." Save for Arab Americans, who felt intimately the aftershock of Americans' reactions to the attacks, Americans should have felt united. But this research shows unequivocally that ethnocultural understandings of the national group matter, even during supposedly unifying times.

The fact that Americans establish both belief-based and demographic-based boundaries on their national group raises interesting questions about how to interpret a belief-based identity. It may well be that the beliefs that are central to being an American tend to be applied only to those who are full members of the national group. Americans' willingness to abrogate the basic civil rights of Arab Americans after 9/11 suggests that Arab Americans no longer "counted" as Americans and therefore could have their rights abridged without much hesitation. Rights belong to Americans, not to those who are not quite American. Similarly, atheistic communists did not deserve their basic rights in the 1950s because they, too, were not quite American. This interpretation could also explain why Americans' belief in equality coincided for much of U.S. history with the unequal treatment of blacks. If African Americans are marginalized, and are therefore not accorded the same rights and freedoms as prototypical Americans, then the belief in equality might be interpreted not to apply fully to African Americans. The same might be true of the belief in economic individualism. No matter how hard blacks work, strong identifiers will not perceive them as living up to the economic individualist ideal, certainly not to the same extent as prototypical Americans.

The work of José Marques and his colleagues is telling in this regard (see, e.g., Marques et al. 2001; Marques, Abrams, and Serodio 2001; Marques and Paez 1994). The "black sheep effect" describes how prototypical group members treat atypical ingroup members more harshly and evaluate them more negatively than outgroup members because "they contribute negatively to the overall image of the ingroup" (Marques et al. 2001: 401). Atypical ingroup members call into question positive group characteristics, and in doing so weaken people's positive evaluations of and social identification with the group. It is not surprising, then, that marginalized group members who do not reflect the ingroup prototype are treated more harshly than outgroup members who do not, and are not expected to, reflect the ingroup prototype. Ingroup members expect outgroup members to be different and to behave in ways that are incongruent with the group's norms. No leeway is given to marginalized ingroup members. In fact, marginalized group members are expected to live up to the group norms even more faithfully than prototypical members, especially when the group is heterogeneous and lacks clear boundaries (Pickett and Brewer 2005). "Subjective rejection of deviates is a mechanism that allows group members to maintain certainty about the validity of ingroup standards and thus the superiority of ingroup identity" (Hogg, Fieldling, and Darley 2005: 196).

The next two chapters empirically test the consequences of national identity both in general and in terms of prototypical versus marginalized group members. The research in this chapter sets up the possibility that the positive consequences of national identity might apply only to prototypical members. Marginalized members, who are held to a higher standard than prototypical members, might be ignored or not deemed worthy of the group's help and loyalty. In Chapter 4, I examine the effect of national identity strength on the sense of obligation to help fellow Americans. In Chapter 5, I focus on loyalty, and in particular reactions to criticisms from ingroup members. These two chapters take the social theory of national identity that I have developed thus far and demonstrate its importance for understanding American national identity and its consequences.

4

The Desire to Help the National Group

When two planes crashed into the World Trade Center and one plane crashed into the Pentagon on September 11, 2001, Americans were shocked and horrified. The initial reaction was to sit in stunned silence, intently watching the news to find out what was going on. But many Americans quickly realized they needed to do something, whatever they could, to help. In Ohio, people donated blood, raised money, and bought flags "to show we're unified." "People were hurting, hundreds of miles away. But it wasn't too far for Northeast Ohioans to do whatever they could … to help" (Albrecht 2001). In Indiana, a mother offered her child-support money, a retired nurse donated food and all of the money she had in her wallet, and local radio stations raised money at the rate of $5,000 per hour because, in the words of a local car dealer, "We're all a part of it" (Kilborn 2001). In Nebraska, young children emptied their piggy banks in an effort to help, and local supermarkets and fast-food restaurants raised thousands of dollars (McCord 2001). And in Utah, a four-year-old girl donated all of the money from her Barbie fund and was hailed as an "example of what a true American is all about" (Burr 2001). Newspapers from across the United States told similar stories in the aftermath of the September 11 terrorist attacks. Americans came together to help their fellow Americans in New York City and Washington, D.C., by doing whatever they could.

The charitable giving in response to the terrorist attacks added up to record-setting numbers. According to the Foundation Center,

$2.8 billion in total private giving was earmarked for 9/11 relief efforts (Foundation Center 2004: 86). Of this, 39 percent came from institutional donors and only about 1 percent came from donors outside the United States. The rest came from individual Americans donating anywhere from small amounts to millions of dollars. Two-thirds of American households were involved in charitable giving of some sort in an effort to help the victims of the attacks (Salamon 2002), and many Americans volunteered their services as well; for example, some delivered sandwiches to rescue workers. The outpouring of compassion toward and effort on behalf of the victims of the terrorist attacks was heralded by many as an awe-inspiring example of the American spirit and of American unity. While some questioned whether the sense of togetherness could last, most commentators focused on the numerous examples of Americans doing whatever they could for their fellow Americans.

Natural disasters similarly kindle Americans' outpourings of sympathy and aid. When four hurricanes hit Florida in 2004, private donations topped $20 million. According to the chief executive officer of the Florida Hurricane Relief Fund, donations poured in from "every state in the union" ("Private Donations Raised $20 Million for Hurricane Relief Fund" 2005). Children in Idaho donated 1,600 books to an elementary school hit hard by Hurricane Charley (Hedberg 2005). A high school in Minnesota raised over $20,000 for a Florida school nearly destroyed by the same hurricane (Mathur 2004). Hurricane Katrina generated even more charitable giving. According to the *New York Times*, "Americans are opening their wallets, homes and hearts to help the victims of Hurricane Katrina" (Wilgoren 2005: A21). The disaster relief effort included celebrity telethons, corporations donating money and goods, cities raising millions of dollars, and school children selling Mardi Gras bracelets to raise money (Wilgoren 2005). Americans all over the United States volunteered time, goods, or money to help the hurricane victims, just as they did to help the victims of the fires that have raged across Southern California, the tornadoes that have torn across the central United States, and the floods and earthquakes that always leave such devastating damage.

Americans' desire to help does not stop with their private giving. They also want to see their government do more to help fellow Americans victimized by a crisis. According to a Pew Research Center for the People and the Press survey administered in October 2005, 80 percent of Americans approved of the $62 billion hurricane relief effort passed by Congress and signed by President George W. Bush in response to Hurricane Katrina. And a plurality of respondents (45 percent) said that too little was being spent on the relief effort (Pew Research Center 2005). A majority of respondents in a variety of polls taken after the hurricane hit said that the government, President Bush, and the Federal Emergency Management Agency (FEMA) had not done a good job responding to the aftermath of Hurricane Katrina, and that they should have done more.

Going out of one's way to help fellow group members, even at great cost to oneself, is a widespread group norm. Groups create a strong sense of community among their members, a community that many believe has a shared fate (Richards and Hewstone 2001; see also Dawson 1994 on linked fate). Since group members believe that what happens to a small portion of the group affects all members, then helping group members in need helps the group as a whole. The norm of feeling obligated to help fellow group members holds across all sorts of groups, but it is perhaps especially strong in national groups where the notion of a shared fate is reinforced daily by politicians who talk about "the American people" as a single entity with a unified response to every event, policy, and outcome. But if national group members are especially likely to hold the helping norm, then why are Americans opposed to welfare spending? Why wouldn't Americans want to have government programs designed to help those fellow Americans who are less fortunate? Why wouldn't they think, "We're all in this together and we need to help each other out," even if that means supporting welfare? Indeed, David Miller (1995) argues that national identity gives diverse peoples a sense of community and a desire to build a strong welfare system to help out fellow nationals. But Americans begrudge welfare spending and are quick to support tax cuts and welfare reform (Gilens 1999). Contrary to Miller, Americans appear on the surface to be dismissive of welfare as a means of helping their compatriots.

I argue in this chapter that national identity is at the heart of understanding Americans' helping behavior. People who identify strongly with their group – in this case, their national group – are much more likely to feel obligated to help their fellow group members (Ellemers,

Spears, and Doosje 2002; Ouwerkerk, Ellemers, and De Gilder 1999). In this sense, national identity has precisely the impact Miller expects. But as I demonstrated in the previous chapter, strong identifiers are more likely to set hard and fast boundaries on who gets included fully as Americans. People who strongly identify with their national group are more likely to set stricter boundaries on who counts as an American and therefore to limit who should receive the benefits of group membership. Strong identifiers want to help prototypical fellow Americans but not those who are marginalized.

The social theory of national identity, I argue, explains the differences in support for certain ways of helping, such as charitable giving and volunteering versus support for welfare spending. When people give money to a charitable organization, they can in many ways pick and choose who will get help. For example, when an American gives money to her church, she knows the money will help people who are like her in important ways. Even choosing to give to a large national charitable organization, such as the American Red Cross, can entail imagining who benefits from the donation. A quick look at the Red Cross web site shows lots of smiling white faces.[1] Welfare, however, is given to anyone who needs it, regardless whether they are considered full members of the group or not. I will provide evidence throughout this chapter that people who strongly identify as Americans are eager to help prototypical Americans but are much more reluctant to help marginalized members. On the other hand, weak identifiers feel less of an obligation to help in any way since they do not feel much of a sense of responsibility to the group. They are less likely to hold group norms and are therefore less likely to feel obligated to help their fellow group members (Terry and Hogg 1996).

WHY DO PEOPLE HELP EACH OTHER?

The group basis of helping has long been recognized by psychologists. Evolutionary understandings highlight the importance of group members helping each other for survival. Assumptions of popular rational choice theories notwithstanding, people tend to be cooperative and

---

[1] This is not to say that the American Red Cross does not help a diverse assortment of people. It certainly does.

want to help each other (Alford and Hibbing 2004; Ridley 1996). The groups most likely to succeed across human history were those that included cooperators (Barkow, Cosmides, and Tooby 1992). If everyone in the group behaved in a self-interested fashion, the group would quickly splinter, fall apart, and decrease chances of survival (Barrett, Dunbar, and Lycett 2002; Buss 1999; Sober and Wilson 1998). Combined with the evolutionary need to categorize quickly ingroup and outgroup members, it is not surprising that even today shared group membership is one of the best predictors of helping behavior (Flippen et al. 1996; Hornstein 1976). People tend to view ingroup members as more attractive and more similar to themselves than outgroup members, both of which are good predictors of prosocial behavior (Dovidio and Morris 1975; Hayden, Jackson, and Guydish 1984), and they feel a stronger sense of empathy and responsibility toward ingroup members (Mullen, Brown, and Smith 1992).

What is perhaps most amazing about helping at the group level is that people are willing to help their ingroup even at personal cost. People want their own group to succeed and to do well, and to that end, they make decisions that benefit the ingroup even when personal costs are high (Brewer and Kramer 1985; Kramer and Brewer 1984). This tendency to be concerned about the group's welfare is especially true when group identity is salient and when people identify strongly with their group. When a group identity is salient, a person's sense of self is as a group member and the group's fortunes are paramount (Ellemers, Spears, and Doosje 1999a; Tajfel 1982). Strong identifiers will do whatever needs to be done to help fellow group members, and benefiting the group becomes more important than individual self-interest. With self-interested behavior set aside, incredible benefits accrue to the group. Group-level prosocial behavior strengthens the group, keeps the group viable, and contributes to group maintenance (see, e.g., Abrams, Hogg, and Marques 2005). When individual identity, or the identity of the self, is salient, on the other hand, individual-level factors, such as humanitarian values or personal self-interest, matter more.

However, not all ingroup members are equally likely to be helped. Group members are significantly more likely to help prototypical members than marginalized members. In part, they help prototypical members more because these are the people in the group who do the most to advance the well-being of the group. Prototypical members most clearly distinguish the ingroup from the outgroup, making the group distinctive (Pickett and Brewer 2005). In addition, prototypical members most clearly exhibit the group's norms and goals and are well liked (Hogg 2001; Hogg and Reid 2006). In contrast, marginalized members are often considered deviants of the group, they contribute to muddying the boundary between the ingroup and the outgroup, and they often bear more of the wrath of the group when things go wrong (Marques, Abrams, and Serodio 2001; Pickett and Brewer 2005). This inequality in the treatment of prototypical and marginalized group members is largely due to the perceived potential damage that a marginalized group member can do to the group's distinctiveness. It is only marginalized group members who experience group wrath and exclusion when norms are broken. Members who deviate from the group norms by adhering to the norms *too* strongly are not treated negatively by fellow group members (Pickett and Brewer 2005).

People who strongly identify with their group should exhibit these differences in helping behaviors the most because they care so much about group maintenance. They want their group to be strong and viable, and helping prototypical members helps do that. Helping marginalized members does not. But strong identifiers are also more likely to help prototypical members because they want to be, and often are, prototypical. Helping prototypical members makes the group stronger but it also contributes to ensuring that strong identifiers will be helped themselves, if they should need the help. And finally, helping prototypical members means helping the members who are most attractive and well-liked. People who only weakly identify with their group are less likely to help the group but are also less likely to distinguish between marginalized and prototypical group members. When they do help, they will help anyone in need. The problem is that they are less likely to help in the first place, approaching the group in a more self-interested, less group-oriented way.

HELPING FELLOW NATIONALS AS A SPECIAL CASE

Most work on prosocial behavior examines either interpersonal instances in which help is needed, such as when a person is having a seizure or needs help contacting a friend, or instances in which help is offered in a small group setting, often using groups concocted by the experimenter. The results from these studies are important and tell us a great deal about helping behaviors, but a question remains concerning what happens when we move the analysis to very large groups where people do not know each other and where helping the group, or a significant segment of the group, becomes a major enterprise. Perhaps only smaller groups elicit strong bonds among members that then lead to prosocial behaviors. Large groups are often amorphous and impersonal and therefore might diminish group effects on helping behavior.

National groups are certainly large, amorphous, and impersonal, and it is quite easy for people to remain anonymous within a national group and to know only a very small number of fellow nationals personally. National groups, however, might create a special attachment that makes this extremely large group differ from most other large groups. Indeed, a case has been made for the idea that people owe a special obligation to their fellow nationals. Robert E. Goodin (1988) lays out the widely accepted argument (although it is one with which he disagrees) that presumes that people have "special duties" toward certain others.[2] A teacher has special duties toward his students, a doctor toward her patients, a mother toward her child, a friend toward a friend, a citizen toward a compatriot. According to this argument, we owe "special 'kindnesses,' 'services,' or 'sacrifices'" to others for whom we hold a special obligation (Goodin 1988: 666).

Miller (1995) pushes this argument further by making the case that people have an especially strong obligation to their national group. He

---

[2] Goodin (1988) argues against this presumption that we owe special duties to compatriots. He points out that not all duties owed to compatriots are positive and that we often owe negative duties to foreigners. For example, we, through elected representatives, can take property away from compatriots if fairly compensated but cannot take property away from foreigners. Goodin develops a theory, what he calls "the assigned responsibility model," that takes into account positive and negative duties and that salvages the universalist argument that people have an obligation to others simply because they are human. He contends that people have an obligation to help others but that certain people are simply assigned responsibility to help certain others. People have the responsibility to help those within their country, whereas people in other countries are responsible for their own. Assigning responsibility makes helping more efficient but doesn't belie the argument that we have an obligation to help all people.

argues that while there is a clear obligation to fellow group members in small, face-to-face groups[3] – for example, family members and workplace colleagues – nations are ethical communities and the "duties we owe to our fellow-nationals are different from, and more extensive than, the duties we owe to human beings as such" (p. 11). These duties or obligations are "unconditional" in that they "arise simply by virtue of the fact that one has been born and raised in that particular community" (p. 42). Even though fellow nationals do not know each other personally, they have an obligation to help each other. It is, in essence, an ethical imperative of being part of a national community. Miller therefore views national identity as a positive force because it brings people together and fosters a strong sense of interdependence and caring. According to Miller, "The potency of nationality as a source of personal identity means that its obligations are strongly felt and may extend very far – people are willing to sacrifice themselves for their country in a way that they are not for other groups and associations" (p. 70).

Miller discusses national identity as a general phenomenon, but perhaps the United States is exceptional, as Samuel Huntington and others have claimed. Americans have long embraced individualism as a core tenet, and this belief in individualism might offset any feeling of obligation to help fellow nationals. Americans don't need to help because people should be able to make it on their own. Alexis de Tocqueville, however, wrote in the early nineteenth century that the combination of individualism and egalitarianism in the United States made Americans more willing to help fellow Americans. Tocqueville, like Lord James Bryce (1891) a half-century later, argued that because Americans interact freely with one another without concern about class or hierarchy, they develop a better understanding of the needs of their fellow Americans. And because Americans are individualistic, he argued, they are well aware that they can succeed or fail themselves, and when they see someone who needs their help, they willingly give it knowing that it could be them next time. This sense of fellowship leads

---

[3] As Miller (1995: 65) says, "Because I identify with my family, my college, or my local community, I properly acknowledge obligations to members of these groups that are distinct from the obligations I owe to people generally. Seeing myself as a member, I feel a loyalty to the group, and this expresses itself, among other things, in my giving special weight to the interests of fellow-members."

to a willingness to help Americans when they are in trouble. "When an American needs the assistance of his fellows, it is very rare for that to be refused, and I have often seen it given spontaneously and eagerly. When there is an accident on the public road, people hurry from all sides to help the victim. When some unexpected disaster strikes a family, a thousand strangers willingly open their purses, and small but very numerous gifts relieve their distress" (Tocqueville 1969 [1835]: 571). Bryce (1891: 682–3) similarly argued that social equality creates a condition where respect for others is developed "and holds up geniality and good fellowship as almost the first of social virtues."

While Miller, Tocqueville, Bryce, and other theorists argue for the special place that national groups hold and the helping that takes place within these national groups, it is clearly the case that some people will help more than others. The people most likely to help their fellow nationals are those who feel a strong sense of commitment to their national group (Ellemers, Spears, and Doosje 2002; Ouwerkerk, Ellemers, and De Gilder 1999). Strong identifiers are more concerned about group viability than weak identifiers and therefore can be expected to feel a greater obligation to help fellow nationals. The group is deeply a part of their sense of self and they view themselves as prototypical, so helping the group helps one's collective self. In general, then, national identity strength is likely to increase helping behaviors within the national group. Weak identifiers, on the other hand, do not believe they are prototypical of a group they hold in low esteem. They are ascriptively members of the group, but they do not feel a positive attachment to the group. Weak identifiers have little motivation to help a group they do not much like and that is not part of their sense of self, which might explain the tendency for weak identifiers to feel less compulsion to put the group's interests above self-interests and to be less willing than strong identifiers to believe they have an obligation to help out their fellow Americans.

Granted, it is difficult to measure self-interested versus group-oriented behavior in a survey, but several questions were asked in the Perceptions of the American People Survey to measure a willingness to be cooperative and helpful toward fellow group members. Survey respondents were asked, in an attempt to get at a self-interested versus a group-oriented perspective, "Would you say that, more often than not, you go after your own self interests when it comes to politics or do you try to get what is best for all Americans, or isn't there a difference between the two?" While few people will admit to purely self-interested motivations (only 19 percent overall), weak identifiers gave much more self-interested responses than strong identifiers. Just under a quarter of weak identifiers (22 percent) said they go after their own self-interests, compared to only 15 percent of strong identifiers. And strong identifiers are more likely than weak identifiers to say they do what is best for all Americans – 63 percent of strong identifiers compared to only 54 percent of weak identifiers say they put group concerns over their own self-interests. While people are likely to give socially desirable responses to this question, and being self-interested is not as socially desirable as the other options, the variation across national identity strength is telling. Presumably social desirability affects all respondents, but strong identifiers are more loath than weak identifiers to say they behave self-interestedly and are more eager to say they want what is best for the national group.

Respondents were also asked about the obligations they felt they owed to fellow Americans:

I am going to read you a list of possible obligations. For each, I want you to tell me if you think this is an obligation you owe or do not owe to fellow Americans ... . How about giving money to charities? ... How about helping when there is a crisis or disaster in the nation? ... How about volunteering in your local community? ... How about paying taxes? ... How about ensuring a basic standard of living for all Americans? ... How about fighting in a war for the U.S.?

Possible responses were not an obligation, somewhat of an obligation, and definitely an obligation. Some of these obligations focused on directly helping ingroup members through individual-choice activities: giving to charities, helping out in a crisis or a disaster, and volunteering in one's local community. Three other obligations were geared toward indirectly helping ingroup members through government-based activities rather than directly helping others. These were ensuring a basic standard of living for all Americans, paying taxes, and fighting in a war for the United States.

Figure 4.1 shows that overall, Americans feel a strong sense of obligation to help fellow Americans who have experienced a crisis or a natural disaster and to pay taxes, with a strong majority of

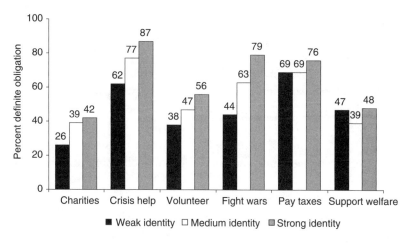

FIGURE 4.1. National identity and the obligation to help fellow Americans

Americans, regardless of national identity, saying they definitely have these obligations. But the results also show that strong identifiers are much more likely than weak identifiers to feel an obligation to help fellow group members in many different ways. The more Americans feel a strong sense of identity with the American people, the more likely they are to feel an obligation to help in a crisis or disaster, give to charities, volunteer in their community, fight in wars, and pay taxes. The only obligation that does not exhibit this same pattern is supporting a strong welfare system, a relationship I will come back to shortly. The message here, though, is that strong identifiers want to help fellow group members and they feel a strong obligation to do so. Weak identifiers feel some obligations, although nowhere near the level of strong identifiers nor for as many types of helping activities.

SUPPORTING GOVERNMENT PROGRAMS AS A WAY TO HELP FELLOW AMERICANS

Helping people by giving money to charity or volunteering in one's community is important, but many problems are large and seemingly intractable, and they demand government action to solve them. Volunteering at a local soup kitchen or donating clothes to the local Goodwill can help feed and clothe some people. However, poverty, even in as wealthy a country as the United States, is widespread, and

its solution, if there is one, lies not in soup kitchens or charitable organizations. Government policies exacerbate or ameliorate poverty and
its problems, which means that solutions often lie at the level of government programs. The taxes that people pay to the government are
used to support programs that deal with poverty, such as food stamps
and welfare programs. Americans can help their fellow Americans
who are impoverished by supporting these programs. When problems
are very big, national groups need government involvement to coor-
dinate efforts to help and they need everyone chipping in to pay for
these programs.

If national identity is based on a shared sense of group membership
and therefore on a sense of community, then helping fellow nationals through the support of national programs simply reflects the
desire to do what one can to help the group. Individual Americans
pay taxes to support programs that help one's compatriots, and this
could well be seen as an obligation that people owe to the other members of the national group. Miller (1995: 73n25) states it well when
he says, "I have a duty *qua* member of this nation to support common projects and to fulfill the needs of fellow members." The obligations that people share to help fellow nationals are formalized by
the government through tax policies and subsequently through social
welfare programs. Miller argues that "obligations of nationality are
strengthened by being given expression in a formal scheme of political
co-operation" (p. 73).

These arguments make sense but do not hold well in the United
States, where support for welfare programs is weak. Countries that
hold the norm of supporting social programs might see a strong relationship between national identity and social program support, but
the United States is not one of those countries. The belief in individualism, according to Miller, explains why Americans do not have
a strong welfare state. Individualism holds that each individual has
an obligation to make it on his or her own. This sense of individual
responsibility has traditionally meant that individuals are "expected to
be self-reliant and to get ahead with little or no help from government
or any other social institution ... since any outside assistance might
engender habits of dependence that would destroy an individual's
incentive to care for himself" (McClosky and Zaller 1984: 267). Any
welfare spending that increases people's dependence on government

or is perceived to contribute to laziness or slothfulness is unacceptable to most Americans. What this has most often meant since the New Deal is that any welfare that "does it all" for people is bad, but welfare that gives people the tools they need to make it on their own is good. In this view, then, allowing people to live on welfare for an extended time undermines individualism, but helping people get an education, for example, bolsters individualism.

Given the widespread belief in individualism, then, it makes sense to expect to find no relationship between national identity and support for social programs in the United States unless people perceive the programs to be a means of giving recipients the tools needed to become self-supporting. When respondents to the national survey were asked about their obligation to ensure a basic standard of living for their fellow Americans (that is, support welfare programs), just under half of both strong and weak identifiers said it was an obligation (see Figure 4.1). In this bivariate analysis, strength of national identity is irrelevant in predicting welfare program support. On the other hand, strong identifiers are somewhat more likely to support paying taxes (see Figure 4.1), which seems contradictory. Of course, taxes can be collected for spending on many different types of programs. Strong identifiers might be more willing to pay taxes not to support welfare spending but to support other government programs. Perhaps strong identifiers want their taxes to be spent on certain groups and not others.

The impact of national identity on beliefs about the appropriate amount of government spending in certain areas tells an interesting story. Respondents were asked, "Now I would like you to think about some issues facing people today in this country, none of which can be solved easily or inexpensively. I'm going to name some of these problems, and for each one I'd like you to tell me whether you think we're spending too much money on it, too little money, or about the right amount." They were then asked about spending on welfare; improving the conditions of blacks; solving the problems in urban areas; improving the nation's education system; and spending on the military, armaments, and defense. Figure 4.2 shows that military spending is the only category for which strong identifiers are more likely than weak identifiers to think spending is too low. There is a highly significant relationship between national identity strength and the belief that the government spends too little on the military: 19 percent

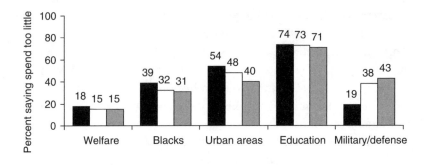

FIGURE 4.2. National identity and the belief that government spending is too low in various areas

of weak identifiers said the government spends too little on the military compared to 43 percent of strong identifiers. Only 11 percent of strong identifiers thought that the government spends too much on the military, compared to 37 percent of weak identifiers.

For the other four types of government spending, national identity is either insignificantly or negatively related to beliefs about the amount of money spent in the area. Close to three-quarters of Americans, regardless of national identity strength, think too little money has been spent on education in the United States. And regardless of national identity strength, relatively few people, less than one-fifth, think too little has been spent on welfare. Indeed, almost half of all respondents believe too much money is spent on welfare. When it comes to spending on blacks and on urban areas, however, we begin to see significant differences across national identity groups and in a direction contrary to Miller's argument. Weak identifiers are significantly *more* likely than strong identifiers to say the government spends too little in these areas, with an 8 percentage point difference between the two groups in spending on blacks and a 14 percentage point difference in urban area spending.

Is Miller wrong? Doesn't national identity increase support for government programs that are designed to help less fortunate compatriots? The results discussed so far suggest it does not. Whether we look at government spending, support for government assistance programs, or support for the welfare system, national identity is either not related to support or is negatively related, in which case strong identifiers are actually less supportive than weak identifiers. Only in the area of military spending are strong identifiers more prone to spend government money. Miller argues that Americans' lack of support for social programs stems directly from their belief in individualism. Americans so strongly believe in the principle that people should "pull themselves up by their own bootstraps" that they cannot bring themselves to support welfare spending. Individualism clearly plays a role in Americans' lack of support for welfare spending and other government assistance programs, but I argue that the bigger issue concerns who is the recipient of the help. This argument makes sense of national identity's relationship with the various ways people can help their compatriots. National identity does increase the desire to help fellow nationals, but who is counted as a fellow national depends on how strictly the boundaries are set on the group.

GROUP BOUNDARIES AND THE HELPING
OF FELLOW NATIONALS

When people give to a charitable organization, they can choose which charity to support, thereby determining in many ways who gets helped. In 2004, religious groups experienced an increase in donations over the previous year and received over one-third of total charitable donations in the United States (Strom 2005). In contrast, human service organizations, such as after-school programs and housing for the homeless, experienced a decrease in giving. According to Lester Salamon, director of the Center for Civil Society Studies, "When people see the overall number for giving in this country, they immediately think to themselves, well, aren't we generous to the poor? ... But services for the poor attract less than 10 percent of total giving, while religious organizations attract the lion's share" (quoted in Strom 2005: A12). When people give to religious organizations, they are helping people who are generally like them in important ways. When people give to human service organizations, they are most often giving to people who differ from them.

Having a choice in who gets helped also holds true for volunteering and helping in a crisis. For example, volunteer groups tend to be homogeneous in terms of age, sex, class, religion, beliefs, and opinion

(Costa and Kahn 2003; George 1990; Levine and Moreland 1998; Magaro and Ashbrook 1985; Skocpol 2002), and group homogeneity might well increase the propensity to help those who are similar to the volunteers. Eric M. Uslaner (2001: 28) argues that, among religious groups, "Religion leads people to do good deeds, but generally only for their own kind." Robert Wuthnow (1998) similarly found that church volunteers were squeamish about helping the needy, who are not like them. Mary, a church volunteer, emphasized the difficulties church volunteers face when dealing with diverse peoples: "It's very hard for them to embrace someone who maybe doesn't look like them or doesn't look like they would like to be a part of their relationships" (quoted in Wuthnow 1998: 148).

When it comes to government programs designed to help people in need, taxpayers both must give money (or pay serious fines or serve possible jail time) and have no control over who gets the money. It is very likely that the latter affects their attitudes toward the former. If people approve of who receives government assistance, they will likely pay their taxes more happily than if they disapprove of the recipients. What we do know is that Americans do not in general support welfare spending and they are especially averse to welfare spending that is traditionally associated with helping African Americans (Gilens 1999). In a clever study, Alberto Alesina, Reza Baqir, and William Easterly (1999) used data from a variety of metropolitan areas to test whether ethnic heterogeneity in a community affected public goods spending. They found a strong and consistent relationship between ethnic heterogeneity and public spending across a range of public goods, including education, roads, and trash pickup. If a white person believes that a public good will be used mainly by blacks, he or she will tend to oppose it because "the identity of the beneficiaries of the public good directly influences the utility level of each individual" (Alesina, Baqir, and Easterly 1999: 1253).

Miller's (1995) argument that a sense of national community increases support for the welfare state makes sense if the national group is a homogeneous one. We might therefore expect to find a stronger welfare system in countries that are ethnically homogeneous (just as Alesina, Baqir, and Easterly 1999 found stronger public services in ethnically homogeneous cities). When the national group is diverse, though, Miller's arguments are less likely to hold true. Prototypical group members will be less willing to provide public goods that will most likely be consumed by marginalized group members. In the United States, the stereotype of the prototypical American is someone who is white, Christian, English-speaking, and native born (see, e.g., Schildkraut 2005 and Chapter 3 in this book). People who do not fit the stereotype are less fully included in the group and therefore are less likely to be helped by their fellow nationals.

In many ways, race is at the center of these concerns. According to Martin Gilens (1995; 1996; 1999), race is the most significant influence on whites' attitudes toward welfare. Individualism is significant as well, but it is the belief that blacks are responsible for their poverty, primarily because of a perceived lack of effort, that most heavily influences opposition to welfare. If blacks would just work harder, the belief goes, they could be as successful as whites. Whites support welfare programs that not only bolster independence but that also are not associated primarily with blacks. For example, a majority of Americans were *not* supportive of spending cuts to the elderly, public schools, or the unemployed, but a vast majority supported spending cuts for food stamps (Gilens 1995: 1009).

It is helpful, I think, to put these findings within the broader framework that I propose. Doing so allows us to explain both attitudes toward government spending and toward individual helping. Blacks are marginalized within the national group by the majority in a way that the elderly are not. Other groups are marginalized as well. American Muslims are a good example. The bottom line is that Americans who strongly identify with their national group have a desire to maintain and protect the group and its boundaries. They are strongly motivated to help their fellow Americans, but they are also more likely to define their group more narrowly. The people they are most willing to help are those who are prototypical. Marginalized members are less likely to receive help from strong identifiers, whether the marginalized members are black, non-Christian, foreign-born, or not English-language speakers. I focus primarily on race in the following analysis because I have the data to do so. Future studies would benefit from analyzing a wider range of marginalized groups within the national group of the American people.

To test whether national identity and group boundaries matter in helping behavior, I examine two sets of dependent variables: helping

behaviors that give the helper a choice of who gets helped and helping behaviors that do not give a choice and that target marginalized Americans. The main independent variables in the analysis are
strength of national identity, the propensity to set hard boundaries on
the national group, and an interaction between these two variables.
When people have a choice in who gets helped, national identity will
be strongly and positively related to helping behavior and the interaction term will be insignificant. The setting of hard boundaries is
irrelevant in these cases because the person can choose whom to help.
It is the desire of strong identifiers to help fellow (prototypical) group
members that matters. When people do not have a choice in who gets
helped, on the other hand, and supporting such help potentially invig-
orates marginalized group members, then strong identifiers can feel
a bit torn. They want to help their fellow nationals, but they do not
want to help if it means helping marginalized group members. I therefore expect it takes the combined effect of national identity and the
setting of hard boundaries to influence significantly people's helping
behavior. The stronger people's national identity *and* the more they
set exclusive hard boundaries on their national group, the less willing
they should be to support government programs that will likely help
marginalized group members.

I also include in the analyses several control variables that likely
affect either or both types of helping behaviors. The most important
control variable is people's belief in individualism. If Miller (1995) is
correct, it is Americans' strong individualism that drives their unwillingness to support government spending on welfare, washing away
what should be a strong relationship between national identity and
welfare support. Research convincingly shows that people who believe
that Americans should pull themselves up by their own bootstraps are
more likely to disapprove of government programs to help the needy
(Hasenfeld and Rafferty 1989; Kluegel and Smith 1986). Any analysis of support for government programs helping the needy needs to
take individualism into account. Doing so is even more important in
this research since strong identifiers are more likely than weak identifiers to be individualistic. I therefore control individualism in the
government-based helping model to see whether national identity
has the effect that Miller predicts once individualism is controlled.
I also include individualism in the individual-choice model. People

who believe that government should do more to help people, rather than leaving it up to the individuals, are less likely to give to charities (Brooks 2006).

Egalitarianism also ought to have an effect: The more people believe in the principle of equality for all, the more they ought to support programs that try to increase equality. Research, however, has often found that egalitarianism is not related to welfare support (Gilens 1995; Kluegel and Smith 1986). Since the logic behind including the variable makes sense, I will include it in my analyses even though its effect has been minimal in past research.

Other political attitudes and predispositions that likely have an effect on the individual- or government-based helping activities are also controlled in the following analyses. In terms of individual helping behaviors where people have a choice, research suggests that ideology matters, as does religiosity. Albert C. Brooks (2006), for example, made quite a splash when his book *Who Really Cares: The Surprising Truth about Compassionate Conservatism* came out providing evidence that conservatives were more likely to give to charities than liberals, contrary to the expectation that soft-hearted liberals would give more. His results, however, suggest that it is more a matter of religion than ideology. Religious conservatives give the most and secular liberals the least, but religious liberals came in right behind religious conservatives. People who are more religious give significantly more to charities than secular people regardless of ideology (Brooks 2006; see also Ladd 1999). Indeed, religiosity is a strong predictor of charitable giving to both religious and secular causes (Schervish and Havens 1997; Brooks 2006) and of volunteering (Ladd 1999). I therefore include religion as a control variable to help explain individual-choice helping behaviors.

Research on Americans' attitudes toward welfare also suggests some important control variables, and these variables might also be important for understanding individual-choice helping behaviors. Democrats and liberals tend to be more in favor of welfare spending than Republicans and conservatives, in part because they tend to be more supportive of government programs in general and are especially likely to support programs that help the needy (Gilens 1999). Interpersonal trust is also likely to be positively related to both types of helping behavior since people high in trust are more likely to think that the recipients of the help are truly needy and not taking the system for a ride.

As an aside, Gilens (1995; 1996; 1999) has shown convincingly that racial attitudes have the strongest impact on welfare support. I do not doubt that he is right, but I place racial attitudes within the broader framework of people's attitudes toward the makeup of their national group.[4] People who set exclusive boundaries on their national group, including the belief that "true" Americans are white, marginalize anyone who does not fit the prototypical group member who is white, Christian, English-speaking, and so on. The previous chapter showed that blacks are especially likely to be marginalized in the United States because of the continued racism in the United States. By setting exclusive boundaries, Americans take their racial attitudes one step further and make African Americans' membership in the national group nominal at best. As the social theory of national identity reveals, people believe they can help their national group both by helping prototypical members and by *not* rewarding marginalized group members. Strengthening the group boundaries is what is important so that the group is distinct from outgroups, and not helping marginalized group members increases the distinctiveness of the boundaries.

The final set of control variables is demographic in nature. People who give to charity or volunteer in the local community tend to be older, better educated, and wealthier than those who do not, whereas the impact of sex on giving is somewhat inconsistent, although overall women tend to be more likely to be involved in these helping behaviors than men (Ladd 1999; Schlegelmilch, Love, and Diamantopolous 1997). Age and income are also related to attitudes toward welfare spending, with older and wealthier people being more opposed, but education does not have a significant impact on support for welfare spending (Gilens 1995; 1996; 1999).

Two types of dependent variables – individual-choice and government-based helping activities – are based on two different types of activities. The individual-choice activities are those where people have

---

[4] I do not have any measures of racism in the survey. As Devos and Banaji's (2005) research suggests, however, there is a strong tendency among white Americans to associate race (being white) with being an American, and this tendency might be deeper and more widespread than racist attitudes.

some say in who gets helped and who does not. People can choose to which charities or crises they wish to devote their resources and which voluntary organizations they will join. These, then, are the measures that were used to create the individual-choice activities scale.[5] As Miller argues, though, people can also help their compatriots by supporting strong welfare programs aimed at helping the neediest of one's national group members. These government programs, supported through taxes, can help a large number of people, but they also remove from the taxpayers any choice concerning who gets helped. In this sense, government assistance programs help many people, many of whom are viewed by some Americans as marginalized group members. I used several different measures to create a scale of support for government-based help. One was the obligations question concerning welfare support. I also used the questions on support for government spending on welfare, blacks, urban areas, and education. Responses to these five questions were used to create the government-based helping scale.[6]

These two scales are the primary dependent variables used in the following analyses. What effect do national identity and the setting of exclusive national group boundaries have on helping behaviors? Is national identity strength all that matters or is it the interaction between national identity and the setting of exclusive boundaries that affects helping behaviors? I argue that it depends on the type of helping behavior. Table 4.1 provides evidence that this expectation is right on target. The impact of national identity, the setting of exclusive, hard boundaries, and the interaction between these two depend on the type of help given. What matters most in predicting whether people give to charities, volunteer in their local community, and help in a crisis is the strength of their national identity. When the setting of hard boundaries is at its mean, people who feel strongly attached to their national

[5] I used the three obligations questions to create the scale. Each of the obligations questions was transformed to range from 0 to 1, and the transformed questions were added together to create the individual-choice activities scale. The coefficient alpha for the scale is .64.

[6] I created an additive scale using these five questions. Each question was transformed to range from 0 to 1 and then these transformed measures were added together to create the scale. The scale ranges from 0, signifying no support for any government programs, to 5, signifying support for all of the government programs. The coefficient alpha for the scale is .65.

TABLE 4.1. *American national identity, hard boundaries, and helping behaviors*

	Individual-choice helping	Government-based helping
American identity (mean centered)	.439*** (.054)	.191*** (.052)
Hard boundaries (mean centered)	.047 (.039)	−.114** (.037)
American identity (mean centered) X hard boundaries (mean centered) interaction	−.140 (.170)	−.406* (.159)
Sex (male)	−.037* (.015)	−.012 (.014)
Age	−.021 (.037)	−.061 (.036)
South	.004 (.016)	−.052*** (.015)
Race (whites excluded category):		
Black	.052* (.025)	.068** (.024)
Hispanic	−.001 (.028)	.079** (.027)
Other race	.074* (.032)	.048 (.030)
Education	.097*** (.027)	.098*** (.026)
Income	−.014 (.031)	−.087** (.030)
Religious	.038 (.020)	−.007 (.019)
Ideology (moderates excluded category):		
Extremely conservative	−.028 (.029)	−.114*** (.028)
Somewhat conservative	.081*** (.022)	.024 (.020)
Somewhat liberal	.066* (.029)	.128*** (.027)
Extremely liberal	.113** (.040)	.141*** (.037)
Party identification (Independents excluded category):		
Strong Republican	.029 (.024)	−.069** (.023)
Weak Republican	.020 (.023)	.014 (.022)
Weak Democrat	.006 (.022)	.028 (.021)
Strong Democrat	−.033 (.022)	.060** (.021)
Individualism	−.014 (.033)	−.096** (.032)
Egalitarianism	.130*** (.032)	.226*** (.030)
Constant	.569*** (.047)	.520*** (.045)
F	7.83***	15.78***
Adj. R²	.14	.27
N	937	864

Source: Perceptions of the American People Survey, 2002
Note: * p < .05; ** p < .01; *** p < .001. Results are from ordinary least squares (OLS) regression analyses. Cell entries are unstandardized regression coefficients with standard errors in parentheses. All of the dependent and independent variables have been transformed to range from 0 to 1. See the appendix for variable details.

group want to do what they can to help their fellow group members, especially those who are prototypical. At the same time, both the setting of hard boundaries on the group and the interaction between identity and exclusive boundaries are insignificant. What generates these individual-choice helping behaviors is feeling a strong sense of attachment and commitment to one's fellow Americans. Since people can choose whom to help, the exclusivity of the boundaries does not matter. Strong identifiers can satisfy their strong sense of obligation to their fellow nationals by helping prototypical group members.

The differences are striking when shifting attention to government-based helping behaviors. American identity continues to have a significant effect on support for government-based helping when the boundaries variable is at its mean. And when American identity is at its mean, the setting of hard boundaries has a significant effect on support – those who set more exclusive boundaries are less likely to support government programs. But the interaction between American identity and the setting of hard boundaries is also significant. People who strongly identify with their national group *and* who set exclusive boundaries on that group are much *less* likely to support government programs that help fellow group members who are in need. The study asked respondents about government assistance programs, specifically for blacks or programs that Americans associate with blacks, such as welfare and programs to support urban areas. Strong identifiers in general want to help, but strong identifiers who set exclusive group boundaries do not want to help marginalized group members, and blacks do not fit the stereotype of the prototypical American. Helping is geared toward those who more closely approximate the prototypical group member.

The full effect of the interaction between American identity and the setting of hard boundaries can be better seen in Figure 4.3. Figure 4.3(a) depicting individual-choice help shows that the setting of hard boundaries is close to being irrelevant for strong identifiers. The line is essentially flat. Among medium and weak identifiers, the setting of hard boundaries has a positive impact on willingness to help, but the impact is decidedly muted. In general, the same cannot be said for Figure 4.3(b). Weak identifiers who set hard boundaries are somewhat more likely to support government programs that help marginalized Americans than weak identifiers who set few boundaries, and the

a. Individual-choice help

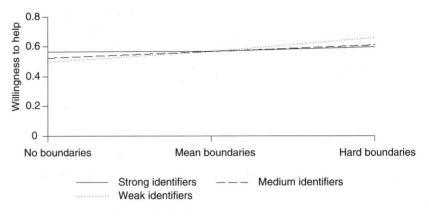

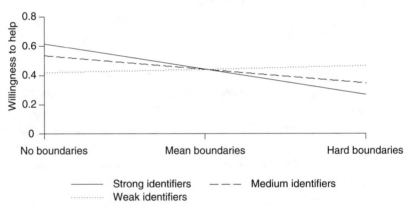

FIGURE 4.3. Willingness to help, national identity, and the setting of hard boundaries

relationship is reversed for medium identifiers, but the lines in both cases are close to being flat. The impact of the setting of hard boundaries on Americans' willingness to support government programs is, however, especially pronounced among strong identifiers. Strong identifiers want to help their fellow Americans, and when these strong identifiers do not set hard boundaries on their national group, they are more likely than anyone else to support government programs that help marginalized Americans. The flip side, though, is that strong identifiers who set hard boundaries on their national group are by far the

least likely to support these government programs. Since strong identifiers tend to set harder boundaries than anyone else, strong identifiers
are much more likely to be unsupportive of government programs that
help marginalized Americans. They set hard boundaries to ensure that
their group is strong and viable. In doing so, they create a situation in
which marginalized group members do not benefit from their membership in the group the way that prototypical members do.

These results for national identity and the setting of boundaries
on the group hold even when important alternative explanations are
controlled. Beginning with individualism and egalitarianism, previous scholars have emphasized individualism as an explanation for
support for government programs and have found egalitarianism not
to have a significant impact. In this research, however, it is egalitarianism that has the bigger impact on both helping behaviors. The
more people believe people ought to be treated equally and that doing
so is better for the country, the more likely they are to try to do something to help the disadvantaged through their own individual efforts
and through support for government programs. Beliefs in equality
are clearly a driving force in promoting the desire to help fellow
Americans. People who hold the individualism norm are significantly
less supportive of government programs designed to help the less fortunate, but these beliefs do not affect support for individual-choice
activities. Miller (1995) argues that Americans' widespread belief in
individualism overshadows the possible positive effects of American
identity on support for welfare. Once individualism is controlled,
national identity does have the positive effect that Miller hopes to
find. But even without individualism controlled, American identity
continues to have a positive effect (data are not shown). What seems
to drive Americans' lack of support for welfare is the individual and
combined effects of commitment and the setting of hard boundaries
more so than individualism.

Some of the other expectations based on past research are also
confirmed. As far as political attitudes are concerned, it is interesting
to note that strong Democrats and liberals tend to be more supportive of government assistance programs whereas strong Republicans
and the extremely conservative are less supportive than Independents
and moderates (the excluded categories). Both liberals and the somewhat conservative, on the other hand, support individual-choice

helping. It is moderates and the extremely conservative who are less inclined to support these activities. Party identification is not related to giving to charities and other individual-choice helping behaviors. Contrary to Brooks' (2006) argument, liberals feel a strong sense of obligation to help their fellow Americans both through individual-choice and government-based helping.

The effects of the demographic variables are less consistent. People from the South are reluctant to support government programs that help marginalized Americans, as are wealthier Americans. The well-educated along with blacks and Hispanics are more supportive of these programs. Blacks and the well-educated are also more supportive of giving to charities, volunteering, and helping in a crisis. Interestingly, religiosity is not significantly related to either type of helping behavior. Contrary to past research, the religious are no more or less likely than the nonreligious to help through individual efforts or to support government programs that help the needy.

The results concerning the main variables of interest, though, are what is important and telling. First, even taking into account the variety of explanations used in past research to explain individual helping behaviors, national identity matters. People who feel deeply a part of their national group are much more likely to want to help fellow group members when they can choose who benefits from their activities. The flip side, of course, is that weak identifiers are more reluctant to want to help. They do not feel the same sense of responsibility for their fellow Americans and do not feel compelled to give to charity, volunteer, or aid in a crisis to help their national group. In the lexicon of research on individual giving, national identity needs to be included as an important explanatory variable. It can hold its own against the other explanations that have been offered in the literature.

Second, there is a big difference between what explains individual-choice and government-based helping behaviors. When marginalized group members are the recipients of the help, or at least are perceived to be the likely recipients of the help, strong identifiers who place strict, almost impermeable boundaries on the national group are significantly less likely to help these fellow Americans through their support of government programs than are weak identifiers and strong identifiers who do not set exclusive boundaries. Strong identifiers who set exclusive boundaries want to know that they are helping prototypical members of the group, not group members who are deviant and who can potentially harm the group by making the distinction between the ingroup and the outgroup less clear. This isn't an issue with individual-choice giving because people can choose whom to help. If nothing else, the people who will decide how to spend the money, and on whom, will be people who are similar to the donor and presumably will share the donor's interests in protecting the group.

If these arguments are right, then we should find that strong identifiers are not opposed to government spending that helps prototypical members and makes the group stronger. Tax monies are used for many different government ventures, some of which help marginalized Americans and others that help prototypical Americans. Some government assistance programs are geared toward helping minorities and the disadvantaged, but others give assistance to, for example, farmers.[7] And some government spending explicitly works to secure the ingroup against possibly hostile outgroups, such as military and defense spending.[8] If my argument is correct, then we should find that it is American identity that best predicts support for government spending on prototypical members or on securing the ingroup from threatening outgroups. The setting of exclusive boundaries and its interaction with American identity should not be relevant since the money is used for helping prototypical ingroup members.

I also examine people's sense of obligation to help fellow Americans by paying taxes. As noted previously, taxes are used by the government to pay for many different programs, not just government assistance programs. If people want to help a wide variety of fellow Americans, they can do so by accepting the need to pay taxes. Taxes are how the government pays for programs that affect many people and for defense. Many Americans, however, are not happy about having to pay taxes. Are they opposed to taxes because of military spending, government assistance programs, or what? We can answer this question by comparing the results of feeling an obligation to pay taxes to the other government spending models (the government-based helping

---

[7] In 2005, the federal government spent $50.7 billion on food assistance programs and $123.3 billion for public assistance programs. In the same year, it spent $26.6 billion for agricultural programs (Commerce 2007).

[8] Again in 2005, the federal government spent $495.3 billion on defense (Commerce 2007).

model in Table 4.1, government assistance for farmers, and support
for spending on the military and defense). What are people thinking
about when they say they do or do not have an obligation to pay taxes?
Are they thinking mostly about tax money that goes to marginalized
or to prototypical Americans?

I used the independent variables listed in Table 4.1 to explain people's responses to three questions: To what extent do people support
government assistance for farmers, support spending on the military
and defense, and view paying taxes as an obligation they owe to fellow
Americans? The results in Table 4.2 are clear. For all three dependent
variables, American identity has a positive impact on support. When
the hard boundaries variable is at its mean, people who strongly identify with the American people are more supportive than weak identifiers of government assistance for farmers (a prototypical group in
the United States), spending on the military and defense (a means
of securing the ingroup), and paying taxes (the source of the money
for these programs). In fact, national identity is by far the best predictor of support for spending on the military. The setting of hard
boundaries and the interaction term are irrelevant when the target
is prototypical farmers. These results look very similar to the results
on individual-choice helping (see Table 4.1), where American identity
was significant and the boundaries variables were not. What matters
in all of these cases is helping the ingroup, and strong identifiers want
to do just that. The setting of hard boundaries is a significant predictor of support for military spending, but in a positive direction. When
American identity is at its mean, people who set exclusive boundaries
on their national group are more inclined to favor military spending,
perhaps because the military helps to secure the ingroup from potentially hostile outgroups.

A very different story concerning hard boundaries emerges when
looking at the obligation to pay taxes. Both the hard boundaries variable and the interaction term are significant and negative (the interaction term is the second best predictor after education). The more
strongly people identify with the American people *and* the more
strictly and exclusively they set the boundaries on the national group,
the less supportive they are of paying taxes as a way to help their fellow Americans. The fact that all three of the key independent variables
are significant in both the government-based helping and the taxes

models suggests that people's opposition to paying taxes is based on their perception that their money is being used to support marginalized group members. If they thought their money was being used to help prototypical members, then American identity should be the only significant variable of the three, as it is in both the individual-choice and the farmers models. Instead, the negative impact of hard boundaries and the interaction term suggest that people's aversion to paying taxes is based on their perception that their money is being spent on group members who are not well liked and who harm rather than strengthen the group. Even though defense spending makes up a vast proportion of government spending – 20 percent in 2005 (Commerce 2007) – and therefore much of people's taxes are going to pay for the military and defense, many people, especially strong identifiers who set exclusive boundaries, instead think of their money going to help disadvantaged, and marginalized, group members.

CONCLUSION

Strong identifiers are highly motivated to want to help their group. The viability of the group is important to them, as are their fellow group members. The group is a community, and strong identifiers want to help their community flourish. The strong bond among group members, even among members who will never meet face to face, is a real one. A national group that is necessarily large and anonymous experiences these same dynamics. Some group members feel a strong sense of attachment to their national group and they rally to help fellow nationals when crises hit, when people are in need, or when the nation needs to be defended. Strong identifiers, who want to have a positive identification with their group, do what they can to ensure the group's progress.

In many ways, the helping behavior of strong identifiers is admirable. We as a nation hold people who help others and who defend the nation in high esteem. To pick just a small handful of newspaper headlines, there is a clear association between helping in a crisis and being considered a hero: "Ham Operators among Katrina's Unsung Heroes," "Amid Ruins, Volunteers Are Emerging as Heroes," "Where Heroes Died; Clarkston Firefighters Visit Ground Zero in NYC," and more generally, "National Make a Difference Day Volunteering

TABLE 4.2. *American national identity, hard boundaries, and their impact on paying taxes and supporting spending on farmers and the military*

	Support government assistance for farmers	Support spending on military/defense	Have obligation to pay taxes
American identity (mean centered)	.133** (.048)	.568*** (.081)	.179** (.064)
Hard boundaries (mean centered)	-.035 (.035)	.128* (.059)	-.091* (.046)
American identity (mean centered) X hard boundaries (mean centered) interaction	-.235 (.153)	-.316 (.257)	-.661*** (.204)
Sex (male)	-.016 (.013)	-.031 (.023)	-.006 (.018)
Age	-.180*** (.034)	.067 (.057)	.092* (.045)
South	.042** (.014)	.023 (.024)	.036 (.019)
Race (whites excluded category):			
Black	-.015 (.023)	-.040 (.038)	-.004 (.030)
Hispanic	.023 (.025)	.016 (.042)	.062 (.034)
Other race	.042 (.029)	.041 (.049)	-.052 (.039)
Education	-.013 (.024)	-.128** (.041)	.131*** (.032)
Income	-.088** (.028)	.011 (.047)	-.079* (.037)
Religious	.018 (.018)	.011 (.029)	-.019 (.023)
Ideology (moderates excluded category):			
Extremely conservative	-.013 (.026)	.000 (.044)	-.012 (.035)
Somewhat conservative	-.009 (.019)	.036 (.033)	.059* (.026)
Somewhat liberal	.082*** (.026)	-.096* (.044)	.085* (.034)
Extremely liberal	.110** (.036)	-.076 (.060)	.050 (.048)

Party identification (Independents excluded category):

Strong Republican	-.003 (.022)	.177*** (.037)	.020 (.029)
Weak Republican	.009 (.021)	.064 (.035)	.037 (.028)
Weak Democrat	-.019 (.020)	.023 (.033)	.026 (.026)
Strong Democrat	.026 (.020)	-.096** (.033)	.012 (.027)
Individualism	-.005 (.030)	-.036 (.050)	.087* (.040)
Egalitarianism	.069* (.028)	-.008 (.048)	-.042 (.038)
Constant	.814*** (.042)	.626*** (.071)	.720*** (.056)
F	4.92***	10.32***	4.27***
Adj. R²	.09	.18	.07
N	932	932	

Source: Perceptions of the American People Survey, 2002

Note: * p < .05; ** p < .01; *** p < .001. Results are from OLS regression analyses. Cell entries are unstandardized regression coefficients with standard errors in parentheses. All of the dependent and independent variables have been transformed to range from 0 to 1. See the appendix for variable details.

Makes Heroes of All of Us Each Day."[9] Anyone who has needed help during a crisis knows how important these helpers are. The national community is richer for their actions. Weak identifiers do not contribute to their community in the same way. They are less willing to extend themselves on behalf of their fellow Americans.

But the helping behavior of strong identifiers comes at a price, a price that is heavy and destructive to the national community they are trying to help. When help is readily given to prototypical Americans but is withheld from marginalized group members, the dynamic exacerbates the feelings of frustration and anger among marginalized group members and further widens the gap between those who are prototypical and those who are marginalized. Marginalized group members are Americans, too. Why shouldn't they get the same group benefits as everyone else? If they are all Americans, why don't they count?

The helping behaviors discussed in this chapter are based on attitudinal measures: feeling an obligation to help, supporting government spending for certain groups, believing that the government should spend more or less in certain areas. I have not examined actual helping behaviors thus far. To remedy this potential problem, I conducted an experiment to test whether marginalized group members get less than prototypical group members from strong identifiers compared to weak identifiers (see the appendix for experiment information). I used a standard one-shot dictator game with a nonstudent adult sample in Lincoln, Nebraska. Participants were told that they would be randomly assigned either to divide $20 between themselves and another participant or to receive whatever amount the divider chose. The supposed randomization process was rigged so that the person chosen as the receiver was actually a confederate of the experiment whereas the participant was always the divider. The two players in the game were brought into a room together to meet each other. They were asked to introduce themselves, with the confederate always going first. The confederate said the same thing to each subject he met: that he was born in Omaha, that he had come to Lincoln to go to the university, and that he had stayed in Lincoln upon graduating to work.

---

[9] The headlines came from the following sources respectively: Ambrose (2001); Sandaine (2001); Konigsmark and Hampson (2005); Prescott (2006).

Two young men acted the role of the confederate, one white and one Arab American. Participants were actually randomly assigned to one of these receivers.

After the introductions and the supposed random assignment to roles, participants were told that they would divide the $20 and that any money they kept would be their only payment for participating in the experiment. Similarly, the money given to the receiver would be the money he would keep. The confederate was then ushered out of the room and the participant was asked to divide the money in private. Once they had made their decision, participants were asked to fill out a short survey and were paid for their participation in the experiment (everyone was actually paid $25).

Research using this dictator game has found that people usually split the money almost in half, with the divider keeping a bit more money than the amount given to the other player, when the two players meet each other face to face (see, e.g., Bohnet and Frey 1999). In this experiment, I take into account both the strength of the national identity of the divider and whether the receiver was white or Arab American.[10] As Figure 4.4 shows, the impact of the interaction between national identity strength and the race of the receiver is telling.[11] Among weak identifiers, the race of the receiver is irrelevant. Whether the receiver was white or Arab American, the divider gave about $9 ($9 for the white receiver, $9.22 for the Arab American receiver) and kept about $11 for himself or herself. The same equality in giving does not hold among strong identifiers. A strong identifier faced with a white receiver divided the money fairly equally, giving an average of $9 to the receiver and keeping $11 – the same distribution as weak identifiers. The amount of money given to the receiver changes dramatically when the receiver is Arab American. Strong identifiers gave only $4.27 to the Arab American receiver and kept an average of $15.73 for himself or herself. Strong identifiers perceive a pronounced difference between prototypical and marginalized Americans and both their attitudes and their behavior reflect this distinction.

---

[10] Since the number of cases is small, I divided national identity into two groups: weak identity and strong identity.

[11] In an analysis of variance (ANOVA), using only white participants, the interaction between identity strength and race of the receiver is significant at the .10 level.

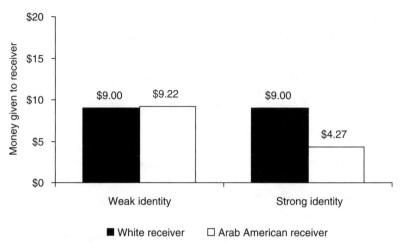

FIGURE 4.4. Amount of money kept by the divider by national identity and race of the receiver

The experiment was set up in such a way that participants had a selfish incentive to keep as much money for themselves as they felt comfortable keeping. They thought they would walk out of the lab with only the money they kept and that the receiver would get only the money he was given. Weak identifiers kept a bit more money for themselves than they gave, but they did so regardless of the ethnicity of the receiver. Strong identifiers also kept a bit more money for themselves when the receiver was a prototypical white American, keeping just over half of the money. They were decidedly ungenerous, however, when the receiver was a marginalized Arab American. The attitudinal differences found using the survey data are replicated using actual behavioral data. Strong identifiers are helpful and generous to prototypical members and at the same time treat marginalized members ungenerously.

I have argued throughout this chapter that strong identifiers are motivated to help their group. Their motivations are not selfish. Rather, they are willing to do whatever it takes to help the group. Their treatment of marginalized group members, however, creates a problem for the very group they want to help. When marginalized group members are not given the same benefits as prototypical members, the inequalities in the system become exacerbated. Prototypical members get helped, marginalized members do not, yet marginalized group members are Americans too. Strong identifiers who define their national group narrowly let marginalized group members know in explicit terms that they are not fully accepted in the national group, that they do not count. When asked about identifying with the American people, the reaction of the African American focus group in Lincoln, Nebraska, was swift:

Tonia: I identify first with African Americans and I am always in a fight. So I guess I have to say I don't identify as closely with Americans as I think I should as an African American. I'm always in a fight – work, church (church is a bunch of African Americans), schools where my kids are concerned. And when I say fight I just mean an issue, not necessarily fisticuffs always.

Kim: I second that. ...

Diane: ... I couldn't go out and be identified with, like you said, quote, unquote, the American people because you get slammed down so quick. Like she said, going to the store, going to my child's school, getting into a conflict.

Vanessa: Amen.

Marginalized group members end up feeling angry and alienated (Abrams, Hogg, and Marques 2005). They potentially withdraw from their national group, their identification with their fellow Americans weakens, and they become much more critical of their national group than they would if they felt themselves fully members of the group. As I will show in the next chapter, strong identifiers view criticism as harmful to the group and want to stifle it. Their treatment of marginalized group members creates precisely the criticisms they so dislike.

5

Loyalty in the Face of Criticism

In the months leading up to the United States' invasion of Iraq in March 2003, both antiwar protesters and prowar activists took to the streets. Antiwar protesters wanted to stop the United States from going to war and to let people at home and around the world know that there was no consensus among Americans concerning the approaching war. These antiwar protesters professed their support for the troops and their love of America, but they wanted the direction of U.S. policy changed. The Reverend Calvin Morris, a protester in Chicago, summed up the protesters' feelings well: "We love America because America is a place where when things are out of order, people can disagree and protest" ("Americans on Both Sides Take to the Streets" 2003). The prowar activists had a very different take on the protesters' motivations. Signs reading "America – Love It or Leave It" that cropped up at the counterprotests were reminiscent of the Vietnam War era. According to the prowar activists, the antiwar protesters could not love America. How could they love America when they were damaging the country? Sherri Tabb, one of the counterprotesters, associated antiwar protests with helping enemies of the United States when she said, "The anti-war protesters ... are aiding and abetting Saddam" ("Thousands Rally in Support of War" 2003).

No one complains or takes offense when people give to charity or help in a crisis as a means of helping fellow group members. The same cannot be said when criticism is the means by which someone tries to help fellow group members. If the group is doing something wrong or needs to do better at something, it helps the group overall to correct the problem. Leaving a problem to fester rather than proactively taking care of the problem is hardly helpful to the group and could lead to the group's downfall. The use of interventions in families and such things as academic program reviews in colleges and universities are designed to find both the strengths *and* weaknesses of a group and to offer constructive criticisms to improve the functioning of the group. Yet it remains a challenge to see criticism in this light.

Accepting criticism is difficult. No one likes to be criticized, and a common response in the face of criticism is for people to become defensive even when it is clear that the criticism is meant to help and even when the criticism is obviously correct (Sherman and Cohen 2006). Group members strike out against the critics, refusing to accept the criticism as accurate and often tightening the bonds among group members, who must stand united against the perceived attack (Branscombe et al. 1999). The criticisms made by antiwar protesters against both the Vietnam War and the Iraq War were not received with openness and warmth by Americans who supported the government's policies. The protesters should "love it or leave it" – that is, keep quiet or move to another country. Protesters who criticize government actions are necessarily bad and shouldn't be part of the group.

Associating critics with being bad group members is a common response. A good group member does not aid and abet the enemy, as Sherri Tabb well knows. When Americans criticize the U.S. government during times of war, they are "un-American" or are helping the enemy (Saddam Hussein, the insurgents in Iraq, al-Qaeda). Bill O'Reilly (2007) said that people "who publicly criticize their country in a time of military crisis" are "bad Americans." Representative Steve King (R-Iowa) criticized war protesters for displaying "un-American values" ("Pro-war Demonstrators Show Support for U.S. Troops" 2003). Trip Baird, an analyst at the Heritage Foundation, referred to a group of students planning a protest against a military response to the attacks on September 11, 2001, as "the most un-American group imaginable" (Beaucar 2001). And a North Platte, Nebraska, radio station joined a boycott of music by the Dixie Chicks because of "un-American comments" made by a member of the group criticizing President George W. Bush ("Some Texas Stations Stop Playing

Dixie Chicks Songs after Bush Remarks" 2003). The message is clear: Criticizing the government makes the critic a bad American. The critic is labeled "un-American" and probably shouldn't be an American at all. Only true Americans (who do not criticize) are accepted fully into the national group. Good Americans are positive about the group and have great pride in what the group has accomplished. Criticism questions the group and its accomplishments and therefore weakens the group.

This chapter examines how national identity affects responses to criticisms directed at the national group. While strong identifiers are significantly more likely than weak identifiers to want to help the group, I argue that strong identifiers are much less likely to accept criticism that could potentially improve the group because they view such criticism as a threat. When a group is attacked physically, group members unite to fight off the attackers. The same response occurs when a group is attacked verbally, that is, when it is criticized. The more strongly people identify with the national group, the more likely they are to view criticisms as an attack on the group and to respond defensively. I use data from the Perceptions of the American People survey to test the relationship between national identity strength and reactions to criticism.

But I also argue that *who* criticizes the group matters. As was shown in the previous chapter, prototypical group members are more likely to be helped than marginalized group members. Prototypical members exemplify the strength of the group. Marginalized group members potentially weaken the group. It makes sense, then, to expect that responses to criticisms from prototypical members will differ from responses to criticisms from marginalized group members. I argue that strong identifiers will view criticisms from prototypical members as more constructive and will therefore be more likely to accept the criticisms as helpful to the group. These same strong identifiers, however, will view criticisms from marginalized group members as a threat to the group and as an attempt to weaken the group itself. Criticisms from marginalized group members will therefore be more likely to be rejected. I use an experimental design to test these arguments.

Before discussing reactions to criticism, however, I will briefly examine positive responses to the group. If "good Americans" express their loyalty to their group in part by being proud of its accomplishments, we should find that strong identifiers are much more likely to experience a sense of pride in their national group than weak identifiers. I examine survey respondents' pride in various proposed accomplishments of the United States and then test in a multivariate analysis the impact of national identity strength on pride. I bring in patriotism since it could be argued that the patriotism norm is driving pride (and reactions to criticism) rather than the social aspect of national identity. Is it love of country that really matters? Or are people primarily motivated by their feeling of shared identity with fellow Americans?

NATIONAL IDENTITY AND PRIDE
IN AMERICAN ACCOMPLISHMENTS

Americans take pride in their country and its accomplishments. Indeed, they consistently rank near the top in national pride over the years (Smith and Kim 2006). While most researchers associate national pride with patriotism (de Figueiredo and Elkins 2003; Kosterman and Feshbach 1989), I argue that it has much to do with national identity and feeling part of the group (see also Smith and Kim 2006). If patriotism is, at its core, loving one's country, then pride in the accomplishments of one's country naturally links to patriotism. But when people feel a strong sense of identity with their national group, they share a sense of linked fate and group pride when fellow nationals do something noteworthy. The question comes down to this: Do people feel pride in their country's achievements or do they feel pride in what their fellow compatriots, past and present, have accomplished, a pride that includes their own sense of self since they are a part of the group? While both are important, I argue that it is the latter that carries more weight in people's national pride.

People widely favor their own group over groups to which they do not belong (Mullen, Brown, and Smith 1992). This does not mean that people are especially mean and nasty to outgroups (Brewer 1999), but they definitely, and automatically, tend to favor their ingroup (Perdue et al. 1990). When faced with a pool of limited resources, they give more to their ingroup than to the outgroup (Brewer 2003: ch. 3). They find ingroup members to be more attractive than outgroup members and they rate ingroup members as more highly accomplished on characteristics that distinguish their ingroup from the outgroup (see, e.g., Hogg and Abrams 1988).

This favorability bias toward the ingroup makes perfect sense if people gain a sense of collective self-esteem from their group membership. Their collective self-esteem is their positive sense of themselves as a member of the group; this sense accrues when their group distinguishes itself, not always positively, from other groups (see, e.g., Spinner-Halev and Theiss-Morse 2003 for an overview of this argument). The actions of the group matter even when people have not been directly involved in the action. Sports fans, for example, "bask in the reflected glory" of their winning team. According to Robert Cialdini, "It becomes possible to attain some sort of respect and regard not by one's own achievements but by one's connection to individuals of attainment" (quoted in McKinley 2000: 1). The more highly fans identify with their team, the more loyal they will be to the team, even when it loses (Wann and Branscombe 1990). Sports fans associate the team's performance with their own performance: They feel elated when their team wins and sad when their team loses, and these reactions are often physiological as well as psychological (Wann 2001). Identifying with a team creates a sense of community among the fans, and that sense of community becomes a strong driving force in fans' reactions to the team's wins and losses.

Since the strength of identification with a sports team matters, we should similarly find that the more strongly people identify with their national group, the more they will react positively to the group's accomplishments, even if an individual group member did not directly contribute to the achievement. Weak identifiers, on the other hand, do not feel as much a part of the community and therefore will not share the same sense of glory that strong identifiers feel in response to the accomplishments of fellow Americans. To test whether this is the case, I used questions asking about survey respondents' pride in various achievements of the United States: "The next questions ask you how proud you are of the United States in a variety of important areas. For each area I mention, please tell me whether you are very proud, somewhat proud, not very proud, or not proud at all." The four achievements analyzed here are the way democracy works in the United States, the United States' political influence in the world,

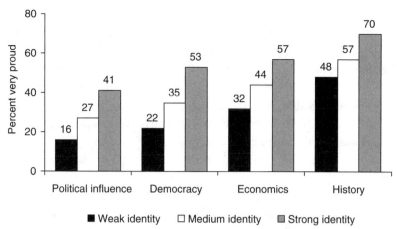

FIGURE 5.1. National identity and pride in U.S. accomplishments

the United States' economic achievements, and the history of the United States.

Figure 5.1 shows that national identity is strongly related to national pride across all four referents. Strong identifiers consistently take more pride than weak identifiers in the proposed achievements of the United States. A majority of strong identifiers feel "very proud" of the United States' democracy (53 percent), its economic achievements (57 percent), and its history (70 percent). Just short of a majority (41 percent) feel "very proud" of the political influence of the United States abroad. Weak identifiers, on the other hand, never reach a majority in feeling "very proud" in any area. While 48 percent of weak identifiers feel very proud of the history of the United States, only 22 percent feel "very proud" of how democracy works and only 16 percent feel that level of pride in the United States' political influence abroad. Strong identifiers are significantly more likely to claim the highest level of pride in the achievements of the United States than weak identifiers.

These results ignore the potential impact of patriotism on pride. It might well be the case that national identity is strongly related to pride only because of its strong relationship with the patriotism norm. Using an additive scale of national pride as the dependent variable, where responses to all four pride questions were added together to create the national pride scale, I ran a regression analysis that included various control variables along with national identity and patriotism. If pride is primarily related to patriotism, then patriotism should be highly significant and much more influential a variable than the social aspect of national identity. Indeed, once patriotism is included in the model, national identity should simply wash out if this argument is right. If, however, pride is primarily related to national identity – such that people's sense of connection with their fellow Americans is what matters and all Americans share in the glory of the successful members – then national identity should have the strongest relationship with national pride and patriotism should have less of an influence.

What explains national pride? Table 5.1 demonstrates convincingly that American national identity is a better predictor of national pride than patriotism. While both variables are highly significant, national identity has almost four times the impact of patriotism on pride. The national pride scale has been transformed to range from 0 (not proud of any achievements) to 1 (very proud of all achievements). A change in patriotism from not patriotic to highly patriotic increases national pride by .12, a highly significant impact. Yet a change in national identity from very weak identity to very strong identity increases national pride by almost half the scale (.46). National identity is by far the strongest predictive variable in the model. People who strongly identify with their fellow Americans take a great deal of pride in the accomplishments of their fellow group members and in their nation's achievements. The accomplishments of group members are reflected in strong identifiers' sense of their collective self. Love of country matters as well, but national identity matters more.

The control variables also tell an interesting story. National pride is higher among the better educated, Republicans of whatever strength, and liberals. African Americans, in contrast, are less likely to feel pride in the United States' accomplishments. The two strongest predictors of national pride after national identity and patriotism, however, are egalitarianism and individualism. Since individualism is a core American value, it comes as no surprise that people who more strongly hold the value exhibit more national pride. A widely held belief in the United States is that America is a great nation because of the willingness of its people to work hard and to make it on their own. The Horatio Alger story is a good example. The American myth of its greatness rests on people pulling themselves up by their own

TABLE 5.1. *American national identity and pride in U.S. achievements*

	Pride in U.S. achievements
American identity	.460*** (.034)
Patriotism	.120*** (.032)
Individualism	.093*** (.020)
Egalitarianism	−.096*** (.018)
Sex (male)	−.006 (.009)
Age	.019 (.021)
Race (whites excluded category):	
Black	−.031* (.014)
Hispanic	.016 (.016)
Other race	−.016 (.019)
Education	.034* (.015)
Political knowledge	.002 (.015)
Ideology (moderates excluded category):	
Extremely conservative	.015 (.017)
Somewhat conservative	−.009 (.012)
Somewhat liberal	.037* (.016)
Extremely liberal	.025 (.024)
Party identification (Independents excluded category):	
Strong Republican	.046*** (.014)
Weak Republican	.026* (.013)
Weak Democrat	.021 (.012)
Strong Democrat	.008 (.013)
Constant	.273*** (.032)
F	36.55***
Adj. R^2	.36
N	1184

Source: Perceptions of the American People Survey, 2002
Note: * $p < .05$; ** $p < .01$; *** $p < .001$. The results are based on ordinary least squares (OLS) regression analyses. Cell entries are unstandardized regression coefficients with standard errors in parentheses. The dependent variable and all of the independent variables have been transformed to range from 0 to 1. See the appendix for variable details.

bootstraps and fulfilling the American dream of attaining wealth and fame. The more that Americans accept this myth as true, the more pride they take in their country's accomplishments. Egalitarianism, in contrast, has a negative effect on national pride. Recall that the egalitarianism measures are worded in such a way that they express dissatisfaction with current levels of equality, that more needs to be done to reach acceptable levels of equality. The more people believe that the United States needs to do more to reach its standard of equality, the less pride they have in the achievements of their nation. If the United States has not reached an acceptable level of egalitarianism, it is hard to accept that its accomplishments are as wonderful as some contend. Looking at it from the other direction, the more that people believe the United States has achieved equality, the more pride they have overall in their nation's achievements.

The major story here, though, is that national identity is strongly related to national pride. The more strongly that people identify with a group, the more positively they evaluate the group and its accomplishments and the more they show favoritism toward their group. People want to be members of groups they evaluate positively, as such positive group membership enhances their collective self-esteem. And the more strongly that people identify with their group, the more positive they need to be. Americans who are strong identifiers view their nation's achievements as something to be very proud of, indeed, as exceptional.

DEALING WITH CRITICISM

People naturally want to be part of a group they evaluate positively, but no group is beyond criticism. Every group can stand to be improved, some more than others. Constructive criticism, then, can be seen as a way to improve the group, to help it by making it better, and therefore to strengthen the group over the long term. But criticism is rarely accepted as constructive and helpful. Criticism is more often viewed as threatening and as an attack on the group. When someone finds fault with a group's performance or the effects of its actions, potential weaknesses of the group are exposed for everyone to see. Such brazen attacks are unacceptable to group members who want their group to be invulnerable. Rather than viewing the critic as helping the group,

group members interpret the critic as attacking the group and weakening it.

Reactions depend, however, on whether the critic is an ingroup or an outgroup member (see, e.g., Hornsey, Oppes, and Svensson 2002). If critics belong to a different group, their negative assessment of the group can be discounted and ignored. These outgroup members, who are attacking the group with their criticism, don't really know anything about the ingroup or have an ulterior motive, perhaps wanting to destroy or weaken the ingroup for their own group's benefit. It is relatively easy to dismiss criticism from an outsider, even if it rankles a bit.

It is much more difficult to dismiss criticisms from insiders, those who *should* be loyal to the group. Ingroup critics are potentially the most dangerous: They know the most about the group, they know best the weaknesses and flaws in the group, and they can do the most damage to the group by exposing these weaknesses and flaws to outsiders. Ingroup critics create real problems for the group. But once again, the status of the ingroup member matters. Marginalized group members are perceived by other group members as more dangerous anyway because they muddy the boundaries between the ingroup and the outgroup. Their loyalty to and place in the group are already questioned. Add these members' criticisms of the group and it becomes clear that these marginalized members cannot be trusted and are potentially dangerous to the group. There certainly is no reason to accept the criticisms as valid or as helpful to the group in any way. Doing so gives legitimacy to their claims. The marginalized group members, as other group members see it, are just trying to hurt the group. They are insiders, so they know the dirt, but they are not good group members and must not be tolerated. If it were possible, they shouldn't be members of the group at all. Unfortunately, they are in the group, but they do not need to be listened to, their message ought to be roundly rejected, and they ought to be silenced if possible.

Imagine, however, if the critic is a prototypical group member. This prototypical member is fully accepted in the group and is viewed as loyal and trustworthy. Criticisms coming from such a person are clearly not meant to be destructive. Since prototypical members can be trusted to want to help and strengthen the group, criticisms coming from a prototypical member must be, by definition, constructive and should therefore be listened to by other group members. If these criticisms are taken seriously, the group will be improved, strengthened, and made more viable. Prototypical members are less likely to criticize anyway, so when they do, the criticism must be serious.

The following analysis will be broken down into two parts. The first part will examine whether national identity strength is related to reactions to criticism or to negative assessments of the national group and its past actions. I will use survey data to test whether national identity is related to reactions to criticisms from foreigners, feelings of shame about U.S. actions, support for the United States whether it is right or wrong, and denial of basic rights to Americans who disagree with what America stands for. I will once again include patriotism in the analyses since people who adhere strongly to the patriotism norm are less likely to accept criticism of their country as well. The analysis will also include the relevant control variables.

In the second part, I directly examine whether group members react differently to criticisms coming from prototypical and from marginalized group members. In an experimental design, participants heard either praise for or criticism of the American people from either a prototypical or a marginalized group member. This experimental design, which will be described in greater detail later, allows me to test whether the status of the ingroup member affects reactions to that member's appraisals of the group.

What If the National Group Isn't So Good?

It is easy to look over a country's history and point to actions taken by the government or its people that are roundly denounced in retrospect. An obvious example is Germany in World War II, but so is the British government's support of opium production in colonized India, Japan and the Bataan Death March, and Serbian ethnic cleansing, to name a few. The United States has its own historical actions that are now considered reprehensible: the treatment of Native Americans, slavery, the internment of Japanese Americans in World War II, the torture of prisoners at Abu Ghraib, and so on. Many of these actions are contrary to the very values that Americans proclaim as their country's own, such as equality and liberty. History suggests that it is relatively easy for governments and their citizens to do things that in retrospect are unacceptable to the country's values.

Yet not all citizens willingly accept what a government or its citizens do during these times. Brave souls raise their voices against such actions, even if those voices are few and far between. Raising criticisms is often perilous for the critic, but the point is that such criticisms give citizens and the government the opportunity to hear the message that what the government and its people are doing is wrong. Scholars have spent considerable effort trying to understand why so many people allow atrocities to continue when critics have pointed out how wrong the actions are (on German bystanders and perpetrators, see Kelman and Hamilton 1989; Staub 1989, 2000; on the McCarthy era, see Gibson 1988). The focus I take here is on people's response to the critics' message. Doing something to right a wrong depends on accepting that a wrong has occurred. And I argue that people who strongly identify with their fellow citizens are much less likely to accept that their government and people have done anything wrong.

Respondents to the Perceptions of the American People Survey were asked several questions about their reactions to negative messages about their country or its people: "When someone from another country criticizes the United States, it doesn't bother me at all," "There are some things about the U.S. today that make me feel ashamed of the U.S.," "Americans should support the U.S. even if it is in the wrong," and "Americans who disagree with what America stands for shouldn't be guaranteed their basic rights." Response options were strongly disagree, disagree, neither agree nor disagree, agree, and strongly agree. Overall, Americans seem willing to accept criticisms of the United States and seem disinclined to shoot the messenger (see Table 5.2). Most Americans say it bothers them when a foreigner criticizes the United States, with only 10 percent agreeing that such criticism does not bother them. For the rest of the measures, it is interesting that only about a third of respondents appear unwilling to accept criticism of the United States. Almost two-thirds of respondents say they have felt ashamed of their country, with just under one-third saying they have not felt ashamed. Only about one-third thinks that people should support the United States even if it is in the wrong, and just under a third thinks that people who disagree with what America stands for should be denied their basic rights. These results suggest that while a

TABLE 5.2. *Facing criticism of the group*

	Criticism from foreigners bothers me – %	Ashamed of the U.S. – %	Support U.S. right or wrong – %	No rights for Americans who disagree – %
Strongly agree	3	15	6	7
Agree	7	49	32	23
Neither agree nor disagree	5	7	12	7
Disagree	49	24	42	46
Strongly disagree	37	6	8	18
Strongly agree and agree	10	64	38	30

Source: Perceptions of the American People Survey, 2002

majority of Americans can accept the notion that the United States has done some bad things, a sizable minority – about one-third of respondents – close off criticism by blindly supporting the United States and punishing those who dare to find fault.

What explains these reactions to criticisms of the national group? Patriotism is likely one explanation. Just as patriotism helps to explain pride in the country's achievements, it could also explain reacting negatively to criticism. People who love their country would be loath to hear negative things about it. Beliefs in core American values could also explain reactions to criticisms. People who are willing to criticize the United States for its falling short of reaching full equality are likely to accept other criticisms about the country and its people as well. People who believe in individualism, on the other hand, might view criticism as an attack on that value itself. When American values are under attack, individualism becomes a target, and strong individualists will not want to entertain such criticisms.

The variable of interest, though, is national identity. If people want to be members of groups that increase their self-esteem, then they will want to see their group in a positive light. Negative messages about the group are dangerous because they say something negative not only about the group but about the members of the group themselves. While people who strongly identify with their group might be bothered by what they hear – that is, strong identifiers might feel bad if a foreigner criticizes Americans – they should be less likely to accept the implications of the message in the first place. Strong identifiers will feel compelled to reject the notion that they ought to feel ashamed of the past actions of the United States. Indeed, they are more likely to say that they support the United States whether it is in the right or it is wrong. And strong identifiers will want to punish those Americans who disagree with what America stands for by taking away their rights. Only Americans loyal to the group should be given their basic civil liberties. Weak identifiers, in contrast, are more likely to be the critics to begin with, and they will therefore be more accepting of critical messages and of those doing the criticizing.

Table 5.3 shows that, in general, national identity is a strong predictor of reactions to criticisms. While strong identifiers are no more or less likely than weak identifiers to say that they would be bothered by criticisms made by foreigners, strong identifiers' reactions to the

TABLE 5.3. *Explaining responses to criticism of the group*

	Not bothered by criticism from foreigners	Ashamed of U.S.	Support U.S. right or wrong	No rights for Americans who disagree
American identity	-.012 (.055)	-.392*** (.068)	.230*** (.065)	.143* (.068)
Patriotism	-.374*** (.052)	-.036 (.063)	.262*** (.060)	-.006 (.063)
Individualism	-.063* (.032)	-.085* (.038)	.045 (.037)	.126*** (.038)
Egalitarianism	-.005 (.030)	.138*** (.036)	.006 (.035)	-.007 (.036)
Sex (male)	.026 (.014)	.022 (.017)	-.040* (.016)	-.002 (.017)
Age	.095** (.034)	-.095* (.041)	.136*** (.039)	.169*** (.041)
Race (people of color)	.065*** (.017)	-.029 (.021)	.011 (.020)	.030 (.021)
Education	.081*** (.023)	.014 (.029)	-.079** (.027)	-.136*** (.029)
Political knowledge	.024 (.024)	.062* (.030)	-.067* (.028)	-.232*** (.030)
Ideology (moderates excluded category):				
Extremely conservative	.058* (.027)	.097** (.033)	.036 (.032)	.018 (.033)
Somewhat conservative	.006 (.019)	.041 (.023)	.015 (.022)	.076*** (.023)
Somewhat liberal	.031 (.012)	-.006 (.032)	-.046 (.031)	-.068* (.032)
Extremely liberal	.064 (.037)	-.024 (.045)	-.015 (.043)	-.008 (.045)
Party identification (Independents excluded category):				
Strong Republican	-.086*** (.022)	-.049 (.027)	.051 (.026)	.019 (.027)
Weak Republican	-.041 (.021)	-.046 (.025)	.027 (.024)	.016 (.025)

Weak Democrat	−.025 (.020)	−.037 (.024)	−.011 (.023)	−.038 (.024)
Strong Democrat	−.016 (.020)	.002 (.025)	−.010 (.024)	−.002 (.025)
Constant	.505*** (.052)	.905*** (.064)	.073 (.061)	.302*** (.064)
F	10.73***	8.18***	10.82***	13.45***
Adj. R^2	.12	.09	.12	.15
N	1194	1197	1194	1190

Source: Perceptions of the American People Survey, 2002

Note: * $p < .05$; ** $p < .01$; *** $p < .001$. The results are based on OLS regression analyses. Cell entries are unstandardized regression coefficients, with standard errors in parentheses. The dependent variable and all of the independent variables have been transformed to range from 0 to 1. See the appendix for variable details.

other three questions are strong and highly predictive. Strong identifiers are significantly less likely than weak identifiers to say that they
have felt ashamed of the United States. When people feel ashamed of
their country, they recognize that their country has done something
wrong and they are ashamed of those actions that the country took.
The fact that strong identifiers are so reluctant to say that they feel
ashamed suggests either that they do not recognize any harmful or
negative past or present U.S. actions – if the U.S. has done nothing
wrong, then people can't feel ashamed – or that they know that the
United States has done bad things but refuse to feel, or admit, any
sense of shame about those actions. Research in social psychology
suggests that the former is the better explanation (Doosje, Ellemers,
and Spears 1999). Strong identifiers "may be less willing to acknowledge the negative aspects of their group's history" and therefore may
experience less guilt when presented with both positive and negative
information about the group's past actions (p. 101). When Dutch students were given positive, negative, or mixed information on the Dutch
colonization of Indonesia, there was no difference between strong and
weak identifiers in the positive and negative conditions – participants
felt guilty when confronted with consistently negative information
and did not feel guilty when confronted with consistently positive
information, regardless of their national identity strength. It was in
the mixed information condition where identity strength mattered a
great deal: Strong identifiers tended to focus on the positive aspects of
their national group and therefore had no need to feel guilty, whereas
weak identifiers responded to the mixed information with height-
ened feelings of collective guilt (Doosje, Ellemers, and Spears 1999).
Respondents to the question about feeling ashamed were not given
information about U.S. history, but their responses suggest that in a
mixed information environment, which is the normal environment in
most countries, strong identifiers choose to focus on the positives and
therefore do not feel ashamed, whereas weak identifiers focus on the
negatives and feel ashamed about the negative actions taken by their
country in the past.

Strong identifiers are also much more likely than weak identifiers
to agree that people ought to support the United States even if it is in
the wrong. The research on Dutch students (Doosje, Ellemers, and
Spears 1999) clearly finds that when strong identifiers are faced with

negative information about their national group, they respond with feelings of guilt. But strong identifiers' reactions to the question about supporting the United States even if it is in the wrong suggest a somewhat different dynamic. When a country does something that everyone can agree is wrong, people might well feel guilt or shame, but they can also withdraw their support from their country or government to show their disapproval of the action. Strong identifiers reject this reaction, claiming instead that people must support their country *even when it has done something wrong.* Being loyal to the group takes precedence over communicating disapproval. Indeed, communicating disapproval is a form of disloyalty because it can weaken the group. The group's dirty laundry must remain hidden.

Finally, what should happen to Americans who question the group's values? The critics in this question are ingroup members, fellow Americans, who "disagree with what America stands for." The punishment for their disloyalty to the national group, a punishment that many would see as extreme, is losing their basic rights. Strong identifiers, who want to keep the group strong and viable, apparently have few qualms about inflicting this punishment on ingroup members who won't accept the group's values. People who are disloyal to the group should not be given the benefits of group membership. They should not be given their basic rights. The interesting paradox, of course, is that one of these basic rights is freedom of speech. It appears that strong identifiers are in favor of removing the right to free speech from those who would use that right to criticize the United States. Free speech is a right only for those who agree with what America stands for.

These results consistently tell the same story. Aside from reactions to foreigners who criticize the United States, strong identifiers are much more likely than weak identifiers to remain consistently loyal to their national group. This loyalty to the group takes the form of refusing to accept the criticism in the first place and of punishing the messenger when criticisms are raised. These results hold even when important control variables are included in the model. Strong identifiers want to believe that their group is good and therefore must process criticisms in a way that allows them to keep their highly positive view of their group intact. Weak identifiers, who distance their sense of self from the group, are much more likely to accept that their national group can do bad things and to take collective responsibility for those actions.

Some of the control variables stand out as intriguing as well. Looking across the four dependent variables, the effects of the patriotism norm can be clearly distinguished from those of national identity. Researchers often define blind patriotism as the uncritical love of and support for one's country (see, e.g., Schatz, Staub, and Lavine 1999). In contrast to constructive patriotism, which holds that true patriots love their country and want to make it better, blind patriots react consistently negatively to criticisms of their country. It is therefore no surprise that patriotism is a better predictor than national identity of reactions to criticisms from a person from another country and of supporting the United States right or wrong. Good patriots of the nonconstructive type don't like to hear anything negative about their country. Even given the strong impact of patriotism on supporting America right or wrong, national identity still has a significant independent effect. More interestingly, patriotism does not significantly predict people's sense of shame concerning the United States or their belief that the basic rights of critics should be taken away, whereas national identity is related to these reactions. Clearly the patriotism norm and national identity can be used to predict different reactions to criticism.

Individualism and egalitarianism have a mixed relationship with the dependent variables. People who are highly individualistic are willing to take away the rights of Americans who disagree with American values (one of those values presumably being individualism), are bothered by criticisms from foreigners, and say that they do not feel ashamed of the United States. Egalitarianism, on the other hand, is only significantly related to feeling ashamed of the United States. Even though egalitarians are themselves critical of the state of equality in the United States, this targeted criticism is not related to reactions to other types of criticism.

Finally, the demographic variables are also telling. Older people are much more likely than younger people to react strongly to criticism and to believe that people should be loyal to and supportive of their country. They are also less likely to feel ashamed by the United States' past actions. The better educated and the more knowledgeable, on the other hand, are accepting of criticism and are very much opposed to the notion of punishing critics by taking away their civil liberties. Perhaps surprisingly, ideology and party identification are not consistently related to the dependent variables. While strong Republicans are more upset than any other partisan group by foreigners criticizing America, partisans do not differ from moderates in any of their other reactions to criticism. The reactions of various ideological groups generally do not differ as well.

National identity is related strongly to various reactions to criticism of the group. Two of the questions address reactions to the United States, but the other two questions focus on who is doing the criticizing, foreigners or Americans. Matthew J. Hornsey's (2005) work on group-directed criticism begins to untangle people's reactions to different critics. Specifically, he examines in a series of experiments the effects of having the critic be a member of the ingroup, an ex-ingroup member, and a member of an outgroup. His results are consistent and strong: When faced with criticism of their nation (Australia), participants rate the ingroup critic more highly than the ex-ingroup critic, who is rated more highly than the outgroup critic. Ingroup critics are considered more constructive in their criticism and participants agree with them more. Group status matters. But what happens when the critic is a prototypical group member rather than a marginalized group member? Not all ingroup members have equal status in the group, and that unequal status could easily affect people's reactions to criticisms coming from these different sources.

Does It Make a Difference If the Critic Is a Prototypical or Marginalized Ingroup Member?

People often view criticism coming from an outgroup member as threatening. Nyla Branscombe and her colleagues (1999) argue that threats to the value of a group identity leads group members to defend the value that has come under attack. When the ingroup is under attack, group members rally to defend it, often by derogating the outgroup that offered the criticism (Hornsey, Oppes, and Svensson 2002). The group does not have to take the criticism seriously, or attempt to make changes to improve the group, if the criticism is unjust and the criticizer a scoundrel. The criticism reflects the outgroup's defect rather than the ingroup's defect. Hornsey and his colleagues found that subjects were significantly more positive toward the message and toward the messenger when criticisms came from an ingroup member than from an outgroup member. Subjects were also more likely to believe that the criticisms were correct when an ingroup member made them than when an outgroup member made them. Much of the reason for these differences in reactions is that "outgroup criticisms arouse more sensitivity because they are seen to be less constructive and less legitimate" (Hornsey, Oppes, and Svensson 2002: 303). Ingroup criticism is not taken as negatively "because it is assumed that ingroup members are saying these things with the best interests of the group at heart" (p. 304).

Reactions to criticisms depend in large part, though, on the level of a person's commitment to the group. It is strong identifiers who energetically denigrate the outgroup when faced with ingroup threat, not weak identifiers. Branscombe and her colleagues (1999) discuss a study of white Americans' reactions to the argument that they have benefited from unearned privileges based on their race. After being confronted with a threat to the image of the ingroup (that whites, the ingroup, have been unfair to and exploitative of other races), experimental subjects who strongly identified as white scored higher on John B. McConahay's (1986) modern racism scale than those in the control condition. These subjects justified whites' past actions by calling into question the deservingness of minorities. Weak identifiers, on the other hand, exhibited significant reductions in self-esteem and no increase in modern racism.

The results of these studies can be applied, I argue, to ingroup members' reactions to prototypical and marginalized members' criticisms of the ingroup. I expect that strong identifiers will be accepting of messages, whether positive or negative, coming from a prototypical ingroup member but will reject negative messages coming from a marginalized ingroup member.[1] Weak identifiers, on the other hand, are less likely to be affected by the group status of the messenger. In fact, we might expect weak identifiers to respond favorably to criticism from

---

[1] Hornsey, Oppes, and Svensson (2002) found that when an outgroup praised the ingroup, people responded positively to the outgroup just as they did to the ingroup. There were no significant differences. In other words, we like to hear positive messages from anybody.

a marginalized member by taking a more critical stance themselves. Weak identifiers are willing to recognize the faults of their national group and to feel guilt about past national transgressions (Doosje, Ellemers, and Spears 1999). They do not feel a need to defend the group's values, actions, or boundaries. People who strongly identify with their national group are likely to react to a critical marginalized ingroup member just as they react to a critical outgroup member: They will express views that move them away from the critical message of the marginalized American and that offer greater support for their ingroup. That is, they will behave in a way to defend the group, its values, and its boundaries.

The data to test these hypotheses come from an experiment I conducted in late 2004.[2] Participants were nonstudent adults from Lincoln, Nebraska. Two weeks prior to the actual experiment, they filled out a pretest questionnaire asking about their national identity and basic demographic and attitudinal information. When they arrived at the experimental site for the actual experiment, about ten participants were ushered into a room and given a short article on Americans' success at the 2004 Olympic Games in Athens, Greece. The purpose of this article was to prime national identity. While participants were waiting for the experimenter to hand out a questionnaire, one of the people in the room, who was actually a confederate posing as a participant, spoke up and either criticized Americans or praised them. The critical remarks were as follows:

You know, this study is about Americans' views of the American people. Let me tell you, I'm embarrassed to be an American. We're so selfish and so ignorant about everything. Just look at what our country is doing in Afghanistan and Iraq – we're making a mess of everything, and for what? Yet Americans just sit around like a bunch of morons watching *Everybody Loves Raymond* and eating jumbo-sized McDonald's. Man, Americans make me sick.

The remarks praising the American people were:

You know, this study is about Americans' views of the American people. Let me tell you, I'm proud to be an American. We think for ourselves and are so helpful to others. Look at what our country is doing in Afghanistan and

---

[2] See the appendix for details on the experiment.

Iraq – we're making those people over there free. Yet Americans don't even blow their own horn about it. They do what's right for the world and don't expect anything in return. Man, Americans are an amazing people.

Just as the confederate finished making his remarks, the experimenter jumped in and said there would be no more talking, thereby preventing anyone else in the room from speaking. The participants then filled out a posttest questionnaire asking about their views of President George W. Bush's handling of various foreign policy concerns, their pride in U.S. history, and whether they have felt ashamed of the United States. Participants were then paid for participating in the study and debriefed.

The main experimental manipulations in this experiment are the race of the confederate and the nature of the message spoken. Half of the participants were randomly assigned to a white confederate. The other half were randomly assigned to a black confederate. Both confederates were in their late twenties and were male. Both confederates said the same short speech praising or criticizing the American people, which was also randomly assigned. No one else in the room was allowed to speak after the confederate had spoken, so no other views were introduced into the room. The only difference in participants' experience in the experiment was the race of the person who spoke and the nature of the message (praise or criticism of the American people).

This experiment is a 2 (black or white confederate) × 2 (praise or criticism) between-groups design. I analyze five dependent variables, all of which were measured in the posttest survey given to the participants after the experimental manipulations. Two of the dependent variables were from the Perceptions of the American People Survey and were discussed earlier in this chapter: whether people have felt ashamed of the United States and how proud they are of U.S. history. The other three dependent variables asked participants to evaluate various aspects of President George W. Bush's foreign policy: "How do you rate the Bush administration's handling of the following problems? Would you say the administration's handling of the problem has been excellent, good, fair, or poor?" They were then asked about President Bush's handling of foreign policy overall, international terrorism, and the situation in Iraq. The responses were coded so that the higher the number, the more positive were subjects' evaluations (not ashamed in the ashamed question, proud in the pride question, and excellent in the three policy questions).

I expect that both weak and strong identifiers will be affected by the race of the confederate but in opposite directions. Weak identifiers feel a greater sense of shame and guilt for the negative aspects of their country's history. One obvious negative aspect of American history is the treatment of blacks. Since weak identifiers are more likely to accept criticisms of their country and its people and to be sympathetic to someone belonging to the mistreated group, I expect to find that weak identifiers are more likely to accept the message of the black confederate than that of the white confederate. If the black confederate criticizes the American people, weak identifiers are likely to become more critical themselves. If, on the other hand, the black confederate praises the American people, weak identifiers will likely become more positive toward the American people and the United States. A marginalized American who praises the United States must mean that America isn't so bad, the thinking goes.

Strong identifiers are also likely to be significantly affected by the race of the speaker but not in the same way as weak identifiers. They are more likely to accept criticism from a prototypical member and will therefore become more negative about the United States when it is the white confederate who is critical. They might also respond favorably to a prototypical member's praise by becoming more positive, although the effects of praise tend to be less strong than the effects of criticism (Hornsey 2005; Hornsey and Imani 2004). When the speaker is a marginalized group member, however, I expect strong identifiers to react as they would to an outgroup member. Strong identifiers are therefore likely to treat the criticism from a marginalized group member as threatening and to react in a defensive manner by moving away from the black speaker's message and becoming more supportive of the president's foreign policy initiatives, less ashamed of the United States, and more proud of U.S. history. If there is an effect for praise, I again expect strong identifiers to move away from the black confederate's positive message by becoming more negative about the United States and its people. In essence, strong identifiers are likely to think that if a marginalized group member says it, it must be wrong, whether the "it" is positive or negative.

I ran analyses of covariance to test these expectations with the ashamed, proud, and foreign policy measures as the dependent variables. The two experimental conditions were included as main effects (white/black speaker by criticism/praise), as was American identity (divided into weak, medium, and strong identity) to test for an interaction effect. I included party identification as a covariate to control for the tendency for Republicans to support Bush's foreign policy and Democrats to oppose it. I also included age and education as covariates. The dynamic of greatest interest is the three-way interaction among strength of national identity, race of speaker, and whether the speaker praised or criticized the American people. The strength of people's national identity should affect their reactions to government actions depending on whether they hear praise or criticism about their national group but also depending on the group status of the person giving praise or criticism. The results, shown in Table 5.4, generally confirm this expectation. National identity has a significant effect almost across the board, and the effect is strong. Strong identifiers are more proud of U.S. history and more supportive of President Bush's foreign policy, including in Iraq and against terrorism. But in three of the five models, the three-way interaction is also significant (proud of U.S. history, not ashamed, and terrorism). The confluence of national identity, hearing praise or criticism, and the group status of the speaker has a significant effect on how people judge their country and its actions.

Figure 5.2 displays visually the three-way interaction effects. Figure 5.2(a) displays reactions to praise coming from the speaker, whereas Figure 5.2(b) shows how participants reacted to hearing criticism from the speaker. The extent to which participants accepted or rejected the black speaker's message was measured based on whether participants were in the praise or criticism condition. Moving in the direction of the message means becoming more positive about the American people and the United States in the praise condition and more negative in the criticism condition. If people who have heard a black person give praise are more positive toward the United States than those who have heard a white person give praise, then overall the black person's message has been more accepted than the white person's message. If people who heard a black person criticize the American people become more negative about the United States than those who heard a white

TABLE 5.4. *Reactions to praise or criticism from a marginalized or prototypical group member*

	Proud of U.S. History	Not Ashamed of U.S.	Bush Foreign Policy	International Terrorism	Iraq
Main Effects					
Praise or criticism	.32	.69	.25	.26	.02
Black or white speaker	1.49	.95	.71	.002	.35
National identity	8.47***	1.80	7.18**	7.89***	6.72**
3-way interaction	4.38*	3.52*	1.48	4.22*	1.26
Covariates					
Party identification	12.86***	40.19***	44.79***	37.93***	42.36***
Age	9.58**	1.32	1.60	5.31*	1.08
Education	2.13	2.43	4.94*	1.57	4.43
R^2	.37	.41	.51	.47	.50
F	4.30***	4.56***	5.67***	6.18***	5.12***

Source: Perceptions of the American People praise/criticize experiment, 2004.

Note: * $p < .05$; ** $p < .01$; *** $p < .001$. The number of cases is approximately eighty for each analysis. The results are based on analyses of covariance. Cell entries are F scores. The two-way interactions have been excluded from the table for ease of presentation. All dependent and independent variables have been transformed to range from 0 to 1.

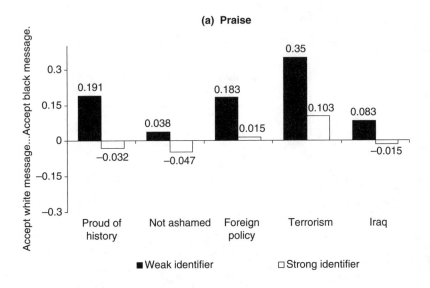

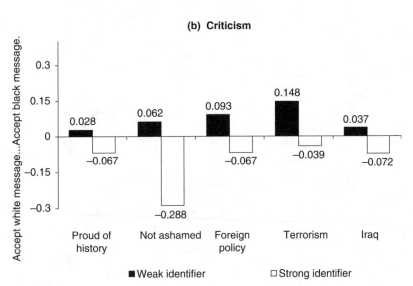

FIGURE 5.2. Acceptance of praise or criticism from a black or white speaker by American identity and its effect on pride, shame, and evaluations of George W. Bush's handling of foreign policy

person criticize Americans, then once again, the black person's message has been more accepted than the white person's. Obviously the opposite is true if people are more accepting of the white person's message. My measure of the effects of speaker race and message focuses on the difference in acceptance of the message depending on the race of the speaker.[3]

Looking first at Figure 5.2(a), the praise condition, note that the story is consistent and clear among weak identifiers. Weak identifiers were much more likely to see their scores on the various dependent variables go up (i.e., become more positive about America) when they heard an African American praise the American people than when they heard a white person give such praise. For all five dependent variables, participants who heard the black speaker give praise had higher scores than participants who heard the white speaker give praise. While the effect is negligible for not feeling ashamed, the effect is very pronounced for judgments about President Bush's antiterrorism policies and is quite strong for being proud of U.S. history and for judgments of President Bush's foreign policy in general.

The results are less clear for strong identifiers in the praise condition. Strong identifiers are more positive about the war on terror and Bush's foreign policy when they have heard a black speaker than when they have heard a white speaker, but they are also more likely to express less shame, feel greater pride, and approve more of Bush's Iraq policy when they have heard a white speaker compared to a

[3] In the praise condition, I subtracted the mean score of all participants who heard praise from the white speaker from the mean score of all participants who heard praise from the black speaker on each dependent variable. A positive score indicates that the mean score on the dependent variable was higher among those who heard the black speaker give praise than among those who heard the white speaker give praise. Hence people who heard the black speaker were more accepting of the positive message than people who heard the white speaker. A negative score, on the other hand, means that participants were more accepting of the white speaker's message than of the black speaker's message. For the criticism condition, I subtracted the black speaker score from the white speaker score so that, once again, positive numbers reflect greater acceptance of the black speaker's message and negative numbers reflect greater acceptance of the white speaker's message. If the score in the white speaker condition is higher than the score in the black speaker condition, then participants were more accepting of the black speaker's critical message because their score is lower. If the score is higher in the black speaker condition, then the black speaker's critical message has not been as accepted as the white speaker's critical message.

black speaker, although some of these effects are again negligible. Nevertheless, strong identifiers clearly do not have consistently positive reactions to the positive message of marginalized over prototypical speakers. Weak identifiers, on the other hand, do.

Moving to Figure 5.2(b), an interesting pattern again emerges. When hearing criticisms of the American people and American foreign policy, strong identifiers this time around are consistent in their reactions. Strong identifiers consistently express more *positive* views of the United States when they have heard a marginalized American offer *criticisms* than when they have heard a prototypical American offer the same criticisms. The most pronounced effect concerns feeling ashamed. Strong identifiers who heard criticisms from a black person express feeling much less shame than those who heard criticisms from a white person. But for all of the dependent variables, strong identifiers are more accepting of negative messages from a white speaker than a black speaker. Weak identifiers, on the other hand, continue to move more in the direction of the black speaker's message than the white speaker's message, but in this case the message is critical. Weak identifiers consistently side with the marginalized American and move away from the message delivered by the prototypical American.

Another way to look at the experimental results is simply to compare the overall mean responses of weak identifiers and strong identifiers across the various conditions. When the means of responses to all five questions making up the dependent variables are compared, the more disapproving responses of weak identifiers stand out (see Figure 5.3). Strong identifiers are consistently more positive about the United States' foreign policy, history, and past actions than weak identifiers. But the important story is the pattern that emerges across the experimental conditions. If participants are persuaded by all messages equally, they should become more positive when hearing praise from any speaker and they should become more negative when hearing criticisms from any speaker. This, however, is not the case. Weak identifiers follow this pattern only when listening to a black speaker: They respond positively when they hear a black person praise the American people (a mean of .37, the highest mean reached by weak identifiers) and negatively when they hear him criticize the American people (a mean of .20). The opposite occurs for the white speaker. When weak

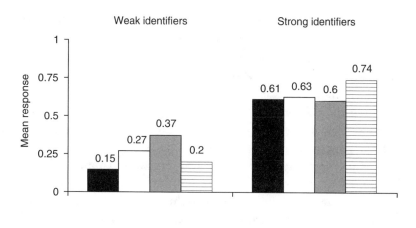

FIGURE 5.3. Mean response of pride, shame, and evaluations of George W. Bush's foreign policy by race of speaker, praise or criticism condition, and American identity strength

identifiers hear a white person praise the American people, weak identifiers give the most negative response (a mean of only .15) and they respond more positively when the white person offers criticisms (a mean of .27).

Among strong identifiers, the pattern is very different. Strong identifiers differ little in their responses when they hear a white person give praise (.61), a white person criticize (.63), or a black person give praise (.60). The only strong reaction occurs when a black person criticizes the American people. In this case, strong identifiers become much more positive, reaching a mean of .74. The race of the speaker does not matter in the praise condition but it matters a great deal in the criticism condition. When under attack by marginalized Americans, strong identifiers react strongly and defensively by becoming much more positive about their country and its people. It is all right to be criticized by prototypical Americans. It is just not all right to be criticized by marginalized Americans. When the latter occurs, strong identifiers shore up their group by becoming significantly more supportive of their country.

Past research has shown that ingroup members treat messages differently depending on whether they come from their ingroup or from an outgroup, with ingroup criticism gaining more positive responses than outgroup criticism. The findings presented here demonstrate that even within the ingroup, the effects of criticism depend on the status of the group member. Strong identifiers rated various aspects of their government more positively when they heard a marginalized ingroup member criticize Americans, perhaps because criticism from marginalized group members is seen as threatening and strong identifiers defensively increase support for the ingroup by reacting contrary to the message. Hornsey, Oppes, and Svensson's (2002) comments about reactions to outgroup members fit reactions to marginalized ingroup members as well: "not only do people think poorly of the outgroup critic, but the criticisms themselves are rejected as unfair and untrue" (p. 304). Strong identifiers treat marginalized ingroup members the same as outgroup members when they hear criticism of their group. Weak identifiers react to the status of ingroup members as well, but contrary to strong identifiers, they shore up their support for marginalized members by being much more accepting of their message than is the case with prototypical members.

CONCLUSION

People who strongly identify with their group want to be fully accepted as members of the group and they want to help the group by doing what they can to make it strong and viable. Helping core members of the group accomplishes this goal. Remaining loyal to the group is another way to accomplish this goal. Americans who strongly identify with their national group don't like to hear criticism of the group, but they also are less likely to take criticism to heart. We know from past research that criticisms from outgroup members are met with skepticism and sometimes outright hostility. Ingroup members, on the other hand, and in particular prototypical ingroup members, are listened to, or at least they are not readily dismissed. Good ingroup members know the group and are perceived to have the best interests of the group in mind when they feel compelled to criticize it. Good ingroup members, those who are prototypical, clearly want to help the group by making constructive criticisms.

Marginalized group members are not given the same benefit of the doubt. Their criticisms are seen as more threatening and destructive to the group, leading to a defensive posture by strong identifiers who want to protect the group from attack. When a marginalized group member criticizes the group, strong identifiers become more supportive of the group and its actions. What this means in practice is that prototypical white Americans can freely criticize their fellow Americans and their comments will not be rejected, nor will such critical Americans be rejected by the group. Marginalized African Americans, on the other hand, are treated as a threat when they criticize their fellow Americans. Their criticisms are not accepted, and strong identifiers are motivated to pull together to support more strongly their national group.

Weak identifiers, in contrast, are less attached to their national group, which allows them to treat marginalized group members differently. Weak identifiers are more likely to feel a sense of collective guilt when faced with mixed information about their group's checkered history (Doosje, Ellemers, and Spears 1999; Ellemers, Spears, and Doosje 1999a). They are also more willing to compensate an outgroup ill-treated by their ingroup (Doosje et al. 1998; Doosje, Ellemers, and Spears 1999). Within the ingroup, weak identifiers are less likely to set hard boundaries in the first place and are less likely to support prototypical members and dismiss marginalized members blindly. Indeed, they seem to be motivated to do just the opposite – dismiss prototypical members and support marginalized members. Why do they do this? The reason might well lie in the weak identifiers' acceptance of their country's past wrongdoings, in their feeling collective guilt about these wrongdoings, and in their desire to compensate groups that have been victimized in the past. African Americans have been treated badly by white Americans across U.S. history. Weak identifiers believe that they have an obligation, then, to listen to African Americans and their criticisms. Rather than seeing such criticisms as a threat to the group, weak identifiers see them as a way to improve a group that has made mistakes, some serious, in the past.

If strong identifiers are indeed motivated by a desire to help their national group in whatever way they can, it is ironic that their reactions to criticism can actually hurt the group in the long run. The lesson from history is that we should learn from past mistakes and not repeat them. This admonition works only if the past actions are accepted as mistakes. Strong identifiers are significantly less willing

than weak identifiers to recognize mistakes and to confront them
directly. In part, they do not have the motivation to do so because
they do not feel ashamed or guilty about what has happened. But they
also refuse to withdraw support when wrongs have been committed
and they want to silence those who dare to criticize. These are not the
reactions of people who want to learn from the criticisms to make the
group stronger and better. Rather, these are defensive actions taken
to keep the status quo in place. The group cannot improve if many of
the criticisms directed at the group are dismissed and the messenger
vilified. The group can in fact become weakened by its unwillingness
to change.

Of course, strong identifiers do not dismiss criticisms from prototypical group members, so it could be argued that these criticisms can
motivate change for the better. The problem, however, is that prototypical members are much less likely to criticize the group, especially
in areas that are important to the group. Criticizing aspects of the
group that are marginal to its identity is not nearly as helpful to the
group's long-term viability as criticisms that lead to positive change in
the group's salient actions. Strong identifiers don't want to admit any
wrongdoing in the group and they want to stifle important criticisms
concerning the group's values. This unwillingness to hear major criticisms can ultimately weaken the group both by not allowing change
and by increasing the number of marginalized group members who
increasingly recognize the problems but are hushed and pushed to
the margins of the group as "un-American." The group's viability is
threatened by the actions of its most loyal supporters.

6

Is National Identity Good or Bad?

During the 2008 presidential election campaign, the question of whether the two major candidates were American enough to be president was raised on the campaign trail and in major media outlets. The questioning of John McCain's Americanness arose from his having been born in the Panama Canal Zone in 1936. The Constitution of the United States says in Article II, Section 1, that "No person except a natural born Citizen ... shall be eligible to the Office of President." Did McCain's circumstances fit the Constitution or the various laws and interpretations that have occurred since the founding of the country? The debate over the issue never became very heated (see, e.g., Hulse 2008a, 2008b; Liptak 2008), and Americans seemed loath to question the Americanness of McCain given his war-hero image. Democrats did not pursue the issue, nor did it have much of a life in the blogosphere.

The same cannot be said of the sometimes explicit, but often implicit, questioning of Barack Obama's Americanness. Jeffrey Frederick, the Virginia GOP chair, rallied his volunteers by associating Obama with Osama bin Laden. The volunteers jumped at the bait: "'And he won't salute the flag,' one woman added, repeating another myth about Obama. She was quickly topped by a man who called out, 'We don't even know where Senator Obama was really born'" (Tumulty 2008). Obama was born in Hawaii, but the "foreigner" tag sticks with him. He is also a Christian, but many Americans believe he is a Muslim and therefore not quite American. A woman at a McCain rally in Minneapolis said, "I don't trust Obama. I have read about him and he's an Arab" (Henny and Hornick 2008). John McCain quickly corrected her but the misunderstanding was persistent. A Pew Research Center poll in July 2008 found that 12 percent of Americans thought that Obama was a Muslim. Almost one in five white evangelical Protestants believed Obama to be a Muslim (Pew Research Center 2008).

None of this would matter much if the questioning of a candidate's Americanness held no consequences. But the consequences are real. Just as Americans are less likely to help or take criticism from marginalized Americans when they identify strongly with their national group, so are they less likely to vote for a candidate they do not believe is quite American enough. Thierry Devos, Debbie S. Ma, and Travis Gaffud (2008) found that when a candidate's race was implicitly made salient, participants in their experiment were more likely to associate Tony Blair, who is white and British, and Hillary Clinton, who is white and American, with being American than Barack Obama, who is black and American. And the more that participants denied the Americanness of Obama, the less likely they were to say that they would vote for him.

The extent to which people view their fellow Americans as prototypical, as fully American, or as marginalized, as sitting on the boundary between the ingroup and the outgroup, has serious consequences. Marginalized Americans are not given the same benefit of the doubt as prototypical Americans. Any help they get is often questioned. Any criticisms they offer are often rejected. And they are less likely to get the support given to prototypical Americans because they don't quite fit what it means to be an American. The social theory of national identity developed throughout this book offers a way to make sense of these group dynamics. I contend that thinking of national identity as a social group identity – that being an American means being part of the group "the American people," that being British means being part of the group "the British people," that being Brazilian means being part of the group "the Brazilian people" – offers a better and more interesting take on a concept that has garnered a great deal of study and little agreement on the concept's meaning. It also opens up many important and fascinating avenues for the study of national identity.

AMERICAN IDENTITY IS NOT EXCEPTIONAL

One avenue concerns shifting our understanding of what national identity is. I am not comfortable with the bifurcated approach to studying national identity that currently seems to reign among many scholars. Why would most countries of the world have one type of national identity – a national identity based on history, culture, language, territory, and religion – whereas the United States has something different? In part, my unease comes from my sense that the United States does have a history, culture, language, territory, and religion, so Americans could therefore have a national identity based on the same things as other countries. Americans have long thought of the United States as a Christian (and historically Protestant) nation that is English-speaking with a culture that is primarily Western European (recognizing the influences of other cultures), a proud history, and a beautiful, expansive, manifest-destiny accrued land. The culture of the United States is heavily influenced by certain principles that are shared by Americans, such as a belief in liberalism, individualism, equality, and so on. But many people in other countries share these beliefs as well. The United States is not exceptional in these regards.

A generalizable theory of national identity is preferable to the bifurcated approach, but the one based on history and culture is not the best approach to take. Every country has a history, culture, language (or languages), and territory. How do these interact to become the incredibly strong force that is national identity? Why are people willing to die and to kill for their nation? Why are the views of an Indian Muslim rioter that, "Riots are like one-day cricket matches where the killings are the runs," and, "The whole honor of your nation depends on not scoring less than the opponent" (Kakar 1996: 15) really not terribly surprising? Basing national identity on a culture, a history, a language, or a set of beliefs doesn't get at the potent dynamic that makes national identity so powerful. That potent dynamic is the social forces that lead people to want desperately what is best for their group.

The best way to conceptualize national identity, then, is in a way that lets these social forces come front and center in a theory of national identity. The social theory of national identity developed throughout this book offers just such a theory. It is generalizable, applying to all national identities, not just some or one. It also offers an important place for history, culture, language, religion, and beliefs in understanding national identity. The prototype people hold of their national group is heavily influenced by all of these things. As seen in Chapter 2, the prototypical American is white (or at least not black), Christian, English-speaking, and individualistic. All of these characteristics have grown out of the history of the United States, are embedded in Americans' collective memory, and have been the fodder for political contestation. The prototype can change over time, but not easily and not quickly. People can even not like that the prototype contains certain characteristics – for example, many Americans likely feel uncomfortable thinking of the prototypical American as white, which is why they often consciously step back from making the association (Devos and Banaji 2005) – but they recognize that the characteristic is widely held to be part of the prototype. And some of these characteristics are explicitly and proudly held, such as the acceptance by many that the United States is a Christian nation. Americans are a collective group of compatriots whose imagining of their group is heavily influenced by all of the forces held to be important in previous research. The social theory of national identity simply brings them together in a way that shows how people use them and how they affect their political attitudes and behaviors. Citizens of all countries hold prototypes of their fellow citizens that are influenced by their history, culture, and political contestation. The United States is not exceptional in these regards either.

THE SOCIAL THEORY OF NATIONAL IDENTITY
RAISES INTRIGUING QUESTIONS

The social theory of national identity also raises a whole host of interesting questions because of its focus on the social dynamics that help us understand why people believe and do what they do. When people's sense of self is deeply embedded in their group membership, they are heavily influenced by the group and its goals. They want to do what is best for the group and they think of themselves in group terms. To say "I am an American," brings with it lots of baggage, including the other 300 million Americans who can make the same claim. Saying,

"I am an American," places the person in a large social group, and this group affects his or her beliefs and behavior.

The research in this book has raised and tried to answer a series of questions that arise from the perspective that an American is part of a large, and largely imagined, group of fellow Americans. One set of questions concerns commitment to the group. Does the strength of people's commitment to their national group matter? Do strong identifiers differ from weak identifiers in their attitudes about the group? Psychologists have in the past largely ignored group commitment, most likely because many psychological studies of group identity used minimal groups put together in the laboratory, where commitment was low, or small, face-to-face groups on college campuses, where commitment was very high. More recently, psychologists have paid greater attention to variations in group commitment, an important step in understanding group identities and their effects (Ellemers, Spears, and Doosje 1999b; Hogg and Reid 2006). Group commitment matters a great deal. For example, strong identifiers are much more likely than weak identifiers to think highly of their fellow Americans, consider their group homogeneous, and feel patriotic.

Focusing on the social dynamics of national identity also raises important questions about who is included in the national group. This is a concern with boundaries. Since the group "the American people" is so large, Americans will meet only a small handful of their fellow compatriots in their lifetime. When confronted with the phrase "the American people," then, they must imagine who is in the group. Boundaries are set between who is an American and who is not an American, thereby distinguishing the ingroup from outgroups, but this process of setting boundaries also acts to place some Americans fully in their national group but to leave out others as not quite fitting. Subtyping allows people to gather up all of those fellow citizens who do not quite fit and place them on the periphery of the group, where they can be ignored or delegitimized (Maurer, Park, and Rothbart 1995; Richards and Hewstone 2001; Rothbart 2001). Boundaries therefore do not simply separate the ingroup from outgroups. They also allow people to distinguish prototypical Americans from marginalized Americans, those who have been placed on the periphery of the group. People who don't quite fit are given a different status within the national group and are treated differently from prototypical group members. The process is not benign and it is not idiosyncratic. The prototypes, which are heavily influenced by history, culture, and politics, act to establish the group boundaries.

Commitment is related to holding the group norms more strongly and setting more exclusive boundaries on the group. Strong identifiers are the most likely to set hard, exclusive boundaries on their national group. They care most about distinguishing their ingroup from outgroups, they want their group to be unique, and they often exhibit a bias toward their ingroup (Brewer 2001; Sedikides and Brewer 2001). Weak identifiers, on the other hand, are less concerned about the group and often feel marginalized themselves. They set soft boundaries on the group but are loath to be exclusive. Just about anyone can be an American if they want to be.

The combination of commitment and the setting of boundaries affects in a profound way Americans' treatment of their fellow Americans. Strong identifiers are much more likely than weak identifiers to help their fellow Americans in a variety of ways. But who counts as a fellow American is much more narrowly defined by strong identifiers than weak identifiers, which means that the people who are most likely to help are also primarily willing to help only fellow Americans who are prototypical, who are Americans like them. Marginalized Americans, who tend to be the most in need of help, do not benefit from their group membership. Strong identifiers who set hard boundaries often consider them not deserving of help because they do not contribute to sustaining the group. The belief in individualism – that Americans should pull themselves up by their own bootstraps, that they should make it on their own without government assistance – is easily applied to people of color on welfare. They are not quite true Americans anyway, and their breaking of the individualism norm is treated harshly. The same norm is not so easily applied, though, to prototypical Americans who get a large amount of government assistance, including farmers, business owners, and the elderly. Strong identifiers do not begrudge prototypical Americans stretching almost to the breaking point the individualism norm. They just begrudge marginalized Americans doing so.

Reactions to criticism are also affected by the combination of commitment and group boundaries. Strong identifiers will take criticism from a prototpyical American, or at least react to it neutrally, but they take a contrary stance when faced with criticism from a marginalized American. When a marginalized American criticizes the American people, strong identifiers become more positive toward and support- ive of their national group and their government's policies. When strong identifiers believe their group is being attacked, even when the attack is verbal, they react defensively but only when the critic is a marginalized American. Prototypical Americans can criticize the group. Perhaps what they have to say is constructive. Marginalized Americans' concerns are not legitimate and must be rejected.

This book has answered several basic questions concerning national identity using the social theory of national identity: Who most strongly identifies with the American people? What characteristics do Americans consider prototypical? Which Americans are the ones to be marginalized? How does national identity affect how Americans treat one another? Answering these questions is enough for one book. But many more questions flow from this social theory that I have not addressed, questions that need to be answered in future research.

- What norms and stereotypes are central to the national group and what norms and stereotypes are peripheral? I have identified some of the norms and stereotypes important to Americans, but a sys- tematic study is essential to understanding why certain norms and stereotypes have the effects they do. Research in social psychology points out the differences in the effects of central norms compared to those that are less important to the group. Norms have latitudes of acceptance, but the latitudes are narrower for central norms. How do these varying latitudes affect prototypical and marginal- ized group members? How are the norms and stereotypes differen- tially perceived by prototypical and marginalized Americans?
- I have focused in this book on the general phenomenon of commit- ment and boundaries, with an emphasis on how strong identifiers react to their fellow Americans. I have spent considerably less effort analyzing marginalized group members. Future research needs to fill this gap. How do these marginalized Americans react to being marginalized? Which marginalized members strive desperately to be prototypical members by holding the group norms more strongly than ever, by identifying with the group strongly, and by setting group boundaries that are more exclusive? Which marginalized

members react to being marginalized instead by disidentifying with the group? Marginalized group members are treated differently from prototypical members, a difference in treatment that marginalized members fully recognize. Some marginalized Americans get fed up with the whole thing and withdraw from the group. They no longer embed their sense of self in the group. Others, however, refuse to give up hope that they can be fully accepted in the group if they just behave and believe more like a "true American." What explains these different reactions from marginalized group members?

- How have people's perceptions of what is prototypical shifted over time? And how has the status of marginalized group members shifted over time? There have been periods in U.S. history when Asian Americans were considered by many to be inferior to white Americans. Now expectations concerning Asian Americans suggest the stereotype that they are in many ways superior – more intelligent, harder working. Asian Americans are still atypical, given that the prototypical American is Caucasian, but with a different valence attached. How has this change happened? What are the effects of this change? Similarly, there has been a significant change for Irish Americans and Italian Americans (and Catholics in general), as they have moved from being marginalized Americans to being fully accepted in the national group. These shifts in the status of certain group members raise important questions about other marginalized Americans. For example, have there been shifts in status among African Americans? What about Latinos and Latinas? Homosexuals? Atheists? Are Arab Americans the most marginalized Americans at this time?

- What roles do leaders play in the social dynamics of the group? What effect do leaders have on who is considered a prototypical American? What effect do leaders have on the treatment of marginalized Americans? How do leaders influence what changes occur in the status of marginalized Americans? These questions are not only relevant to the United States. The impact of leaders on group inclusion and exclusion matters internationally as well – in the former Yugoslavia, in Rwanda, in Somalia. Political leaders can use their positions of power to effect changes in the status of group members by defining who is prototypical and who is not. Since people, and in particular strong identifiers, have a natural tendency to want to make their group strong by pushing marginalized group members away from the core of the group, group leaders can play a key role in advocating such actions and in providing the resources to execute them.

NORMATIVE CONCERNS RAISED BY THE
SOCIAL THEORY OF NATIONAL IDENTITY

The social theory of national identity raises interesting and important empirical questions, but it also allows us to address important normative concerns. The social theory of national identity brings to light deep normative issues that quickly become paramount. I began this research thinking that strongly identifying with one's national group would naturally have negative consequences. My assessment of strong identifiers has gone up and down over the course of doing this research and I now view strong identifiers in somewhat more conflicted terms. On the one hand, strong identifiers feel a strong sense of community and they want to do what is right for the group. They are willing to give to the group in ways that weak identifiers are not. Being willing to help out the group even at great expense to oneself is good and important for the group. Strong identifiers are the ones who are the most likely to give to charity, volunteer in their local communities, help in crises, and fight in wars. These actions are taken to benefit their fellow Americans because strong identifiers hold such a deep sense of group attachment. Strong identifiers do these things because they want to help the group.

Anyone who has ever worked in a group knows how important these strong identifiers are to its well-being. In any political science department across the country, there are faculty, staff, and students who do much more than their share in making the department a pleasant place to work and in promoting the department's interests, often over their own. These people benefit the group a great deal, more than many people realize. The national group benefits as well when strong identifiers help their fellow Americans. Weak identifiers, in contrast, can in some ways be free riders. Since they care less about what happens to the group, they are more likely to put their own self-interests above the group's interests. Weak identifiers are in general less likely to help than strong identifiers but they are also less likely to set exclusionary boundaries on their national group. So while they help less than strong identifiers, they help everyone equally.

There is a dark side to strong identifiers that creates the normative conflict, a conflict not experienced with weak identifiers. Strong identifiers who are inclusive are the most helpful of anyone, going out of their way to help prototypical and marginalized Americans alike. The problem is that inclusive strong identifiers are a rare phenomenon. Strong identifiers have a definite tendency to be exclusionary and narrow. These far more typical exclusionary strong identifiers want to help the group but end up hurting it. They marginalize atypical group members, they do not help fellow Americans most in need, and they refuse to accept criticism that could make the group a better one. They are significantly more likely than weak identifiers to withdraw basic rights, constitutional rights, from those who disagree with what they believe America stands for. They are much more likely to treat marginalized Americans, such as Arab Americans, unequally, even though Americans supposedly hold a belief in equality. They are much more likely to apply the group's basic principles unevenly depending on the status of the group member.

While the benefits that accrue from strong identifiers holding such a pronounced sense of community are important, the exclusionary nature of strong identifiers' pro-group behavior is unacceptable. Marginalized Americans resent not being fully included in the national group. They are Americans and ought to be treated the same as other Americans. The Chevy Silverado truck ads featuring John Mellencamp singing "Our Country" in which white, hard-working, cowboy-styled males proclaim that America is their country is, from this perspective, difficult to stomach. More insidious than these psychological reactions, though, are the political uses of identity.

There are many instances in U.S. history when politicians have targeted marginalized group members to advance their political goals and to gain or maintain power (Stuckey 2004). Tali Mendelberg's (2001) important book *The Race Card* demonstrates convincingly that when African Americans are used in implicit race appeals, white Americans' racial resentment is activated and they are more likely to vote for Republican candidates. The infamous Willie Horton ad, for example, focused on the issue of crime but implicitly raised the issue of race and its association with crime. Americans' reactions to these ads helped elect George H. W. Bush to office. Senator Joseph McCarthy targeted American communists as a means of advancing his own Senate career. His actions eventually led to his downfall, but his rise in power from being simply a junior senator from Wisconsin to one of the most powerful men in Washington was swift and clearly connected to his targeting certain marginalized Americans. Fletcher Bowron, mayor of Los Angeles when the Japanese attacked Pearl Harbor, whipped up hysteria against native-born Japanese Americans by suggesting that even seemingly loyal Japanese Americans were worshiping the Japanese emperor at Shinto temples in Los Angeles and had sent their children to Japan to be "steeped in the Japanese way of life and in the Japanese philosophy" and that these children are "now living in our midst" ("Bowron Asks Removal of All Japanese Inland" 1942).

Politicians are not the only people who target marginalized Americans. Americans frequently target marginalized Americans, their fellow ingroup members, for discrimination and for scapegoating. African Americans are a clear example, but many other groups have been targeted as well. In the aftermath of the September 11, 2001, terrorist attacks, the Reverend Jerry Falwell blamed the attacks on a variety of Americans, many of whom are marginalized:

I really believe that the pagans, and the abortionists, and the feminists, and the gays and the lesbians who are actively trying to make that an alternative lifestyle, the A.C.L.U., People for the American Way, all of them who have tried to secularize America, I point the finger in their face and say, "You helped this happen" (Goodstein 2001: 15).

Hate crimes against Arab Americans increased after the attacks and relatively few Americans have expressed loudly any serious concerns about Arab Americans' loss of basic civil liberties since 2001.

When asked about the trade-off between promoting security and protecting civil liberties, Americans overwhelmingly supported promoting security after the September 11 terrorist attacks. According to a Pew Research Center report, Americans' attitudes concerning this trade-off have remained quite steady. Respondents to the Pew survey were asked which was a bigger concern: that the United States had not gone far enough to protect the country or that the United

States had gone too far in restricting civil liberties. In 2004, just under half (49 percent) of the respondents said the United States had not gone far enough to protect the country and 29 percent said the United States had gone too far restricting civil liberties. Two years later, in 2006, the percentages were very similar (with 46 percent siding with security and 33 percent siding with civil liberties) (Pew Research Center 2006). When talking about this trade-off in class, the common response among students who support security over civil liberties is that the restrictions on civil liberties apply only to people who are likely guilty. The government is not going to wiretap "people like me," it is going to wiretap people who have done something wrong. Prototypical Americans have nothing to worry about, and their civil liberties are not in jeopardy. Marginalized Americans, especially Arab Americans but also Muslims in general and people who criticize the government, are likely to see restrictions on their civil liberties, but that is all right. It's a small price to pay for a more secure country, the argument goes.

Justifying the mistreatment of American citizens by labeling those whose rights are restricted as somehow deserving of the unequal treatment is not new. The social theory of national identity offers an interesting take on the dynamics behind these attitudes. The Constitution provides basic rights to those who are "true Americans." Anyone who is under suspicion and whose rights have been curtailed is not a "true American" and therefore is not of great concern to those who cannot imagine themselves ever being under suspicion. Bad Americans lose their rights, not good Americans, and curtailing their rights helps the group as a whole. Security for the group as a whole is more important than protecting the rights of bad Americans.

Many political theorists argue for the positive effects of national identity – that it increases self-esteem (see Spinner-Halev and Theiss-Morse 2003 for an overview), that it creates a community of obligation (Miller 1995), and that it unites diverse peoples (Walzer 1992). But all of these potential positives have a negative side as well. Increased self-esteem can come at the expense of increased intergroup rivalry. An increased sense of obligation to the community can be applied only to those fully in the community and lead to exclusion. And diverse peoples can be united within the national group, but the prototypical members, who reflect those who are dominant, are still the only ones who are considered fully included in the group and they are the ones who set the rules. Contrary to Horace Kallen's (1924) arguments, the state is not neutral. Government offices, including the U.S. Post Office, are not open for business on Sundays. Nor are they open on Christmas or the Monday after Easter. They often are open, however, on non-Christian religious days: Yom Kippur, Rosh Hashanah, Eid ul-Fitr, Eid ul-Adha, and Diwali, to name a few. The non-neutrality of the state privileges certain people's practices and beliefs over those of others. The dominant prototypical members are the ones who benefit. Marginalized group members must try to work around a system that does not give them the same benefits.

The normative implications of national identity are therefore complex, but the positive effects of national identity come at a great price. If it were possible to pull out only the positive side of national identity, there would be no normative problem. Group identities, though, are natural and powerful, and their dynamics do not allow for only the good to emerge. People have a strong motivation to make their group strong and distinctive. These dynamics lead to both the good and the bad, which seem to go hand in hand. But is there any way to salvage the good without taking all the bad as well?

IS THERE A SOLUTION?

Can national identity be good, as many scholars wish it to be, without being bad too? I will end this book by discussing some possibilities for making national identity benign. Unfortunately, solutions that do not take into account the group dynamics of national identity are not likely to work. The social dynamics of national identity are strong and must be faced for any meaningful solutions to have the desired effect.

Solutions That Likely Will Not Work

Superordinate Identities

One solution that appears on its surface to have great potential when two or more groups are hostile and intergroup relations are fractious is the promotion of a superordinate identity that brings all of the groups under the umbrella of one large, overarching group identity. According to the Common Ingroup Identity Model (Gaertner et al. 1993; Gaertner and Dovidio 2000), people who think of their ingroup and an outgroup as "us" versus "them" can shift to thinking of everyone as "we" when the two groups are placed within a common superordinate group. For example, people from France and Germany might view their own national group as the ingroup and the other national group as the outgroup, but when they are placed within the context of the European Union, they are all Europeans. Other intergroup differences might then become salient, such as Europeans against Americans, but the original French and German identities are no longer key in guiding behavior.

Since groups are rarely homogeneous and there are often subgroups within any given group, the overarching identity serves the purpose of uniting disparate people within the superordinate identity. Animosities are quelled and people within the common identity are less likely to "make sharp distinctions between their own and others' welfare" (Kramer and Brewer 1984: 1045). We could therefore expect that the various subgroup identities within the United States, including those of different races and religions, would take a back seat to the overarching American national identity when national identity is salient. Subgroup differences and interests would be less important than doing what is best for the national group as a whole.[1]

---

[1] This is precisely what John Transue (2007) found in his important study of race and American national identity in the Twin Cities area. People with a salient national identity were willing to support increased taxes to pay for public schools whether the money went to public education in general or to minorities in particular. When national identity was not salient, people were less willing to support increased taxes to improve education for minorities than for education in general. There are good reasons for why our results and arguments appear to differ. One is methodological. Transue asked respondents in the national identity treatment how close they feel to other Americans. In my research, I measure all three components of group identity (cognitive, affective, and evaluative) when measuring American identity. I also used a national random sample rather than a Twin Cities sample. The second reason is more important and suggests that our arguments and results are actually quite similar. In Chapter 4, I showed that American identity strength was not significantly related to support for more education spending. About three-quarters of respondents, regardless of identity strength, thought the United States spent too little on education. In previous work, I found that results concerning attitudes toward education spending were much more similar to results on individual-choice helping behaviors than to results on attitudes toward welfare and toward helping African Americans. Americans often associate education with individualism – regardless of one's race, everyone needs a good education to give them what it takes to pull themselves up by their own bootstraps. Transue's results support this interpretation.

The Common Ingroup Identity Model offers an important theory, and the empirical results of studies using the model are telling. I argue, however, that people still distinguish between prototypical and marginalized group members even within the larger group. The empirical results reported throughout this book support this argument. And the stronger that people hold their superordinate identity, the more likely they are to make this distinction. What this suggests is that a strong superordinate identity cannot erase the effects of subgroup differences. People who hold a strong national identity want their national group to be distinct regardless how many subgroups are part of the national group. Any subgroup that muddies the boundaries between the ingroup and outgroups must be pushed to the periphery, and this holds true in small groups, big groups, and extremely large superordinate groups.

The dominant people within a group determine to a large extent what the prototype of the group is (Sidanius and Pratto 1999), which is partly what makes changing the prototype so difficult. Dominant group members do not want to give up their dominance and they do not want to be pushed to the periphery. Marginalized group members have little influence on the setting of group boundaries. Superordinate groups do not somehow eradicate these social dynamics that exist in all groups. Superordinate groups have boundaries, just as subgroups do, and these boundaries are also set by the dominant group members. Some members of the superordinate group will be marginalized just as some will be prototypical.

The European Union remains a good example. Much has been written about how national identities fit with an overarching European identity (see, e.g., Breakwell and Lyons 1996; Herrmann, Risse-Kappen, and Brewer 2004). What haven't been studied are perceptions of what constitutes a prototypical European and who becomes marginalized in the process. Does the superordinate European identity make subtyping disappear? Probably not. It is more likely that certain Europeans are not counted as fully European whereas others are (perhaps Eastern Europeans fit in the former category whereas Germans, the French, and other Western Europeans fit into the latter). The important point, though, is that it is likely that not all Europeans are considered equally European, meaning that a superordinate identity does not erase boundaries between subgroups and cannot stop

dominant members from marginalizing those who are not prototypical. Certainly Jacques Chirac's comments to Eastern European
countries that publicly expressed their support for a U.S. invasion of
Iraq – that they were "badly brought up" and that they had missed
"an opportunity to keep quiet" (Smith 2003) – smacked of condescen-
sion and an unwillingness to listen to those whom he perhaps viewed
as being on the periphery of the European Union.

Superordinate identities can play a positive role in some circumstances, but they will not take care of the group dynamics that often
unconsciously drive group behavior. A serious external threat, such as
the 9/11 attacks, can pull people together in important and meaningful
ways under their superordinate national identity, but the effects do not
necessarily last long and fissures remain even in groups united against
a common enemy. External threats unite people, but the differences
between prototypical and marginalized group members remain.

Patriotism

Another possible solution is to play up patriotism and to downplay
national identity. Patriotism refers to love of country, without the
additional negative assessments of other countries (what political
psychologists call nationalism), and therefore could potentially be a
benign influence. Perhaps emphasizing patriotism at the expense of
national identity would lead to more positive outcomes. People would
still want to do whatever they could to help their country, but they
wouldn't engage in the social dynamics that marginalize certain
Americans. Perhaps patriotism takes all of the good from national
identity and leaves behind the bad.

The problem with this solution is that patriotism tends not to
get rid of the bad and doesn't do anything towards promoting the
good of national identity. Chapter 3 showed that strong identifiers
are much more likely than weak identifiers to set hard boundaries on
their national group (see Table 3.2). I didn't include patriotism in that
analysis, but when I substitute patriotism for national identity, patriotism mimics national identity in that it is positively and significantly
related to setting hard boundaries as well (b = .278, p <.001).[2] Patriots

---

[2] When both national identity and patriotism are included in the regression analysis
shown in Table 3.2, the substantive results remain unchanged. American identity

are therefore more likely than the less patriotic to view their national group boundaries in exclusive terms, which means that patriotism does not move us away from the effects of exclusion.

If patriots are much more likely to help their fellow Americans, though, perhaps their significant but weaker relationship with setting exclusive boundaries will be offset. However, this is not the case. When patriotism is included in the regression analysis displayed in Table 4.1, patriots are no more likely than the unpatriotic to feel an obligation to help their fellow Americans by giving to charity, volunteering, or helping in a crisis (b = .051, p = .372). The strong sense of obligation to help fellow Americans, a driving motivation among strong identifiers, is not felt by the highly patriotic. Loving one's country is different from feeling attached to one's fellow nationals, and only the latter leads to a sense of obligation to help. Patriotism is also not related to support for government programs that help the needy, which means it cannot be superior to national identity on that front either.

Promoting Other Identities over National Identity

A third solution is to make national identity less salient and to have people strengthen their identities with other groups. Since national groups have so many resources at their disposal that can be used in a discriminatory way, perhaps it would be better to have people hold weaker national identities. Other identities could easily fill the void. And if people hold many cross-cutting identities, then they would be less likely to hold such strong ingroup biases and would be more likely to emphasize only the positive aspects of their group identities. Prototypical members of one group might well be marginalized members of another group. Experiencing different group statuses would potentially make people more empathetic and thereby decrease the negative treatment of marginalized group members.

It is unlikely, though, that people could be persuaded to stop identifying with their national group (just as it would be difficult to persuade them to stop loving their country). National identities tend to be

and patriotism continue to be strong predictors of the setting of hard, exclusive boundaries on the American people, and all of the other significant variables remain so at the level depicted in the table.

strong and stable. They are one identity for which people are willing to die. And they take on a sense of moral superiority. Marilynn B. Brewer (1999: 435) discusses large, institutionalized groups, but she could easily be talking about national groups: "As ingroups become larger and more depersonalized, the institutions, rules, and customs that maintain ingroup loyalty and cooperation take on the character of moral authority. When the moral order is seen as absolute rather than relative, moral superiority is incompatible with tolerance for difference." National identities cannot simply be turned off when they become destructive. For this very reason, it is also not possible to turn off national identity and turn on various other identities, such as racial or ethnic identities, gender identities, or superordinate group identities.

Solutions That Hold More Promise

It is much easier to criticize possible solutions than it is to come up with ones that might work, especially if the solution has to work within the parameters of the group dynamics that drive and motivate all group identities, as I argue it must. It is impossible to get rid of people's group identities – people will even create group identities based on such inanities as who presumably counted more or fewer dots or who prefers the paintings of Klee or Kandinsky (Tajfel et al. 1971) – and national identities are especially strongly held. It is also impossible to get rid of many people's desire for inclusion and differentiation, a desire that is fulfilled by being a member of an exclusive group that is difficult to join and has hard, exclusive boundaries (Brewer 2003). Finally, it is impossible in heterogeneous groups not to have some members be less prototypical than other members. Stereotypes and norms develop within all groups, and some people fit the stereotypes and norms better than others. All of these factors must be taken into account when trying to find a solution to the problems of intragroup relations. I offer three solutions to the negative effects of national identity that acknowledge the group dynamics that underlie social identities. None of these solutions, however, is without problems. They all have drawbacks, some more serious than others, but they offer ways to think through how to overcome the negatives of national identity.

Change the Stereotype of the National Group

When Americans are asked to characterize the American people, they can do so readily. Much of the stereotype of an American has historical roots – for example, the founders and most early inhabitants of the United States were white, Northern European, Protestant, and English-speaking – and is therefore heavily embedded in how people think about their fellow Americans. But these stereotypes can change, and these changes have occurred over American history (see Reimers 1998). Italian Americans and Irish Americans are fully accepted as being "true Americans" today, whereas this wasn't the case not that long ago. Catholics are widely accepted now, whereas even fifty years ago many Americans questioned whether a Catholic could legitimately be the president of the United States. And the valence surrounding Americans' perceptions of Asian Americans has shifted over the past century or so, from perceiving them negatively to perceiving them as superior in important ways. These shifts in stereotypes of the American people suggest that shifts will occur in the future as well.

One place to look for possible changes in the American stereotype is among youth. The attitudes of young Americans toward ethnocultural and racial differences are more inclusive, as are their attitudes toward homosexuality, and they are less likely than their elders to place religious beliefs front and center in their political beliefs (Pew Research Center 2007). Young Americans are also much more positive about the effects on American society of immigration (Pew Research Center 2007). If these attitudes are not simply due to life-cycle effects, then the differences in social and political attitudes between young Americans and older Americans might well presage a change in the stereotype of who counts as an American. Just as Italian Americans and Irish Americans became "just like us," various racial, ethnic, and social groups might well become "just like us" in the future given the more inclusive attitudes of youth in America today.

The increased percentage of Hispanics and Latinos in the U.S. population might also affect the national stereotype. In 1980, Hispanics and Latinos made up just over 6 percent of the U.S. population. The percentage of Hispanics and Latinos increased to 9 percent in 1990, to 12.5 percent in 2000, and to 14.4 percent in 2005, and it is expected to be at 16.6 percent by 2015 (Commerce 1980, 1994, 2007). As Hispanics and Latinos make up more of the group "the American people," the stereotype of Americans as Northern European is likely to shift. Not only will young Americans have different views of who are "true Americans," so will an increasing proportion of the rest of the American population.

The problem with any solution that relies on a significant change in the American stereotype is that change must necessarily be slow and some of the prototypical characteristics might not change for an extremely long time. African Americans remain burdened by the legacy of slavery and the deep-seated racism that has existed in the United States over its history. If Americans perceive the American people to be white and this perception is often unconscious (Devos and Banaji 2005), it is difficult to assume that change in this stereotype will come quickly. It is too early to tell if Barack Obama's election to the presidency will have a positive effect on this national stereotype. It is also not clear that the perception that Americans are Christian will change any time soon. The belief that America is a Christian nation and that Americans are a Christian people is often publicly acclaimed with few people raising their voices against this characterization. When there is little desire to change a stereotype, it is unlikely that the "American = Christian" association will be transformed. Many Western Europeans have increasingly viewed themselves as secular, but the same shift has not occurred in the United States, where three-quarters of Americans say they are Christians.

Change the Group Norms

Another opening for a possible solution comes with how group members treat intragroup differences. Everyone is not the same, but that does not mean the prototypical members must necessarily treat the marginalized group members less well. We know from research on intergroup relations that the norms of a group influence these relations. If a group holds norms that are hostile and discriminatory toward outgroups, then it will treat outgroups just that way. But if a group holds norms that are caring and fair toward others, then group members will be reluctant to treat outgroups pejoratively. Stephen Reicher and Nick Hopkins (2001: 34) are right when they argue that norms of "dominance, affluence and aggression" will lead to very different intergroup behaviors than norms of generosity and caring. Group norms are likely to affect not only intergroup relations but intragroup relations as well. If group norms allow for discrimination against and the mistreatment of marginalized group members, then it is no surprise that such behaviors are prevalent. If, on the other hand, group norms insist that everyone in the group – regardless of how prototypical they are – be treated charitably and generously, then it is likely that intragroup relations will shift accordingly.

If a norm is central to the group, then prototypical members are expected to follow the norm closely. The latitude of acceptance is relatively narrow, giving group members little leeway in how they interpret and apply the norm. Prototypical members can then play a key role in applying rigorously the new norm since these members are expected to adhere closely to the norm. When Bill Clinton was president of the United States, he made a conscious and very public effort to be more inclusive of African Americans, to bring them into the fold as equal partners. Such inclusiveness and appreciation of diversity can have significant effects on people's willingness to accept marginalized group members as full members of the group.

The group dynamic here is difficult, though. Most people who promote the norms of inclusiveness and appreciation of diversity focus on creating an open and inclusive multi-ethnic and multiracial society. People of all ethnicities and races are welcome. What happens, though, to Americans who prefer to view their group as homogeneous and who refuse to be inclusive? Group members who refuse to follow the strongly held norm are atypical and pushed to the group's periphery. People who are not inclusive and accepting of diversity will be marginalized. How are they to be treated?

The tolerance literature argues that to be tolerant, people must give groups they strongly dislike their basic civil liberties (see, e.g., Marcus et al. 1995; Sullivan, Piereson, and Marcus 1982). The Ku Klux Klan should be allowed to hold a rally just as groups that are well liked can. Giving an abhorrent group their basic rights is not easy – they will say horrible things, things that people who are not, for example, racist do not want to hear. But holding the principled belief that everyone should be given their basic rights means not discriminating against those who want to exercise those rights. Everyone has a right to free speech and assembly. Does the same hold true for the application of group norms concerning inclusivity and appreciation of diversity? Must group members treat equally those who want to be unfair? Group dynamics play out whether the marginalized group members are African Americans, homosexuals, critics of the United States, Christian fundamentalists, or racists. When the norms insist on Americans being inclusive and open to diversity, then all diversity must be acknowledged. But does everyone need to be treated generously? Once it becomes acceptable to marginalize and mistreat some group members, the door opens to marginalizing and mistreating many others.

Make People More Aware of Group Dynamics
The final solution I propose is that simply making people aware of the dynamic that certain Americans are marginalized because they do not fit the prototypical American can create changes in how people respond to these marginalized Americans, especially among those who weakly identify with their national group. Weak identifiers are less likely to feel strong obligations to their national group, but they are eager to defend those who have been marginalized, as the experiment in Chapter 5 demonstrated. If weak identifiers can be persuaded that marginalized group members are treated differently from prototypical Americans, then they might well become proactive on behalf of marginalized Americans.

A good place to start making people more aware is to frame issues – such as welfare support – in terms of inclusiveness. The tolerance literature again offers relevant evidence. Framing civil liberties as a positive norm increases tolerance scores significantly compared to a neutral frame (the control group) or a negative norm frame (Marcus et al. 1995). Deborah Schildkraut (2005) has shown that Americans hold a norm of inclusiveness. If helping fellow Americans were framed with a positive inclusiveness norm, many Americans, perhaps even strong identifiers, would shift their attitudes and behaviors. Since norms often compete with each other, emphasizing the inclusiveness norm could lead to Americans feeling an obligation to help all Americans and not just those who are prototypical. They might also react differently to criticism – all group members want to help the group, not just prototypical members.

It might even work to teach people directly the negative and positive effects of group dynamics. John Hibbing and I have argued elsewhere that teaching people to appreciate democratic processes – the need for debate, conflict, and compromise – could increase Americans' appreciation for democracy as it works in the U.S. political system (Hibbing and Theiss-Morse 2002). Civic education classes could address national identity and the potent combination of commitment and setting group boundaries. If students learned how setting exclusive boundaries on who counts as an American transforms the positive motivations of those who hold a strong national identity to negative outcomes, they might well try to change their attitudes and behaviors. If students are encouraged to consider what helps the national group in the long term, they should conclude that being exclusive is detrimental to this goal. Of course, research would need to be done to determine whether such a civics curriculum would have the desired effects.

None of these three solutions is perfect, but they all take into account how group dynamics work and the positive and negative aspects of holding a strong national identity. Strong identifiers want their group to be strong and viable, but these desires lead them to place group solidarity above the best interests of the group overall. The solutions that could possibly work attempt to break down the setting of exclusive boundaries while keeping intact the sense of community that leads to good group outcomes. As long as group exclusivity plays such an important role in national groups, the desire of strong identifiers to strengthen their group will actually end up harming it.

I am skeptical, however, that these solutions can work. Groups powerfully affect their members' attitudes and behaviors. Often these effects are unconscious. Since groups will always have prototypical members and members who do not fit the prototype, and since group members want to optimize their distinctiveness, the atypical group members will be subtyped and, very likely, treated differently from prototypical members. During times of threat, the group will come together, but the same dynamic that unites people can set off the desire to discriminate against fellow group members who can easily be made scapegoats. Unity, solidarity, the sense of community – all have inherent within them the need for exclusion. National identity is not a panacea that will bring together diverse peoples in a community of obligation. National identity carries deep within it the fundamental forces that bring people together *and* that tear them apart.

Appendix

NATIONAL SURVEY

The data sets used throughout this book are part of the Perceptions of the American People project funded by the National Science Foundation (Grant SES-0111887). The survey was administered by the Ohio State University's Center for Survey Research. Households in the forty-eight contiguous states and the District of Columbia were randomly chosen using random-digit dialing. An English-speaking respondent within the household was randomly chosen using the "last birthday" selection technique (Lavrakas 1993). Only U.S. citizens were included in the sample. A total of 1,254 interviews were completed between May 29, 2002, and July 21, 2002. The response rates were as follows: American Association for Public Opinion Research (AAPOR) Response Rate 5, 34 percent; AAPOR Cooperation Rate 3, 39 percent; and Modified AAPOR Cooperation Rate 3, 74 percent. The average length of the interviews was 31 minutes and the data are weighted to match the sample with the population based on the 2000 U.S. Census.

The survey items and scales used as independent and dependent variables in the regression analyses in Chapters 2 through 5 were standardized to range from 0 to 1, making comparisons easier. See Gary King (1986) and Robert Luskin (1991) for a discussion of how to interpret scales using this method of standardizing variables.

AGE: "In what year were you born," recoded to be age in years and transformed to range from 0 to 1 (mean = .35 [mean age = 45 years old], sd = .23).

AMERICAN IDENTITY: Created using responses to four questions: "Do you identify with the American people?" (response options ranged from 1 = not part of the group to 7 = very strongly part of the group); "I am a person who feels strong ties to the American people"; and, "Being an American is important to the way I think of myself as a person" (response options ranged from 1 = strongly disagree to 5 = strongly agree); and, "I would like you to tell me what you think of the American people as a group. Let's think about being informed about politics. If 1 is extremely uninformed and 7 is extremely informed, with 2 through 6 in between, where would you place the American people? ... unselfish or selfish, tolerant or intolerant, and untrustworthy or trustworthy?" (response options ranged from 1 = negative description to 7 = positive description). Each of these variables was transformed to range from 0 to 1 and then added together to create the scale, which was transformed to range from 0 to 1 (alpha = .65, mean = .73, sd = .15). Using factor analysis, all four items loaded on only one factor, with 50 percent of the variance explained by that factor.

CHRISTIAN/RELIGIOUS: "What is your religious preference, or do you not have one?" Response options were Protestant (26 percent), Catholic (21 percent), Jewish (2 percent), Muslim (.1 percent), Orthodox (.2 percent), Other (33 percent), and None or no preference (18 percent). For the Christian variable, 1 = Protestant, Catholic, or Other (80 percent), and 0 = else (20 percent). I included "Other" with Christians after an analysis of the open-ended responses revealed that the vast majority of those who answered "Other" were Christian. When asked to explain what their religion was, many of these respondents volunteered Christian denominations, such as Lutheran, Baptist, or Episcopalian. For the "Religious" variable, 1 = Protestant, Catholic, Jewish, Muslim, Orthodox, or Other (82 percent), and 0 = No religion (18 percent).

EDUCATION: "What is the highest grade or year of school you have completed?" Coded 0 = less than high school (16 percent); 1 = high school graduate (33 percent); 2 = associate certificate (8 percent); 3 = some college (19 percent); 4 = bachelor's degree (17 percent); and 5 = post-graduate degree (8 percent).

GOVERNMENT ASSISTANCE FOR FARMERS: "Many people in America could potentially get some government assistance, like student loans, food stamps, welfare, farm subsidies, business subsidies, and so on. There is a limit, though, on how much money the government can give out. I'm going to read you a list of groups in the United States. Please tell me if you think the group should have the chance to get government assistance or not. How about farmers?" Response options ranged from 0 = definitely no (1 percent), 1 = no (7 percent), 2 = depends (4 percent), 3 = yes (59 percent), to 4 = definitely yes (29 percent).

GOVERNMENT-BASED HELPING: One obligations question and four spending questions were used to create this scale. The obligations question was: "I am going to read you a list of possible obligations. For each, I want you to tell me if you think this is an obligation you owe or do not owe to fellow Americans. ... How about ensuring a basic standard of living for all Americans?" Response options were 0 = not an obligation, 1 = somewhat of an obligation, and 2 = definitely an obligation. The four spending questions were: "Now I would like you to think about some issues facing people today in this country, none of which can be solved easily or inexpensively. I'm going to name some of these problems, and for each one I'd like you to tell me whether you think we're spending too much money on it, too little money, or about the right amount ... improving the nation's education system ... welfare ... improving the conditions of blacks ... solving the problems in urban areas." Response options were 0 = spending too much, 1 = spending about the right amount, and 2 = spending too little. All of these variables were transformed to range from 0 to 1, added together, and transformed to range from 0 to 1 (alpha = .62, mean = .58, standard deviation = .24). Using factor analysis, the four items loaded on only one factor with 45 percent of the variance explained by that factor.

HARD GROUP BOUNDARIES: "Some people say each of the following things is important for being truly American. Others say they are not important. How important do you think each of the following is? ... to have been born in the United States ... to have U.S. citizenship ... to have lived in the U.S. for most of one's life ... to be able to speak English ... to be a Christian ... to be White." Response options were 1 = not important at all, 2 = not very important, 3 = fairly important, and 4 = very important. I created an additive scale from these variables, transformed to range from 0 to 1 (alpha = .78, mean = .65, standard deviation = .22). Using factor analysis, all six items loaded on only one factor with 49 percent of the variance explained by that factor.

IDEOLOGY: "When it comes to politics, some people think of themselves as liberal, and others think of themselves as conservative. How would you describe yourself?" Extremely conservative was coded 1 = extremely conservative (7 percent) and 0 = else. Somewhat conservative was coded 1 = somewhat conservative (15 percent) and 0 = else. Somewhat liberal was coded 1 = somewhat liberal (7 percent) and 0 = else. Extremely liberal was coded 1 = extremely liberal (4 percent) and 0 = else. Moderate was the excluded category and included everyone who said moderate or middle-of-the-road.

INCOME: "Approximately what was your total household income from all sources, before taxes for 2001? Would you please tell me if it was. ... " Coded 0 = $0 to $10,000 (8 percent); 1 = $10,001 to $20,000 (13 percent); 2 = $20,001 to $30,000 (15 percent); 3 = $30,001 to $40,000 (14 percent); 4 = $40,001 to $50,000 (12 percent); 5 = $50,001 to $60,000 (9 percent); 6 = $60,001 to $75,000 (11 percent); 7 = $75,001 to $100,000 (12 percent); 8 = $100,001 to $150,000 (5 percent); and 9 = more than $150,000 (2 percent).

INDIVIDUAL-CHOICE HELPING: "I am going to read you a list of possible obligations. For each, I want you to tell me if you think this is an obligation you owe or do not owe to fellow Americans ... .How about giving money to charities? ... How about helping when there is a crisis or disaster in the nation? ... How about volunteering in your local community?" Response options were 0 = not an obligation, 1 = somewhat of an obligation, and 2 = definitely an obligation. I created an additive scale, transformed from 0 to 1 (alpha = .58, mean = .71, standard deviation = .23). Using factor analysis, the three items loaded on only one factor with 55 percent of the variance explained by that factor.

INDIVIDUALISM: "Any person who is willing to work hard has a good chance of succeeding." Response options ranged from 0 = strongly disagree to 4 = strongly agree. The variable was transformed to range from 0 to 1 (mean = .78, standard deviation = .22).

EGALITARIANISM: "If people were treated more equally in this country, we would have many fewer problems," and, "One of the big problems in this country is that we do not give everyone an equal chance." Response options ranged from 0 = strongly disagree to 4 = strongly agree. I created an additive scale from these two questions, transformed to range from 0 to 1 (alpha = .64, mean = .61, standard deviation = .25). Using factor analysis, both items loaded on only one factor with 74 percent of the variance explained by that factor.

INTEREST: "How interested are you in politics and national affairs? Are you very interested, somewhat interested, slightly interested, or not at all interested?" Coded 0 = not at all interested (9 percent), 1 = slightly interested (18 percent), 2 = somewhat interested (47 percent), and 3 = very interested (26 percent).

INTERPERSONAL TRUST: Two questions were used to create this variable: "Do you think most people would try to take advantage of you if they got a chance, or do you think they would try to be fair?" (Response options were 0 = try to take advantage if they got the chance and 1 = try to be fair.) "Generally speaking, would you say that most people can be trusted, or would you say that you can't be too careful in dealing with people?" (Response options were 0 = can't be too careful in dealing with people and 1 = most people can be trusted.) These two variables were added together and transformed to range from 0 to 1 (alpha = .64, mean = .49, standard deviation = .42).

NATIVE-BORN: "Were you born in the United States?" Coded 0 = no (4 percent) and 1 = yes (96 percent).

OBLIGATION TO PAY TAXES: "I am going to read you a list of possible obligations. For each, I want you to tell me if you think this is an obligation you owe or do not owe to fellow Americans .... How about paying taxes?" Response options were 0 = not an obligation (5 percent), 1 = somewhat of an obligation (24 percent), and 2 = definitely an obligation (71 percent).

PARTY IDENTIFICATION: "Generally speaking, do you think of yourself as a Democrat, a Republican, an Independent, or something else?" For those who answered Democrat or Republican, respondents were asked whether they would call themselves a strong or not very strong Democrat/Republican. Strong Republican was coded 1 = strong Republican (14 percent) or 0 = else. Weak Republican was coded 1 = not very strong Republican (15 percent) or 0 = else. Weak Democrat was coded 1 = not very strong Democrat (17 percent) or 0 = else. Strong Democrat was coded 1 = strong Democrat (16 percent) or o = else. Independent was the excluded category and included everyone who said Independent or something else.

PATRIOTISM: "I feel proud to be an American," "Generally the U.S. is a better country than most other countries," and, "I cannot think of another country in which I would rather live." Response options ranged from o = strongly disagree to 4 = strongly agree. An additive scale was created and transformed to range from o to 1 (alpha = .68, mean = .83, standard deviation = .16). Using factor analysis, all three items loaded on only one factor with 62 percent of the variance explained by that factor.

POLITICAL KNOWLEDGE: "What job or political office does Dick Cheney now hold?" (70 percent correct); "What job or political office does Tony Blair now hold?" (45 percent correct); "Who has the final responsibility to decide if a law is constitutional or not? Is it the President, Congress, or the Supreme Court?" (53 percent correct); and, "Which party currently has the most members in the U.S. House of Representatives?" (51 percent correct). Responses were coded o = incorrect or 1 = correct. An additive index was created and transformed to range from o to 1 (mean = .55, standard deviation = .33).

PRIDE IN U.S. ACCOMPLISHMENTS: "The next questions ask you how proud you are of the United States in a variety of important areas. For each area I mention, please tell me whether you are very proud, somewhat proud, not very proud, or not proud at all. ... The way democracy works in the United States. ... The United States' political influence in the world. ... The United States' economic achievements. ... The history of the United States." Response options were 1 = not proud at all, 2 = not very proud, 3 = somewhat proud, and 4 = very proud. An additive scale was created and transformed to range from o to 1 (alpha = .69, mean = .76, standard deviation = .18). Using factor analysis, the four items loaded on only one factor, with 52 percent of the variance explained by that factor.

RACE: "What race or races do you consider yourself?" Response options were 1) Alaskan Native; 2) American Indian/Native American; 3) Asian; 4) African American or Black; 5) Hispanic/Latino/Latina/ Chicano/Chicana; 6) Pacific Islander; 7) White/Caucasian; and o) Other. Hispanic suboptions were 1 = Hispanic/Latino/Latina/Chicano/ Chicana (7 percent) or o = else. Black suboptions were 1 = African American or Black (13 percent) or o = else. Other race suboptions were

1 = Alaskan Native, American Indian/Native American, Asian, Pacific Islander, or Other (5 percent) or 0 = else. White was the excluded category and included everyone who answered White/Caucasian (74 percent).

REACTIONS TO CRITICISM: Effect of criticism from foreigners: "When someone from another country criticizes the United States, it doesn't bother me at all." Ashamed of the United States: "There are some things about the U.S. today that make me feel ashamed of the U.S." Support for the U.S. right or wrong: "Americans should support the U.S. even if it is in the wrong." No rights for Americans who disagree: "Americans who disagree with what America stands for shouldn't be guaranteed their basic rights." Response options ranged from 1 = strongly disagree to 5 = strongly agree.

SEX: Coded 0 = female (51.7 percent of the sample) or 1 = male (48.3 percent).

SOFT GROUP BOUNDARIES: "Some people say each of the following things is important for being truly American. Others say they are not important. How important do you think each of the following is? ... to respect the U.S.'s political institutions and laws ... to feel American ... to value freedom and equality." Response options were 1 = not important at all, 2 = not very important, 3 = fairly important, and 4 = very important. I created an additive scale from these variables, transformed to range from 0 to 1 (alpha = .46, mean = .90, standard deviation = .14). Using factor analysis, the three items loaded on only one factor, with 50 percent of the variance explained by that factor.

SOUTH: 1 = people living in the deep South states (33 percent) or 0 = else (67 percent).

SPENDING ON MILITARY/DEFENSE: "Now I would like you to think about some issues facing people today in this country, none of which can be solved easily or inexpensively. I'm going to name some of these problems, and for each one I'd like you to tell me whether you think we're spending too much money on it, too little money, or about the right amount ... the military, armaments, and defense." Response options were 0 = spending too much (21 percent), 1 = spending about the right amount (46 percent), and 2 = spending too little (33 percent).

TENDENCY TO IDENTIFY WITH GROUPS: "Let's begin with people in your racial or ethnic group. With '1' meaning you do not feel part of the group at all and '7' meaning you feel very strongly part of the group, while 2 through 6 indicate something in between. How strongly do you feel part of, or identify with, people in your racial or ethnic group ... people who are the same sex as you ... people who do the same work as you ... people who share your religious beliefs ... people from your region of the country ... people from your state." Response options ranged from 1 = not part of the group at all, to 7 = feel very strongly part of the group. Responses to these questions were added together and then transformed to range from 0 to 1 (alpha = .83, mean = .74, standard deviation = .21). Using factor analysis, all six items loaded on only one factor, with 55 percent of the variance explained by that factor.

TYPICALITY: "When I think of the American people, I think of people who are a lot like me," "I would feel good if I were described as a typical American," "In many respects, I am different from most Americans" (reverse coded), and, "On the important issues, I find I often agree with the American people." Response options ranged from 0 = strongly disagree to 4 = strongly agree. An additive scale was created and transformed to range from 0 to 1 (alpha = .56, mean = .62, standard deviation = .18). Using factor analysis, all four items loaded on only one factor, with 44 percent of the variance explained by that factor.

WISDOM OF THE VOTE: "How much trust and confidence do you have in the wisdom of the American people when it comes to making choices on Election Day – a great deal, some, a little, or none?" Coded 0 = none (7 percent), 1 = little (26 percent), 2 = some (52 percent), and 3 = a great deal (15 percent).

FOCUS GROUPS

The four focus groups sessions were conducted in February 2002 in three communities: Lincoln, Nebraska; Rogers, Arkansas; and Fort Smith, Arkansas. Each focus group consisted of five to ten participants who were recruited by advertisements, flyers, random telephone calls, and announcements at various civic and social meetings. One of the focus groups held in Lincoln, Nebraska, consisted of only African American participants. One of the focus groups, in Rogers, Arkansas, had only white participants. The other two focus groups were a mix of races and ethnicities, although mostly white. Each session lasted approximately one and a half hours. Participants were paid $40 or $50 for their participation.

The moderator used a question protocol to guide the discussion. All of the main questions were asked at some point in the focus groups but not always in the same order. An assistant tape-recorded the sessions and kept track of participants' comments with pen and paper. The transcripts were later transcribed and analyzed.

Focus Group Protocol

1. I want to begin by asking you, when you think of the American people, how would you describe them? Are they intelligent? Knowledgeable about politics? Open-minded? Selfish or altruistic? Lazy or hard-working? Tolerant of differences?
   a. What kinds of political values do the American people hold? Let's start with tolerance. Do you think Americans are tolerant of groups they dislike? Do they support people's freedoms (of speech, religion, etc.)? Do they believe in equality, etc.?
   b. What about their beliefs in democracy? Do they believe in democracy? Do they support democratic processes, such as debate, compromise, elections, the rule of law? Do they approve of the government? Do they appreciate how democracy works?
   c. Overall, would you say Americans are all pretty much alike or are they very different? In what ways are they alike? In what ways are they different?
2. There are lots of different groups with which you could identify – gender, race, professional/work, sports, and so on. I'd like to find out a couple of things. First, I'd like to know whether or not you identify with the American people as a group. And second, I'd like to know how your feelings about identifying with the American people compares to your identification with other groups.
   a. Is your identification with the American people stronger or weaker than your identification with other groups? Why?
   b. What does it mean to you to identify with the American people?

3. Do you think the American people have power in the U.S.? What power do they have?

    a. How does their power compare to the power of other groups – e.g., business people, blacks, Hispanics, men/women, elected representatives, Catholics, Southerners?

4. Finally, I'd like to discuss some attitudes or behaviors about the American people. Do you think you owe a special obligation to help fellow Americans versus people who are not fellow Americans? Do we owe something to each other that we don't owe to others?

    a. How much do you think you can trust the American people?

    b. Do you think it is possible for the American people to work toward the common good? Do the American people know what is in the nation's best interest?

    c. Given your view of the American people, what kind of political system do you think would work best? Should we leave decision making up to public officials? Should we give more decision-making power to the people?

EXPERIMENTS

The experiments were conducted at the University of Nebraska–Lincoln. Participants in the experiment were recruited from the non-student, adult population in Lincoln, Nebraska, and surrounding areas. Recruitment procedures included a mailing sent to staff (not faculty or students) at the university, classified ads in the local newspaper, flyers placed around Lincoln, an ad placed on a screen at a local movie theater, and a runner on the local weather channel.

The experiment discussed in Chapter 4 was a small experiment with forty-six participants. A total of eighty-nine people participated in the experiment discussed in Chapter 5. In both experiments, the participants, while not randomly chosen, reflected a broad range of the Lincoln, Nebraska, adult population. All participants in both experiments were paid $25 for their involvement in the study. The experimental designs are described in Chapters 4 and 5.

The national identity, party identification, age, and education variables used in Table 5.4 were measured in the same way as the survey variables. The dependent variables are based on a series of questions concerning George W. Bush's foreign policy: "How do you rate the Bush administration's handling of the following problems? Would you say the administration's handling of the problem has been excellent, good, fair, or poor? ... Overall foreign policy ... International terrorism ... The situation in Iraq." Responses were coded 1 = poor, 2 = fair, 3 = good, and 4 = excellent. The "ashamed" variable is the same as the one used in the survey.

References

Abrams, Dominic, Michael A. Hogg, and José M. Marques. 2005. *The Social Psychology of Inclusion and Exclusion*. New York: Psychology Press.

Abrams, Dominic, Margaret Wetherell, Sandra Cochran, Michael A. Hogg, and John C. Turner. 1990. "Knowing What to Think by Knowing Who You Are: Self-Categorization and the Nature of Norm Formation, Conformity and Group Polarization." *British Journal of Social Psychology* 29:97–119.

Albrecht, Brian E. 2001. "Patriotism on Display in NE Ohio." *Plain Dealer*, 13 September, A16.

Alesina, Alberto, Reza Baqir, and William Easterly. 1999. "Public Goods and Ethnic Divisions." *Quarterly Journal of Economics* 114 (4):1243–84.

Alford, John R., and John R. Hibbing. 2004. "The Origin of Politics: An Evolutionary Theory of Political Behavior." *Perspectives on Politics* 2 (4):707–23.

Allport, Gordon W. 1954. *The Nature of Prejudice*. Cambridge, MA: Addison-Wesley.

Alwin, Duane F., Ronald L. Cohen, and Theodore M. Newcomb. 1991. *Political Attitudes over the Life Span: The Bennington Women after Fifty Years*. Madison: University of Wisconsin Press.

Ambrose, Jean. 2001. "National Make a Difference Day Volunteering Makes Heroes of All of Us Each Day." *Charleston Gazette*, 22 October, P5A.

2003. "Americans on Both Sides Take to the Streets." FoxNews.com. 17 March. http://www.foxnews.com/story/0,2933,81227,00.html (accessed 7 November 2007).

Anderson, Benedict. 1991. *Imagined Communities: Reflections on the Origins and Spread of Nationalism*. 2nd ed. London: Verso.

Andrews, Molly. 1991. *Lifetimes of Commitment: Aging, Politics, Psychology*. Cambridge: Cambridge University Press.

Aronson, Elliot, Timothy D. Wilson, and Robin M. Akert. 2002. *Social Psychology*, 4th ed. Upper Saddle River, NJ: Prentice Hall.

Asch, Solomon E. 1958. "Effects of Group Pressure Upon the Modification and Distortion of Judgments." In *Readings in Social Psychology*, 3rd ed., ed. E.E. Maccoby, T.M. Newcomb and E.L. Hartley. New York: Henry Holt.

Ashmore, R. D, L. Jussim, and David Wilder, ed. 2001. *Social Identity, Intergroup Conflict, and Conflict Reduction*. Oxford: Oxford University Press.

Barkow, Jerome H., Leda Cosmides, and John Tooby. 1992. *The Adapted Mind: Evolutionary Psychology and the Generation of Culture*. New York: Oxford University Press.

Barrett, Louise, R.I.M. Dunbar, and John Lycett. 2002. *Human Evolutionary Psychology*. Princeton: Princeton University Press.

Bar-Tal, Daniel, and Ervin Staub. 1997. "Introduction: Patriotism: Its Scope and Meaning." In *Patriotism: In the Lives of Individuals and Nations*, ed. D. Bar-Tal and E. Staub. Chicago: Nelson-Hall.

Beaucar, Kelley O. 2001. "Coming Protests Are Principled to Some, 'Un-American' to Others." FoxNews.com. 24 September. http://www.foxnews.com/story/0,2933,34879,00.html (accessed 11 September 2007).

Billig, Michael. 1995. *Banal Nationalism*. London: Sage.

Blank, Thomas, and Peter Schmidt. 2003. "National Identity in a United Germany: Nationalism or Patriotism? An Empirical Test with Representative Data." *Political Psychology* 24 (2):289–312.

Bodvarsson, Orn B., and William A. Gibson. 1997. "Economics and Restaurant Gratuities: Determining Tip Rates." *American Journal of Economics and Sociology* 56 (2):187–204.

Bohnet, Iris, and Bruno S. Frey. 1999. "Social Distance and Other-Regarding Behavior in Dictator Games: Comment." *American Economic Review* 89 (1):335–9.

"Bowron Asks Removal of All Japanese Inland." 1942. *Los Angeles Times* (1886–Current File), ProQuest Historical Newspapers, http://o-proquest.umi.com.library.unl.edu/pqdweb?index=48&did=414380641& SrchMode=1&sid=5&Fmt=10&VInst=PROD&VType=PQD&RQT =309&VName=HNP&TS=1195583182&clientId=14215 (accessed 20 November 2007), 6 February: 1.

Boyd Bell, Gregory. 2004. "Go, Canada! Northern Lights Look Bright to 'Dubya Dodgers'." *Newsday*, 10 November, A41.

Branscombe, Nyla R., Naomi Ellemers, Russell Spears, and Bertjan Doosje. 1999. "The Context and Content of Social Identity Threat." In *Social Identity: Context, Commitment, Content*, ed. N. Ellemers, R. Spears and B. Doosje. Oxford: Blackwell.

Breakwell, Glynis M., and Evanthia Lyons, ed. 1996. *Changing European Identities: Social Psychological Analyses of Social Change*. Oxford: Butterworth-Heinemann.

Brewer, Marilynn B. 1999. "The Psychology of Prejudice: Ingroup Love or Outgroup Hate?" *Journal of Social Issues* 55 (3):429–44.

2001. "Ingroup Identification and Intergroup Conflict: When Does Ingroup Love Become Outgroup Hate?" In *Social Identity, Intergroup Conflict, and Conflict Reduction,* ed. R.D. Ashmore, L. Jussim and D. Wilder. Oxford: Oxford University Press.

2003. *Intergroup Relations,* 2nd ed. Buckingham: Open University Press.

2004. "What Does It Mean to Be an American? Patriotism, Nationalism, and American Identity after 9/11." *Political Psychology* 25 (5):727–39.

Brewer, Marilynn B., and Donald T. Campbell. 1976. *Ethnocentrism and Intergroup Attitudes: East African Evidence.* Beverly Hills, CA: Sage.

Brewer, Marilynn B., and Roderick M. Kramer. 1985. "The Psychology of Intergroup Attitudes and Behavior." *Annual Review of Psychology* 36:219–43.

Brooks, Arthur C. 2006. *Who Really Cares: The Surprising Truth about Compassionate Conservatism.* New York: Basic.

Brown, Rupert. 2000. *Group Processes,* 2nd ed. Oxford: Blackwell.

Bruner, Jerome S. 1957. "On Perceptual Readiness." *Psychological Review* 64:123–51.

Bryce, James. 1891. *The American Commonwealth.* 2 vols. Vol. 2. London: Macmillan.

Burr, Thomas. 2001. "4-Year-Old Praised Anew for Sept. 11 Fund Donation." *Salt Lake Tribune,* 22 November, B3.

Buss, David M. 1999. *Evolutionary Psychology: The New Science of the Mind.* Boston: Allyn and Bacon.

Caporael, Linnda R. 2001. "Parts and Wholes: The Evolutionary Importance of Groups." In *Individual Self, Relational Self, Collective Self,* ed. C. Sedikides and M.B. Brewer. Philadelphia: Psychology Press.

Cialdini, Robert B. and Melanie R. Trost. 1998. "Social Influence: Social Norms, Conformity, and Compliance." In *Handbook of Social Psychology* Vol. 2, D.T. Gilbert, S.T. Fiske, and G. Lindzey, Eds., pp. 151–92. Boston, MA: McGraw-Hill.

Citrin, Jack. 1990. "Language Politics and American Identity." *Public Interest* (99):96–109.

Citrin, Jack, Ernst B. Haas, Christopher Muste, and Beth Reingold. 1994. "Is American Nationalism Changing? Implications for Foreign Policy." *International Studies Quarterly* 38 (1):1–31.

Citrin, Jack, Beth Reingold, and Donald P. Green. 1990a. "American Identity and the Politics of Ethnic Change. *Journal of Politics* 52 (4):1124–54.

Citrin, Jack, Beth Reingold, Evelyn Walters, and Donald P. Green. 1990b. "The 'Official English' Movement and the Symbolic Politics of Language in the United States." *Western Political Quarterly* 43 (3):535–59.

Citrin, Jack, Cara Wong, and Brian Duff. 2001. "The Meaning of American National Identity: Patterns of Ethnic Conflict and Consensus." In

Social Identity, Intergroup Conflict, and Conflict Reduction, ed. R.D. Ashmore, L. Jussim and D. Wilder. Oxford: Oxford University Press.

Commerce, U.S. Department of. 1980. *Statistical Abstract of the United States 1980*. http://www2.census.gov/prod2/statcomp/documents/1980-01.pdf (accessed 21 September 2007).

——— 1994. *Statistical Abstract of the United States 1994*. http://www2.census.gov/prod2/statcomp/documents/1994-01.pdf (accessed 21 September 2007).

——— 2007. "Federal Government Finances & Employment: Federal Budget – Receipts, Outlays, and Debt." *Statistical Abstract of the United States 2007*. http://www.census.gov/compendia/statab/federal_govt_finances_employment/federal_budgetreceipts_outlays_and_debt/ 2007 (accessed 21 September 2007).

Costa, Dora L., and Matthew E. Kahn. 2003. "Civic Engagement and Community Heterogeneity: An Economist's Perspective." *Perspectives on Politics* 1 (1):103–11.

Darley, John M., and Bibb Latané. 1968. "Bystander Intervention in Emergencies: Diffusion of Responsibility." *Journal of Personality and Social Psychology* 8:377–83.

Dawson, Michael C. 1994. *Behind the Mule: Race and Class in African-American Politics*. Princeton: Princeton University Press.

de Figueiredo, Rui J.P., Jr., and Zachary Elkins. 2003. "Are Patriots Bigots? An Inquiry into the Vices of In-group Pride." *American Journal of Political Science* 47 (1):171–88.

Deaux, Kay. 2000. "Models, Meanings and Motivations." In *Social Identity Processes: Trends in Theory and Research*, ed. D. Capozza and R. Brown. London: Sage.

Delli Carpini, Michael X., and Scott Keeter. 1996. *What Americans Know about Politics and Why It Matters*. New Haven: Yale University Press.

Devine, Patricia G. 1989. "Stereotypes and Prejudice: Their Automatic and Controlled Components." *Journal of Personality and Social Psychology* 56 (1):5–18.

Devos, Thierry, and Mahzarin R. Banaji. 2005. "American = White?" *Journal of Personality and Social Psychology* 88 (3):447–66.

Devos, Thierry, Debbie S. Ma, and Travis Gaffud. 2008. "Is Barack Obama American Enough To Be The Next President?" Poster presented at the IXth Annual Meeting of the Society for Personality and Social Psychology, Albuquerque.

Diamond, Jared M. 1997. *Guns, Germs, and Steel: The Fates of Human Societies*. New York: W. W. Norton.

Doherty, Carroll. 2006. "Attitudes Toward Immigration: In Black and White." In *Pew Research Center Publications: Pew Research Center for the People & the Press*. http://pewresearch.org/pubs/21/attitudes-toward-immigration-in-black-and-white (accessed 15 October 2007).

Doob, Leonard W. 1964. *Patriotism and Nationalism: Their Psychological Foundations*. New Haven: Yale University Press.

Doosje, Bertjan, Nyla R. Branscombe, Russell Spears, and Antony S. R. Manstead. 1998. "Guilty by Association: When One's Group Has a Negative History." *Journal of Personality and Social Psychology* 75:872–86.

Doosje, Bertjan, Naomi Ellemers, and Russell Spears. 1999. "Commitment and Intergroup Behaviour." In *Social Identity: Context, Commitment, Content*, ed. N. Ellemers, R. Spears and B. Doosje. Oxford: Blackwell.

Dovidio, John F., and W. N. Morris. 1975. "Effects of Stress and Commonality of Fate on Helping Behavior." *Journal of Personality and Social Psychology* 31:145–9.

Ellemers, Naomi, Russell Spears, and Bertjan Doosje. 1999a. "Introduction." In *Social Identity: Context, Commitment, Content*, ed. N. Ellemers, R. Spears and B. Doosje. Oxford: Blackwell.

———. 1999b. *Social Identity: Context, Commitment, Content.* Oxford: Blackwell.

———. 2002. "Self and Social Identity." *Annual Review of Psychology* 53:161–86.

Esses, Victoria M., John F. Dovidio, Lynne M. Jackson, and Tamara L. Armstrong. 2001. "The Immigration Dilemma: The Role of Perceived Group Competition, Ethnic Prejudice, and National Identity." *Journal of Social Issues* 57 (3):389–412.

Feshbach, Seymour, and Noboru Sakano. 1997. "The Structure and Correlates of Attitudes Toward One's Nation in Samples of United States and Japanese College Students: A Comparative Study." In *Patriotism: In the Lives of Individuals and Nations*, ed. D. Bar-Tal and E. Staub. Chicago: Nelson-Hall.

Flippen, A. R., H. A. Hornstein, W. E. Siegal, and E. A. Weitzman. 1996. "A Comparison of Similarity and Interdependence as Triggers for Ingroup Formation." *Personality and Social Psychology Bulletin* 22:882–93.

Foundation Center. 2004. "September 11: The Philanthropic Response." New York: Foundation Center.

Freeman, Stephen, Marcus R. Walker, Richard Borden, and Bibb Latané. 1975. "Diffusion of Responsibility and Restaurant Tipping: Cheaper by the Bunch." *Personality and Social Psychology Bulletin* 1 (4):584–7.

Gaertner, Samuel L., and John F. Dovidio. 2000. *Reducing Intergroup Bias: The Common Ingroup Identity Model.* Philadelphia: Psychology Press.

Gaertner, Samuel L., John F. Dovidio, Phyllis A. Anastasio, Betty A. Bachman, and Mary C. Rust. 1993. "The Common Ingroup Identity Model: Recategorization and the Reduction of Intergroup Bias." *European Review of Social Psychology* 4 (1):1–26.

Gellner, Ernest. 1983. *Nations and Nationalism.* Ithaca: Cornell University Press.

George, Jennifer M. 1990. "Personality, Affect, and Behavior in Groups." *Journal of Applied Psychology* 75:107–16.

Gibson, James. 1988. "Political Intolerance and Political Repression During the McCarthy Red Scare." *American Political Science Review* 82 (2):511–29.

2006. "Do Strong Group Identities Fuel Intolerance? Evidence From the South African Case." *Political Psychology* 27 (5):665–705.

Gibson, James L., and Amanda Gouws. 2003. *Overcoming Intolerance in South Africa: Experiments in Democratic Persuasion.* Cambridge: Cambridge University Press.

Gilens, Martin. 1995. "Racial Attitudes and Opposition to Welfare." *Journal of Politics* 57 (4):994–1014.

_____. 1996. "'Race Coding' and White Opposition to Welfare." *American Political Science Review* 90 (3):593–604.

_____. 1999. *Why Americans Hate Welfare: Race, Media, and the Politics of Antipoverty Policy.* Chicago: University of Chicago Press.

Goodin, Robert E. 1988. "What Is So Special about Our Fellow Countrymen?" *Ethics* 98 (4):663–86.

Goodstein, Laurie. 2001. "After the Attacks: Finding Fault; Falwell's Finger-pointing Inappropriate, Bush Says." *New York Times*, 15 September, A15.

Green, Donald P., Bradley Palmquist, and Eric Schickler. 2002. *Partisan Hearts and Minds: Political Parties and the Social Identities of Voters.* New Haven: Yale University Press.

Greenfeld, Liah. 1992. *Nationalism: Five Roads to Modernity.* Cambridge: Harvard University Press.

Hamilton, Alexander, James Madison, and John Jay. 1961. *The Federalist Papers.* Edited by C. L. Rossiter. New York: New American Library.

Hasenfeld, Yeheskel, and Jane A. Rafferty. 1989. "The Determinants of Public Attitudes toward the Welfare State." *Social Forces* 67:1027–48.

Hayden, S. R., T. T. Jackson, and J. N. Guydish. 1984. "Helping Behavior of Females: Effects of Stress and Commonality of Fate." *Journal of Psychology* 117:233–7.

Hedberg, Kathy. 2005. "Students Replace What Charley Took; Lewiston Elementary Students Send 1,600 Books to School in Florida Wrecked by Hurricane." *Lewiston Morning Tribune*, 5 January, 1A.

Held, David. 1996. *Models of Democracy, 2nd ed.* Stanford: Stanford University Press.

Henny, Ed, and Ed Hornick. 2008. "Rage Rising on the McCain Campaign Trail." CNN, 11 October, http://www.cnn.com/2008/POLITICS/10/10/mccain.crowd/index.html?iref=newssearch (accessed 14 October 2008).

Herrmann, Richard K., Thomas Risse-Kappen, and Marilynn B. Brewer, ed. 2004. *Transnational Identities: Becoming European in the EU.* Lanham, MD: Rowman & Littlefield.

Hewstone, Miles, Mark Rubin, and Hazel Willis. 2002. "Intergroup Bias." *Annual Review of Psychology* 53:575–604.

Hibbing, John R., and Elizabeth Theiss-Morse. 2002. *Stealth Democracy: Americans' Beliefs about How Government Should Work.* Cambridge: Cambridge University Press.

Hill, Lawrence. 2001. *Black Berry, Sweet Juice: On Being Black and White in Canada.* Toronto: HarperCollins.

Hilton, James L., and William von Hippel. 1996. "Stereotypes." *Annual Review of Psychology* 47:237–71.

Hoffman, Elizabeth, Kevin McCabe, and Vernon L. Smith. 1996. "Social Distance and Other-Regarding Behavior in Dictator Games." *American Economic Review* 86 (3):653–60.

Hoge, Warren. 2002. "Britain's Nonwhites Feel Un-British, Report Says." *New York Times*, 4 April, 13A.

Hogg, Michael A. 2001a. "Social Categorization, Depersonalization, and Group Behavior." In *Blackwell Handbook of Social Psychology: Group Processes*, ed. M. A. Hogg and S. Tindale. Oxford: Blackwell.

2001b. "Social Identity and the Sovereignty of the Group: A Psychology of Belonging." In *Individual Self, Relational Self, Collective Self*, ed. C. Sedikides and M. B. Brewer. Philadelphia: Psychology Press.

2005. "All Animals Are Equal But Some Animals Are More Equal Than Others: Social Identity and Marginal Membership." In *The Social Outcast: Ostracism, Social Exclusion, Rejection, and Bullying*, ed. K. D. Williams, J. P. Forgas and W. von Hippel. New York: Psychology Press.

Hogg, Michael A., and Dominic Abrams. 1988. *Social Identifications: A Social Psychology of Intergroup Relations and Group Processes*. London: Routledge.

Hogg, Michael A., Kelly S. Fielding, and John M. Darley. 2005. "Fringe Dwellers: Processes of Deviance and Marginalization in Groups." In *The Social Psychology of Inclusion and Exclusion*, ed. D. Abrams, M. A. Hogg and J. M. Marques. New York: Psychology Press.

Hogg, Michael A., and Scott A. Reid. 2006. "Social Identity, Self-Categorization, and the Communication of Group Norms." *Communication Theory* 16:7–30.

Hornsey, Matthew J. 2005. "Why Being Right Is Not Enough: Predicting Defensiveness in the Face of Group Criticism." *European Review of Social Psychology* 16:301–34.

Hornsey, Matthew J., and Armin Imani. 2004. "Criticizing Groups from the Inside and the Outside: An Identity Perspective on the Intergroup Sensitivity Effect." *Personality and Social Psychology Bulletin* 30 (3):365–83.

Hornsey, Matthew J., Tina Oppes, and Alicia Svensson. 2002. "'It's OK If We Say It, But You Can't': Responses to Intergroup and Intragroup Criticism." *European Journal of Social Psychology* 32:293–307.

Hornstein, Harvey A. 1976. *Cruelty and Kindness: A New Look at Aggression and Altruism*. Englewood Cliffs, NJ: Prentice-Hall.

Huddy, Leonie. 2001. "From Social to Political Identity: A Critical Examination of Social Identity Theory." *Political Psychology* 22 (1):127–56.

Huddy, Leonie, Stanley Feldman, Theresa Capelos, and Colin Provost. 2002. "The Consequences of Terrorism: Disentangling the Effects of Personal and National Threat." *Political Psychology* 23 (3):485–509.

Huddy, Leonie, Stanley Feldman, Charles Taber, and Gallya Lahav. 2005. "Threat, Anxiety, and Support of Antiterrorism Policies." *American Journal of Political Science* 49 (3):593–608.

Huddy, Leonie, and Nadia Khatib. 2007. "American Patriotism, National Identity, and Political Involvement." *American Journal of Political Science* 51 (1):63–77.

Hulse, Carl. 2008a. "McCain's Canal Zone Birth Prompts Queries about Whether That Rules Him Out." *New York Times*, 28 February, A21.

2008b. "Senate Says McCain Is Eligible." *New York Times*, 1 May, A22.

Huntington, Samuel P. 1997. "The Erosion of American National Interests." *Foreign Affairs* 76 (5):28–49.

2004. *Who Are We?: The Challenges to America's Identity*. New York: Simon & Schuster.

Hurwitz, Jon, and Mark Peffley. 1990. "Public Images of the Soviet Union: The Impact on Foreign Policy Attitudes." *Journal of Politics* 52 (1):3–28.

Ignatieff, Michael. 1994. *Blood and Belonging: Journeys into the New Nationalism*. 1st American ed. New York: Farrar Straus and Giroux.

Isenberg, D.J. 1986. "Group Polarization: A Critical Review and Meta-analysis." *Journal of Personality and Social Psychology* 50:1141–51.

Jetten, Jolanda, Tom Postmes, and Brendan J. McAuliffe. 2002. "'We're All Individuals': Group Norms of Individualism and Collectivism, Levels of Identification and Identity Threat." *European Journal of Social Psychology* 32:189–207.

Kakar, Sudhir. 1996. *The Colors of Violence: Cultural Identities, Religion, and Conflict*. Chicago: University of Chicago Press.

Kallen, Horace. 1924. *Culture and Democracy in the United States*. New York: Boni and Liveright.

Kaplan, Joel. 2005. *One Nation Under Law*. http://bnaibrith.org/pubs/bnaibrith/pov/050513_kaplan_pov.cfm 1 April 2005 (accessed 26 May 2005).

Kelman, Herbert C., and V. Lee Hamilton. 1989. *Crimes of Obedience: Toward a Social Psychology of Authority and Responsibility*. New Haven: Yale University Press.

Kilborn, Peter T. 2001. "After the Attacks: Voices; Fellow Americans Opening Hearts, Wallets, Veins." *New York Times*, 13 September, A19.

King, Gary. 1986. "How Not to Lie with Statistics." *American Journal of Political Science* 39:666–87.

Kinket, Barbara, and Maykel Verkuyten. 1997. "Levels of Ethnic Self-Identification and Social Context." *Social Psychology Quarterly* 60 (4):338–54.

Kluegel, James R., and Eliot R. Smith. 1986. *Beliefs About Inequality: Americans' Views of What Is and What Ought to Be*. New York: A. de Gruyter.

Konigsmark, Anne Rochell, and Rick Hampson. 2005. "Amid Ruins, Volunteers Are Emerging as Heroes; as Government Agencies Delay,

Non-Profits Are Energizing Rebuilding Efforts on Gulf Coast – and Giving Hope." *USA Today*, 22 December, 1A.

Kosterman, Rick, and Seymour Feshbach. 1989. "Toward a Measure of Patriotic and Nationalistic Attitudes." *Political Psychology* 10 (2):257–74.

Kramer, Roderick M., and Marilynn B. Brewer. 1984. "Effects of Group Identity on Resource Utilization in a Simulated Commons Dilemma." *Journal of Personality and Social Psychology* 46:1044–57.

Labaton, Stephen. 2007. "McCain Casts Muslims as Less Fit to Lead." *New York Times*, 30 September, 22.

Ladd, Everett Carll. 1999. *The Ladd Report*. New York: Free Press.

Lakoff, George. 1987. *Women, Fire, and Dangerous Things: What Categories Reveal about the Mind*. Chicago: University of Chicago Press.

Large, Jerry. 2005. "Katrina: Race and Class Separate Yet Connected." *Seattle Times*, 18 September, M1.

Larimer, Christopher W. 2003. "Behavior a Function of Publicity." Paper presented at the annual meeting of the Human Behavior and Evolution Society, Lincoln, Nebraska.

Latané, Bibb. 1981. "The Psychology of Social Impact." *American Psychologist* 36:343–56.

Lavrakas, Paul J. 1993. *Telephone Survey Methods: Sampling, Selection, and Supervision*. 2nd ed. Newbury Park, CA: Sage.

Levine, John M., and Richard L. Moreland. 1998. "Small Groups." In *The Handbook of Social Psychology, 4th ed.*, ed. D.T. Gilbert, S.T. Fiske and G. Lindzey. New York: McGraw-Hill.

Li, Qiong, and Marilynn B. Brewer. 2004. "What Does It Mean to Be an American? Patriotism, Nationalism, and American Identity after 9/11." *Political Psychology* 25 (5):727–39.

Lipset, Seymour Martin. 1996. *American Exceptionalism: A Double-Edged Sword*. New York: W. W. Norton.

Liptak, Adam. 2008. "A Hint of New Life to a McCain Birth Issue." *New York Times*, 11 July, A11.

Lodge, Milton, and Charles Taber. 2000. "Three Steps toward a Theory of Motivated Political Reasoning." In *Elements of Reason: Cognition, Choice, and the Bounds of Rationality*, ed. A. Lupia, M. McCubbins, and S. Popkin. Cambridge, UK: Cambridge University Press.

2005. "The Automaticity of Affect for Political Leaders, Groups, and Issues: An Experimental Test of the Hot Cognition Hypothesis." *Political Psychology* 26: 455–82.

Lodge, Milton, Charles Taber, and Inna Burdein. 2003. "The Impact of Self-Identifications on Political Attitudes: An Experimental Test Employing Subliminal Priming." Paper presented at the annual meeting of the Midwest Political Science Association, Chicago.

Luskin, Robert. 1991. "Abusus non tollit usum: Standardized Coefficients, Correlations, and R2s." *American Journal of Political Science* 35:1032–46.

Mackie, Diane M., and Joel Cooper. 1984. "Attitude Polarization: Effects of Group Membership." *Journal of Personality and Social Psychology* 46:575–85.

Magaro, Peter A., and Richard M. Ashbrook. 1985. "The Personality of Societal Groups." *Journal of Personality and Social Psychology* 48:1479–89.

Mahtani, Minelle. 2002. "Interrogating the Hyphen-Nation: Canadian Multicultural Policy and 'Mixed Race' Identities." *Social Identities* 8 (1):67–90.

Marcus, George E., John L. Sullivan, Elizabeth Theiss-Morse, and Sandra Wood. 1995. *With Malice toward Some: How People Make Civil Liberties Judgments.* Cambridge, UK: Cambridge University Press.

Markus, Hazel Rose, and Shinobu Kitayama. 1994. "A Collective Fear of the Collective: Implications for Selves and Theories of Selves." *Personality and Social Psychology Bulletin* 20 (5):568–79.

Marques, Jose M., Dominic Abrams, Dario Paez, and Michael A. Hogg. 2001. "Social Categorization, Social Identification, and Rejection of Deviant Group Members." In *Blackwell Handbook of Social Psychology: Group Processes*, ed. M. A. Hogg and S. Tindale. Malden, MA: Blackwell.

Marques, Jose M., Dominic Abrams, and Rui G. Serodio. 2001. "Being Better by Being Right: Subjective Group Dynamics and Derogation of In-Group Deviants When Generic Norms Are Undermined." *Journal of Personality and Social Psychology* 81:436–47.

Marques, Jose M., and Dario Paez. 1994. "The 'Black Sheep Effect': Social Categorization, Rejection of Ingroup Deviates and Perception of Group Variability." *European Review of Social Psychology* 5:37–68.

Mathur, Shruti L. 2004. "In Brief; Orono; Hurricane Fund Doubles Goal." *Minneapolis Star Tribune*, 3 November, 3W.

Maurer, Kristin L., Bernadette Park, and Myron Rothbart. 1995. "Subtyping Versus Subgrouping Processes in Stereotype Representation." *Journal of Personality and Social Psychology* 69 (5):812–24.

McCarthy, Joseph R. 1950. "Enemies from Within." Speech given in Wheeling, West Virginia, 9 February, at History Matters, http://historymatters .gmu.edu/d/6456 (accessed 25 October 2007).

McClosky, Herbert, and Alida Brill. 1983. *Dimensions of Tolerance: What Americans Believe about Civil Liberties.* New York: Russell Sage Foundation.

McClosky, Herbert, and John Zaller. 1984. *The American Ethos: Public Attitudes toward Capitalism and Democracy.* Cambridge, MA: Harvard University Press.

McConahay, John B. 1986. "Modern Racism, Ambivalence, and the Modern Racism Scale." In *Prejudice, Discrimination, and Racism*, ed. J. F. Dovidio and S. L. Gaertner. Orlando, FL: Academic Press.

McCord, Julia. 2001. "Across the Midlands, People Open Their Hearts, and Wallets; Everyone from Kids to Corporations Digs Deep to Help

Victims of the Sept. 11 Terrorist Attacks." *Omaha World Herald*, 27 September, 6B.

McKinley, James. 2000. "Sports Psychology; It Isn't Just a Game." *New York Times*, 11 August, 1.

Meacham, Jon. 2007. "Op-Ed: A Nation of Christians Is Not a Christian Nation." *New York Times*, Section 4, page 15.

Mendelberg, Tali. 2001. *The Race Card: Campaign Strategy, Implicit Messages, and the Norm of Equality*. Princeton: Princeton University Press.

Milgram, Stanley. 1974. *Obedience to Authority: An Experimental View*. New York: Harper Colophon.

Miller, David. 1995. *On Nationality*. Oxford: Oxford University Press.

Mink, Gwendolyn. 1986. *Old Labor and New Immigrants in American Political Development: Union, Party, and State, 1875–1920*. Ithaca: Cornell University Press.

Mlicki, Pawel P., and Naomi Ellemers. 1996. "Being Different or Being Better? National Stereotypes and Identifications of Polish and Dutch Students." *European Journal of Social Psychology* 26 (1):97–114.

Moscovici, S., and M. Zavalloni. 1969. "The Group as a Polarizer of Attitudes." *Journal of Personality and Social Psychology* 12:125–35.

Mullen, Brian, Rupert J. Brown, and C. Smith. 1992. "Ingroup Bias as a Function of Salience, Relevance, and Status: An Integration?" *European Journal of Social Psychology* 22:103–22.

Mummendey, Amelie, Andreas Klink, and Rupert Brown. 2001. "Nationalism and Patriotism: National Identification and Out-group Rejection." *British Journal of Social Psychology* 40:159–72.

Myers, D. G., and H. Lamm. 1976. "The Group Polarization Phenomenon." *Psychological Bulletin* 83:602–62.

Nathanson, Stephen. 1997. "Should Patriotism Have a Future?" In *Patriotism: In the Lives of Individuals and Nations*, ed. D. Bar-Tal and E. Staub. Chicago: Nelson-Hall.

Newcomb, Theodore M. 1943. *Personality and Social Change: Attitude and Social Formation in a Student Community*. New York: Dryden Press.

Newcomb, Theodore M., Kathryn E. Koenig, Richard Flacks, and Donald P. Warwick. 1967. *Persistence and Change: Bennington College and Its Students after Twenty-five Years*. New York: Wiley.

Newsweek Poll. 2007. www.pollingreport.com/terror.htm. 11–12 July (accessed 5 May 2008).

Oakes, Penelope J. 2003. "The Root of All Evil in Intergroup Relations? Unearthing the Categorization Process." In *Blackwell Handbook of Social Psychology: Intergroup Processes*, ed. R. Brown and S. L. Gaertner. Malden, MA: Blackwell.

O'Reilly, Bill. 2007. "Talking Points: 'Bill Moyers, the Far Left, and Blatant Dishonesty.'" FoxNews.com. 27 April. http://www.foxnews.com/story/0,2933,268979,00.html (accessed 11 September 2007).

Ouwerkerk, Jaap W., Naomi Ellemers, and Dick De Gilder. 1999. "Group Commitment and Individual Effort in Experimental and Organizational Contexts." In *Social Identity: Context, Commitment, Content*, ed. N. Ellemers, R. Spears and B. Doosje. Oxford: Blackwell.

Packer, George. 2001. "The Way We Live Now: 9-30-01; Recapturing the Flag." *New York Times*, 30 September, 15.

Pappu, Sridhar. 2007. "Walking a Hard Line on Campaign Trail in Iowa; Can Anti-Immigration Fervor Keep Tancredo in the Race?" *Washington Post*, 11 August, C01.

Perdue, C.W., John F. Dovidio, M.B. Gurtman, and R.B. Tyler. 1990. "'Us' and 'Them': Social Categorization and the Process of Intergroup Bias." *Journal of Personality and Social Psychology* 59:475–86.

Perreault, Stephane, and Richard Y. Bourhis. 1999. "Ethnocentrism, Social Identification, and Discrimination." *Personality and Social Psychology Bulletin* 25 (1):92–103.

Petrocik, John R. 1974. "An Analysis of Intransitivities in the Index of Party Identification." *Political Methodology* 1:31–47.

Pew Forum on Religion & Public Life. 2006. "Many Americans Uneasy with Mix of Religion and Politics." http://pewforum.org/docs/?DocID=153 (accessed 5 May 2008.)

Pew Research Center. 2005. "Katrina Relief Effort Raises Concern over Excessive Spending, Waste: Growing Number Sees U.S. Divided between 'Haves' and 'Have-Nots'." http://people-press.org/reports/display.php3?ReportID=260 2005 (accessed 13 March 2006).

— 2006. "Americans Taking Abramoff, Alito and Domestic Spying in Stride: Democrats Hold Huge Issue Advantage." Washington: Pew Research Center for the People and the Press. 11 January. http://people-press.org/reports/display.php3?ReportID=267 (accessed 21 November 2007).

— 2007. "How Young People View Their Lives, Futures and Politics: A Portrait of 'Generation Next'." Washington: Pew Research Center for the People and the Press. 9 January. http://people-press.org/reports/pdf/300.pdf (accessed 21 November 2007).

— 2008. "12% – Still Think Obama Is Muslim." Washington: Pew Research Center for the People and the Press. http://pewresearch.org/databank/dailynumber/?NumberID=509 (accessed 14 October 2008).

Phillips, Timothy L. 1996. "Symbolic Boundaries and National Identity in Australia." *British Journal of Sociology* 47 (1):113–34.

Pickett, Cynthia L., and Marilynn B. Brewer. 2005. "The Role of Exclusion in Maintaining Ingroup Inclusion." In *The Social Psychology of Inclusion and Exclusion*, ed. D. Abrams, M.A. Hogg and J.M. Marques. New York: Psychology Press.

Prescott, Jean. 2006. "Ham Operators among Katrina's Unsung Heroes; Radio Amateurs Lauded for Handling Hundreds of Messages after Disaster." *Contra Costa Times*, 1 May, F4.

"Private Donations Raised $20 Million for Hurricane Relief Fund." 2005. *Associated Press State & Local Wire*, 15 August, BC cycle.

Prothro, James W., and Charles W. Grigg. 1960. "Fundamental Principles of Democracy: Bases of Agreement and Disagreement." *Journal of Politics* 22 (2):276–94.

"Pro-war Demonstrators Show Support for U.S. Troops." 2003. FoxNews. com. 23 March. http://www.foxnews.com/story/0,2933,81936,00.html (accessed 11 September 2007).

Reicher, Stephen, and Nick Hopkins. 2001. *Self and Nation: Categorization, Contestation, and Mobilization*. London: Sage.

Reimers, David M. 1998. *Unwelcome Strangers: American Identity and the Turn against Immigration*. New York: Columbia University Press.

Reno, Raymond R., Robert B. Cialdini, and Carl A. Kallgren. 1993. "The Transsituational Influence of Social Norms." *Journal of Personality and Social Psychology* 64:104–12.

Renshon, Stanley A. 2005. *The 50% American: Immigration and National Identity in an Age of Terror*. Washington: Georgetown University Press.

Richards, Zoe, and Miles Hewstone. 2001. "Subtyping and Subgrouping: Processes for the Prevention and Promotion of Stereotype Change." *Personality and Social Psychology Review* 5 (1):52–73.

Ridley, Matt. 1996. *The Origins of Virtue*. New York: Penguin.

Rothbart, Myron. 2001. "Category Dynamics and the Modification of Outgroup Stereotypes." In *Blackwell Handbook of Social Psychology: Intergroup Processes*, ed. R. Brown and S.L. Gaertner. Malden, MA: Blackwell.

Saad, Lydia. 2006. "Anti-Muslim Sentiments Fairly Commonplace: Four in Ten Americans Admit Feeling Prejudice against Muslims." Gallup News Service. http://www.gallup.com/poll/24073/AntiMuslim-Sentiments-Fairly-Commonplace.aspx (accessed 5 May 2008).

Salamon, Lester M. 2002. "What Really Matters about September 11." *Chronicle of Philanthropy* 14 (22):47.

Sandaine, Kerri. 2001. "Where Heroes Died; Clarkston Firefighters Visit Group Zero in NYC." *Lewiston Morning Tribune*, 28 November, 1A.

Schatz, Robert T., Ervin Staub, and Howard Lavine. 1999. "On the Varieties of National Attachment: Blind versus Constructive Patriotism." *Political Psychology* 20 (1):151–74.

Schervish, Paul G., and John J. Havens. 1997. "Social Participation and Charitable Giving: A Multivariate Analysis." *Voluntas* 8 (3):235–60.

Schildkraut, Deborah J. 2003. "American Identity and Attitudes toward Official-English Policies." *Political Psychology* 24 (3):469–99.

2005. *Press One for English: Language Policy, Public Opinion, and American Identity*. Princeton: Princeton University Press.

Schlegelmilch, Bodo B., Alix Love, and Adamantios Diamantopoulos. 1997. "Responses to Different Charity Appeals: The Impact of Donor

Characteristics on the Amount of Donations." *European Journal of Marketing* 31 (8):548–60.

Schlesinger, Arthur M. 1993. *The Disuniting of America: Reflections on a Multicultural Society*. New York: W. W. Norton.

Schwartz, Barry. 2000. *Abraham Lincoln and the Forge of National Memory*. Chicago: University of Chicago Press.

Sedikides, Constantine, and Marilynn B. Brewer. 2001. *Individual Self, Relational Self, Collective Self*. Philadelphia: Psychology Press.

Sherif, Carolyn W., Muzafer Sherif, and Roger E. Nebergall. 1965. *Attitudes and Attitude Change*. Philadelphia: Saunders.

Sherif, Muzafer. 1958. "Group Influence upon the Formation of Norms and Attitudes." In *Readings in Social Psychology*, 3rd ed., ed. E. E. Maccoby, T. M. Newcomb and E. L. Hartley. New York: Holt, Rinehart, and Winston.

Sherif, Muzafer, and Carl I. Hovland. 1961. *Social Judgment: Assimilation and Contrast Effects in Communication and Attitude Change*. New Haven: Yale University Press.

Sherif, Muzafer, and Carolyn W. Sherif. 1969. *Social Psychology*. New York: Harper and Row.

Sherman, David K., and Geoffrey L. Cohen. 2006. "*The Psychology of Self-Defense: Self-Affirmation Theory*." In *Advances in Experimental Social Psychology*, Vol. 38, ed. M. P. Zanna. San Diego: Academic Press.

Sidanius, Jim, Seymour Feshbach, Shana Levin, and Felicia Pratto. 1997. "The Interface between Ethnic and National Attachment: Ethnic Pluralism or Ethnic Dominance?" *Public Opinion Quarterly* 61 (1):102–33.

Sidanius, Jim, and John R. Petrocik. 2001. "Communal and National Identity in a Multiethnic State: A Comparison of Three Perspectives." In *Social Identity, Intergroup Conflict, and Conflict Resolution*, ed. R. D. Ashmore, L. Jussim and D. Wilder. Oxford: Oxford University Press.

Sidanius, Jim, and Felicia Pratto. 1999. *Social Dominance: An Intergroup Theory of Social Hierarchy and Oppression*. Cambridge, UK: Cambridge University Press.

Skocpol, Theda. 2002. "From Membership to Advocacy." In *Democracies in Flux*, ed. R. D. Putnam. New York: Oxford University Press.

Smith, Craig S. 2003. "Threats and Responses: Brussels; Chirac Scolding Angers Nations That Back U.S." *New York Times*, 19 February, A1.

Smith, H. J., and Tom R. Tyler. 1997. "Choosing the Right Pond: The Impact of Group Membership on Self-Esteem and Group-Oriented Behavior." *Journal of Experimental Social Psychology* 33 (2):146–70.

Smith, Rogers M. 1988. "The 'American Creed' and American Identity: The Limits of Liberal Citizenship in the United States." *Western Political Quarterly* 41 (2):225–51.

Smith, Tom W., and Seokho Kim. 2006. "National Pride in Comparative Perspective: 1995/96 and 2003/04." *International Journal of Public Opinion Research* 18 (1):127–36.

Sniderman, Paul M., Pierangelo Peri, Rui J. P. de Figueiredo, Jr., and Thomas Piazza. 2000. *The Outsider: Prejudice and Politics in Italy.* Princeton: Princeton University Press.

Sober, Elliott, and David Sloan Wilson. 1998. *Unto Others: The Evolution and Psychology of Unselfish Behavior.* Cambridge, MA: Harvard University Press.

"Some Texas Stations Stop Playing Dixie Chicks Songs after Bush Remarks." 2003. FoxNews.com. 16 March. http://www.foxnews.com/story/0,2933,81177,00.html (accessed 11 September 2007).

Spears, Russell. 2001. "The Interaction between the Individual and the Collective Self: Self-Categorization in Context." In *Individual Self, Relational Self, Collective Self,* ed. C. Sedikides and M. B. Brewer. Philadelphia: Psychology Press.

Spears, Russell, Bertjan Doosje, and Naomi Ellemers. 1999. "Commitment and the Context of Social Perception." In *Social Identity: Context, Commitment, Content,* ed. N. Ellemers, R. Spears and B. Doosje. Oxford: Blackwell.

Spinner-Halev, Jeff, and Elizabeth Theiss-Morse. 2003. "National Identity and Self-Esteem." *Perspectives on Politics* 1 (3):515–32.

Staub, Ervin. 1989. *The Roots of Evil: The Origins of Genocide and Other Group Violence.* Cambridge, UK: Cambridge University Press.

2000. "Genocide and Mass Killing: Origins, Prevention, Healing and Reconciliation." *Political Psychology* 21 (2):367–82.

Stone, Andrea. 2007. "Poll: Founders Intended Christian USA; Survey Shows Limits Public Sees on Freedoms of Religion, Press." *USA Today,* 12 September, 2A.

Strom, Stephanie. 2005. "Giving in '04 Was Up 2.3% in Rebound." *New York Times,* 14 June, A12.

Stuckey, Mary E. 2004. *Defining Americans: The Presidency and National Identity.* Lawrence: University Press of Kansas.

Sullivan, John L., Amy Fried, and Mary G. Dietz. 1992. "Patriotism, Politics, and the Presidential Election of 1988." *American Journal of Political Science* 36 (1):200–34.

Sullivan, John L., James Piereson, and George E. Marcus. 1982. *Political Tolerance and American Democracy.* Chicago: University of Chicago Press.

Sun, Key. 1993. "The Implications of Social Psychological Theories of Group Dynamics for Gang Research." *Journal of Gang Research* 1 (3):39–44.

Tajfel, Henri. 1978. *Differentiation between Social Groups: Studies in the Social Psychology of Intergroup Relations.* London: Academic Press.

1982. *Social Identity and Intergroup Relations.* Cambridge, UK: Cambridge University Press.

Tajfel, Henri, Michael Billig, R. P. Bundy, and Claude Flament. 1971. "Social Categorization and Intergroup Behavior." *European Journal of Social Psychology* 1:149–78.

Tajfel, Henri, and John C. Turner. 1986. "The Social Identity Theory of Intergroup Relations." In *The Psychology of Intergroup Relations*, ed. S. Worchel and W. G. Austin. Chicago: Nelson-Hall.

Tajfel, Henri, and A. L. Wilkes. 1963. "Classification and Quantitative Judgement." *British Journal of Psychology* 54 (2):101–14.

Taylor, Charles. 1998. "The Dynamics of Democratic Exclusion." *Journal of Democracy* 9 (4):143–56.

Terry, Deborah J., and Michael A. Hogg. 1996. "Group Norms and the Attitude-Behavior Relationship: A Role for Group Identification." *Personality and Social Psychology Bulletin* 22:776–93.

Theiss-Morse, Elizabeth. 1993. "Conceptualizations of Good Citizenship and Political Participation." *Political Behavior* 15:355–80.

Thompson, Suzanne C., Jeffrey C. Kohles, Teresa A. Otsuki, and Douglas R. Kent. 1997. "Perceptions of Attitudinal Similarity in Ethnic Groups in the U.S.: Ingroup and Outgroup Homogeneity Effects." *European Journal of Social Psychology* 27:209–20.

"Thousands Rally in Support of War." 2003. FoxNews.com. 22 February. http://www.foxnews.com/story/0,2933,79333,00.html (accessed 7 November 2007).

Tocqueville, Alexis de. 1969. *Democracy in America*. Translated by G. Lawrence. Edited by J. P. Mayer. Garden City, NY: Anchor.

Transue, John E. 2007. "Identity Salience, Identity Acceptance, and Racial Policy Attitudes: American National Identity as a Uniting Force." *American Journal of Political Science* 51 (1):78–91.

Trew, Karen, and Denny E. Benson. 1996. "Dimensions of Social Identity in Northern Ireland." In *Changing European Identities: Social Psychological Analyses of Social Change*, ed. G. M. Breakwell and E. Lyons. Oxford: Butterworth-Heinemann.

Tumulty, Karen. 2008. "In Battleground Virginia, a Tale of Two Grand Games." *Time*, 12 October, http://www.time.com/time/politics/article/0,8599,1849422,00.html (accessed 14 October 2008).

Turner, John C. 1999. "Some Current Issues in Research on Social Identity and Self-Categorization Theories." In *Social Identity: Context, Commitment, Content*, ed. N. Ellemers, R. Spears and B. Doosje. Oxford: Blackwell.

Tyler, Tom R., and Steven Blader. 2000. *Cooperation in Groups: Procedural Justice, Social Identity, and Behavioral Engagement*. Philadelphia: Psychology Press.

Uslaner, Eric M. 2001. "Volunteering and Social Capital: How Trust and Religion Shape Civic Participation in the United States." In *Social Capital and Participation in Everyday Life*, ed. P. Dekker and E. M. Uslaner. London: Routledge.

Verba, Sidney, Kay Lehman Schlozman, and Henry E. Brady. 1995. *Voice and Equality: Civic Voluntarism in American Politics*. Cambridge, MA: Harvard University Press.

Walzer, Michael. 1992. *What It Means to Be an American*. New York: Marsilio.

Wann, Daniel L. 2001. *Sport Fans: The Psychology and Social Impact of Spectators*. New York: Routledge.

Wann, Daniel L., and Nyla R. Branscombe. 1990. "Die-Hard and Fair-Weather Fans: Effects of Identification on BIRGing and CORFing Tendencies." *Journal of Sport and Social Issues* 14 (2):103–17.

Weisberg, Herbert F., and Edward B. Hasecke. 1999. "The Psychological Underpinnings of Party Identification." Paper presented at the annual meeting of the American Political Science Association, Atlanta, 2–5 September.

Wilgoren, Jodi. 2005. "In a Multitude of Forms, the Offers of Help Pour In." *New York Times*, 2 September, A21.

Worchel, Stephen, and Dawna Coutant. 1997. "The Tangled Web of Loyalty: Nationalism, Patriotism, and Ethnocentrism." In *Patriotism: In the Lives of Individuals and Nations*, ed. D. Bar-Tal and E. Staub. Chicago: Nelson-Hall.

Wuthnow, Robert. 1998. *Loose Connections: Joining Together in America's Fragmented Communities*. Cambridge, MA: Harvard University Press.

Zerubavel, Yael. 1995. *Recovered Roots: Collective Memory and The Making of Israeli National Tradition*. Chicago: University of Chicago Press.

Index